| | | | | | | 2<br>He<br>Helium |
|---|---|---|---|---|---|---|

| 5<br>B<br>Boron | 6<br>C<br>Carbon | 7<br>N<br>Nitrogen | 8<br>O<br>Oxygen | 9<br>F<br>Fluorine | 10<br>Ne<br>Neon |
|---|---|---|---|---|---|

| 13<br>Al<br>Aluminum | 14<br>Si<br>Silicon | 15<br>P<br>Phosphorus | 16<br>S<br>Sulfur | 17<br>Cl<br>Chlorine | 18<br>Ar<br>Argon |
|---|---|---|---|---|---|

| 28<br>Ni<br>Nickel | 29<br>Cu<br>Copper | 30<br>Zn<br>Zinc | 31<br>Ga<br>Gallium | 32<br>Ge<br>Germanium | 33<br>As<br>Arsenic | 34<br>Se<br>Selenium | 35<br>Br<br>Bromine | 36<br>Kr<br>Krypton |
|---|---|---|---|---|---|---|---|---|
| 46<br>Pd<br>Palladium | 47<br>Ag<br>Silver | 48<br>Cd<br>Cadmium | 49<br>In<br>Indium | 50<br>Sn<br>Tin | 51<br>Sb<br>Antimony | 52<br>Te<br>Tellurium | 53<br>I<br>Iodine | 54<br>Xe<br>Xenon |
| 78<br>Pt<br>Platinum | 79<br>Au<br>Gold | 80<br>Hg<br>Mercury | 81<br>Tl<br>Thallium | 82<br>Pb<br>Lead | 83<br>Bi<br>Bismuth | 84<br>Po<br>Polonium | (85) | 86<br>Rn<br>Radon |
| (96) | (97) | (98) | (99) | (100) | | | | |

| 64<br>Gd<br>Gadolinium | 65<br>Tb<br>Terbium | 66<br>Dy<br>Dysprosium | 67<br>Ho<br>Holmium | 68<br>Er<br>Erbium | 69<br>Tm<br>Thulium | 70<br>Yb<br>Ytterbium | 71<br>Lu<br>Lutetium |
|---|---|---|---|---|---|---|---|

PERIODIC TABLE OF THE ELEMENTS
BEFORE WORLD WAR II

# ADVENTURES IN

# THE ATOMIC AGE

# ADVENTURES IN

# THE ATOMIC AGE

## FROM WATTS

## TO WASHINGTON

## GLENN T. SEABORG

WITH ERIC SEABORG

**FARRAR, STRAUS AND GIROUX**

NEW YORK

Farrar, Straus and Giroux
19 Union Square West, New York 10003

Distributed in Canada by Douglas and McIntyre Ltd.
Printed in the United States of America
First edition, 2001

Library of Congress Cataloging-in-Publication Data
Seaborg, Glenn Theodore, 1912–1999
    Adventures in the atomic age : from Watts to Washington / Glenn T. Seaborg with Eric
Seaborg.— 1st ed.
        p. cm.
    Includes index.
    ISBN 0-374-29991-9 (hardcover : alk. paper)
    1. Seaborg, Glenn Theodore, 1912–1999.  2. Science and state—United States.
3. Nuclear energy—Government policy—United States.  4. Science consultants—United
States—Biography.  5. Chemists—United States—Biography.  I. Seaborg, Eric, 1954–
II. Title

QD22.S436 A32 2001
327.1′74′092—dc21
[B]
                                                                        00-049522

Photo credits appear on pages 299–300

Designed by Jonathan D. Lippincott

*To Helen and Ellen, whose love and support made it all possible*

# CONTENTS

# ADVENTURES IN

# THE ATOMIC AGE

ONE

# A MICHIGAN BOYHOOD

Congressional hearing rooms are arranged to mimic a courtroom, with the members of Congress looking down like judges from high wooden benches. The arrangement leaves no doubt as to who is in charge. I found myself looking up at these platforms one day in the 1960s. As chairman of the U.S. Atomic Energy Commission, I'd been summoned to explain to the Joint Committee on Atomic Energy why budget cuts were forcing the agency to lay off machinists at the Oak Ridge National Laboratory.

The laboratory was a major employer in Tennessee, and I'd enjoyed generally cordial relations with Senator Albert Gore Sr. (whose son would grow up to become Vice President). But faced with the prospect of jobless constituents, the senator was determined to do what he could to defend them. He grilled me about the reasons for the layoffs and our choice of whom to lay off, finally growling, "Dr. Seaborg, just what do you have against machinists?"

It was the best question I could have hoped for. "Senator, I don't have anything against machinists," I responded. "As a matter of fact, my father was a machinist." After that sank in, I continued, "And my grandfather was a machinist . . . and my *great*-grandfather was a machinist." I looked up at him. "And if I'd had any talent for it, I would have been a machinist myself."

Everyone in the room broke into laughter, including Senator Gore. The laughter broke the tension, and the hearing soon ended. Gore's question, though, brought into focus a thought I've long had about the relationship between my path as a scientist and my forebears' paths as machinists. To be a creative machinist was as close to being a scientist as their restricted worlds would allow, and they laid the groundwork that allowed me the good fortune of a world with broader horizons.

My great-grandfather was the master mechanic at the ironworks in Hällefors, Sweden. He was the first to carry the name Sjöberg, abandoning the traditional Swedish patronymic of Olsson.

His son, Johan Erik Sjöberg, also became a machinist at Hällefors before leaving for America. Nineteenth-century Sweden's population boom, coupled with recurring hard times, fueled waves of migration—only Ireland sent a higher proportion of her people to the United States. To escape the hardships brought on by a series of crop failures, Johan set sail in 1867 at the age of twenty-three.

My father told me the story of this trip. The cheapest tickets were in steerage, belowdecks and near the rudder, a rough place to ride. When the ocean grew turbulent, the vomit of seasick passengers lubricated the deck and the luggage would slide around with the rolling of the ship. Johan would stretch out his legs to keep from being crushed against the wall.

As far as we know, it was an immigration official at Ellis Island who Anglicized his name to Seaborg. Like many of his countrymen, he headed for the Upper Peninsula of Michigan, where the climate was reminiscent of his homeland's and his skills were in demand at the iron mines. At the Cleveland Cliffs Mining Company, in the little town of Ishpeming, he built a reputation as a fabulous machinist.

He and his family knew so little of this new land that his mother wrote, asking, "We wonder if they celebrate Christmas in America." Johan wrote home in amazement at the country he found, where if his employer didn't give him a raise he could find a job somewhere else, because "you don't have to kowtow to anyone" and people were independent: "The railroad here goes in all directions, so we can go wherever we want to. People here have no more furniture than they can take in two or three horseloads to the station, and they can travel wherever they want." And you could buy an insurance policy that the company would pay off even if you died a day later. "You might not believe this, but I know it is the truth. A man here died the year after he was insured, and his wife got the money right away."

Johan saved enough money to bring his mother, three sisters, and two brothers to this land of opportunity. He married a twenty-two-year-old Swedish immigrant, Charlotta Wilhelmina Johnson, whose family came to Ishpeming in 1869. Of their ten children, four died in infancy.

My father, Herman Theodore, who was called Ted, was the oldest surviving child of this union, and he became a foreman in the machine shop of the Cleveland Cliffs Company. He and his siblings all finished high school, quite an achievement for working-class people in that day. Johan died young, and it fell to my father to hold the family together, so his education ended after high school. My Uncle Henry received a teaching degree from Northern Michigan College and became a high school shop teacher on the recommendation of the mining company, with the understanding that his skills would be available to them to work on intricate problems; my Uncle Lawrence graduated from Michigan Tech with an engineering degree. This first American generation of Seaborgs made the most of their educational opportunities, and their investment paid off.

Ishpeming was an ethnic town, with groups of Finns, Italians, and Cousin Jacks (as we called the Cornish) in addition to Swedes, all holding on to their traditions and celebrations. At one of these festivals, a picnic on Midsummer Day, my father met Selma Erickson.

She'd immigrated four years earlier, at the age of seventeen, fleeing the proverbial wicked stepmother who treated her stepchildren like servants. Her uncle had already emigrated to America, and when he came back to Sweden for a visit, he suggested that she return to America with him. An inheritance from her mother gave her enough money to buy a ticket and still have ten dollars in her pocket. Immigrants needed forty dollars in cash for entry at Ellis Island, a requirement that her uncle circumvented by claiming she was his daughter. She lived with her uncle's family in Ishpeming, until hired by a well-to-do family as a live-in maid.

As she later told the story, my father pursued her at the Midsummer Day picnic, but she avoided him because he was drunk. Asked later why she had further dealings with him if she found his drunkenness distasteful, she said, "The Seaborgs had a reputation for being smart."

And that's how I came to be born in Ishpeming in 1912. My sister Jeanette filled out the family two years later. Jeanette and I learned Swedish before we learned English. My American-born father was perfectly bilingual, but my mother never lost her Swedish accent. Throughout their lives, they would move seamlessly between the two languages in conversation. Swedish so predominated in the neighborhood where we lived that when neighbors heard we'd be called Glenn and Jeanette, some asked my mother, "Are those names?" In fact, my mother never did get the hang of pronouncing the *J* in my sister's name, and she remained Yeanette.

But aside from these American names, Swedish customs prevailed in our home. For Christmas Eve dinner, my mother would cook a traditional Swedish smorgasbord, with pickled herring, lutfisk, saffron buns and bread made with glacéed fruits, gingersnaps cut into fanciful shapes, lingonberries, and a dessert of rice pudding topped with cinnamon, cream, and sugar.

My parents expressed pride in our Swedish heritage. We would hear about the accomplishments of people like Alfred Nobel and the monopolistic owner of a huge company, of whom my father observed, "Even the biggest crook in the world is a Swede."

Our family led a comfortable existence in a modest house, and my memories of Ishpeming are pleasant ones. We kept a pig in the backyard, at least during World War I. Sugar was rationed then, and you could buy it in proportion to the amount of cereal you bought. My parents bought the cereal and fed it to the pig—that way my mother could have more sugar for her baking, and for her coffee *kalas*, a neighborhood club in which housewives would invite each other over and bake with a covert competitiveness.

On my first day of school, my mother took my hand and walked me down the street. As we passed each doorway, the lady of the house would ask, "Oh, is Glenn starting school today?" and my mother would respond with dignity that I was. I felt very proud, and I think it impressed on me the importance that my family placed on education more effectively than any other gesture. In school, however, I was too shy even to raise my hand to ask to be excused to go to the bathroom. My mother made arrangements with my teacher that allowed me to absent myself without asking.

When I was eight years old and wanted to earn spending money, I started caddying at the nearby country club's nine-hole golf course. The golfers would line us up to see if we were tall enough to keep the bag from dragging on the ground, and because of my height I was usually one of the first chosen. Caddies were paid twenty cents, or twenty-five by more affluent clients. An even better job was to open the gate to the country club. The drivers would toss you a penny or two, a nickel, even a dime, and you could make a dollar or more. The spot was so lucrative that sometimes we'd sleep out on the Friday night before a tournament to claim the job on Saturday morning.

One day, when I was seven, the Green Bay Packers came to town. It was their first year of existence and, representing the Indian Packing Company, they played our local Ishpeming town team of rugged iron miners. Curly Lambeau, their captain, coach, runner, and quarterback, later recalled: "The game at Ishpeming was an odd one. They had a tough team, and on our first three running plays, three of our men went out with broken bones. We never ran again—we passed on every play and we beat them 33–0. It was that day we realized the value of the forward pass." Of course, in our isolated world we considered this newly invented forward pass close to cheating.

And indeed Ishpeming was an isolated world of its own. Its unpaved streets were tinged red from iron ore. A lone streetcar ran the three miles to the neighboring town of Negaunee, where it reversed and came back on the same track. A train ran the twelve or fourteen miles to Marquette, on Lake Superior. We read of the outside world in the Marquette *Mining Journal* and the Sunday Chicago *Tribune*. But in my ten years in Ishpeming, I never talked on a telephone or heard the word "radio." Santa Claus would spice our Christmas stockings with an orange, an exotic delicacy from far to the south.

In this company town, my parents owned our house, but Cleveland Cliffs owned the land it stood on. And that was leverage that the company used to keep workers in line. My father used to tell us that when he was young there'd been a person in town whom everyone called the Democrat, the only one who'd admit to being one in public, since the company expected you to vote Republican. If a foreman found it inconvenient to have too many crew members named Anderson, he might tell some of them to change their names, and they would. If you were injured, you were out of work and out of luck. Workmen's compensation was an idea of the future. And if your friend suffered an accident in the mine shaft, your pay was docked for the time you were away from your job helping him to the surface.

Our family friends the Engstroms moved to California and wrote urging my parents to join them in the promised land. My mother was eager to go. Part of her motive was to escape the harsh Michigan winters, with snows so deep I can recall strapping on my skis and skiing out our second-story window. But more important was her dissatisfaction with the limited opportunities in such a place; she wanted to expand her children's horizons.

I imagine that if it had been up to my father, he would have stayed in Ishpeming. Pa was easygoing, not particularly ambitious, and more gregarious than my mother. As foreman of the machine shop where he'd established a solid reputation, he was guaranteed a satisfactory job. And it must have been difficult for a forty-two-year-old man to pull up roots from the only town he'd ever known. But he was very proud of my mother and completely devoted to her; if he ever resisted her impulse to move, I never heard about it.

Ma was the leader of the family. Considering her shy and reserved nature, and her prospects and resources when she arrived in this country, she was remarkable in her determination to build a better life for us. When I asked her once about the fear she must have felt immigrating to a strange land, she said that she hadn't thought about that, only about what she was getting away from. She inspired her sister and brother to come to America, and her sister would follow her to California.

In the fall of 1922, my parents sold our house and furniture for $1,200, and we boarded the train with one-way tickets for California. It's easy to see how provincial my Ishpeming experience was from a wide-eyed letter about our trip I wrote to my cousins: "In Denver we went up in a tower fifteen stories high and the people on the ground looked like ants. In Minneapolis I seen a building eighteen stories high. Down town of the big citys theres a street car running on nearly every street. They have two street car lines on one street, one line for the cars going up the street and the other line for cars going down the street."

And the mild climate of California was an exotic change from the Upper Peninsula, where November signaled the onset of winter. "They took us out for a car ride around the orange groves. I've had all the fruit I've wanted since I came out here."

# CALIFORNIA HERE WE COME

Like immigrants to a new land, we moved in with our friends the Engstroms while getting a start. They lived in a new subdivision called Home Gardens in the town that would soon become South Gate, just south of Los Angeles. Home Gardens, growing at a boomtown pace, was still a crude place, with unpaved streets and no sidewalks.

My parents bought three lots across the street from the Engstroms for $295 apiece and hired Mr. Engstrom, a carpenter, to build as much house as we could afford. In our several weeks with them, the Engstroms served overcooked cabbage every day, a dish my father swore he'd never eat again, so he was relieved when we could move into what was still little more than a roof over unfinished outside walls. Heavy tar paper tacked onto two-by-threes delineated the four future rooms. One day the Santa Ana winds blew so hard that we had to call our neighbors over to help us as we leaned against the walls to keep them from falling in. Mr. Engstrom added bracing the next day. A faucet by the side of the house, bringing water from the Home Gardens well, was the only plumbing. We carried water in by bucket, and used a privy in the backyard. There was a gas light in the kitchen, and no electricity.

My mother's sister brought her family out from Minneapolis, and the ten of us shared this little house while they built one of their own across the street. When Aunt Hilda died of a thyroid condition just a few years later, Ma became a substitute mother of their five young children as much as she could.

Our house got its plumbing in a style in which families often did things in those days. My father's sister, who was married to a plumber, brought her family out from Detroit the following year and lived with us while they tried to get started in California. My father bought the pipes, toilet, and other materials, and my uncle installed them. My uncle never did find steady work in California, however, and he ended up moving back to Detroit.

My father's luck was only slightly better. He found work as a machinist, but nothing so reliable or lucrative as being foreman in Ishpeming. It took three or four years to save enough money to finish the inside of the house.

Carl Sandburg described his father as a "black Swede," a description that fit my father too. His black hair framed a complexion so dark that Mexicans would walk up to him on the street and speak Spanish. He was six feet tall, a spare but strong man who'd been champion of the local firehouse boxing club in Ishpeming. He handed his paycheck over to Ma every week, and she managed our finances. She even rationed his beer and cigarettes, partly to spare her lungs from the smoke and largely as an economy measure. She rolled his smokes herself, then parceled out his allotment a day at a time. If he wanted money, he would have to ask her for it, which was probably a good thing for the family, because he was generous enough to give it all away—what was his was yours. As far as we could tell, he had no problem with this arrangement. His adoration for Ma was no doubt sparked in part by the way she embodied the qualities of discipline he lacked. An outgoing raconteur to whom making people laugh came naturally, he could have been an entertainer. Perhaps Ma's difficult childhood made her more serious and ambitious.

We had no money to spare, but life was comfortable enough. We weren't poor so much as we just didn't have money—the same as almost everyone in the neighborhood. My mother was an excellent seamstress and made my sister's clothes—Jeanette didn't feel too poor because her clothes were nicer than those of her friends. Ma prepared a big Sunday dinner each week, always making enough to feed another family in case the neighbors dropped by, which they often did.

String beans, potatoes, and beets from our vegetable garden were welcome supplements to Pa's paycheck. A chicken coop provided eggs and meat for our table and hours of cleaning chores for me. I would make the rounds of the neighborhood selling string beans and tomatoes from a bucket. As a teenager, I made money working as a church janitor and for a friend who had a lawn-mowing and landscaping business.

The greater worldliness of the Los Angeles area struck me immediately. Though I'd never even heard of a radio in Ishpeming, in Home Gardens one of our neighbors had already built a crystal set, and I was soon at work building my own. Almost every weekend my friends and I could be found in a South Gate arena where the Shelley Players presented two shows a night under a large tent. We couldn't afford tickets, but when the gates were opened at the first intermission to let patrons stretch their legs, we'd wander back in with them, then stay for the second show.

We could catch a free jitney bus to a streetcar line that ran though Huntington Park and into the metropolis of Los Angeles. We could even thumb a ride out to the ocean.

We spent hours outdoors in the mild southern California climate. I joined a Boy Scout troop and went to camp in the San Bernardino Mountains. A patrol leader and Life Scout, I fell one merit badge short of Eagle Scout status because there was no swimming pool where I could practice lifesaving.

When baseball season neared, the neighborhood boys would gather in the open field behind our house and hoe the weeds all day until we could lay out a diamond. Our sandlot football team played teams from other neighborhoods. I played end to take advantage of my height. It seemed that anything I ate went into vertical growth, and nothing into girth. If we had a dinner invitation, Ma would feed me before we went so I wouldn't embarrass her with my appetite. But I remained so thin that later in life a doctor advised me to *gain* thirty pounds. I was never good enough to play on the school teams—the year I tried out for track they pronounced me too slow for the sprints and too lacking in stamina for the distance events—but a lifelong love of sports started on those fields.

I was drawn to the competition of sports, and that competitive trait was evident from early childhood. I can remember sitting at the kitchen table in Ishpeming when I came home for lunch and having my mother test me in spelling. I was the usual winner of the periodic spelling bees.

One time, the teacher tried to rig it so someone else could win. When a girl and I were the final contestants remaining, the teacher said we'd draw straws to determine the winner. As the girl drew her straw, the teacher declared her the winner. But the teacher's intentions had never occurred to me, and to her annoyance I pointed out that I was holding the longer straw.

When the South Gate Methodist Church announced a contest in which the first child who could learn all the names of the books of the Old and New Testaments would win a Bible, I went home and memorized them. The next Sunday I came ready to recite them. The church elders were chagrined—they'd planned on a long-running contest.

The area was growing so fast that the authorities were having a hard time building schools quickly enough. The Home Gardens Elementary School was so crowded that each room held two classes divided by an imaginary line down the center, with the teacher oscillating between the two halves. I skipped a grade soon after coming out to California, which created a mild problem in that I missed being introduced to decimals. I couldn't figure out why they were putting periods, which you use at the end of sentences, into these numbers, and I was too shy to ask. Eventually, I must have figured it out.

I loved learning. On one of my forays to Long Beach, I saw a used encyclopedia for sale for six dollars. I enlisted the aid of a friend and we went back and claimed it, making an arduous trip toting the heavy volumes. But I took hours of pleasure just reading the encyclopedia. I enjoyed novels as well; *Arrowsmith*, Sinclair Lewis' tale of a scientist's adventures, held me spellbound—a reaction I later found I shared with other scientists of my generation.

The closest high school was a two-mile bus ride away, David Starr Jordan High, in Watts. It was so new that the athletic field was planted in cauliflower, and the first physical education classes consisted of clearing and leveling the ground with hoes and shovels.

Jordan's diverse mix of four hundred students included blacks (called "colored" back then), Mexicans, Filipinos, Asians, and Anglos. I made many friends from different ethnic groups, and learned to take them as individuals without judging them by their race or ethnicity. Moreover, I saw firsthand the insidious irrationality of racism and the restraints it placed on my black friends. When it came time for them to find a job, their only option seemed to be "railroading," as they called it.

Jordan students chose majors according to their future plans, and my mother urged me to follow the commercial track. She thought that could lead to a white-collar job in an office, such as bookkeeping or account-ing, which was her idea of the greatest success I could hope for. But I wanted to go to college, so I took the college preparatory literary course.

I liked history and English, and had an obvious aptitude for math. By the time I got to trigonometry, the teacher himself would occasionally get lost in a proof or problem and turn to me and say, "Glenn, you show them how to do it." (My parents had named me "Glen," but in California I added another *n* to my name because I thought it looked better.)

I had no interest in the school's science offerings. The general science and biology taught in the freshman and sophomore years sounded deathly dull. As I planned for my junior year, a school counselor pointed out that I needed at least one science laboratory class to fulfill college re-quirements. Forced to take a science class, I signed up for the subject that happened to be offered that year, chemistry.

My Berkeley colleague physicist Luis Alvarez wrote that "every sci-entist can recall the teacher who aroused his interest in a field." For me, that teacher was Dwight Logan Reid. Mr. Reid taught chemistry with the charisma and enthusiasm of an old-fashioned preacher. His eyes would light up and he'd tell stories that brought the subject alive. He made the great chemists of the day human and drew my interest to the controversies of the subject in a way that made me want to know the an-swers.

I liked the fact that in chemistry the problems had definitive solu-tions. You could conduct an experiment, and there was physical evidence of a right answer. The logic of the scientific method greatly attracted me.

I started a diary when I was fourteen, and have scarcely missed a day writing in it since. On February 3 of my junior year, I recorded: "I like Chemistry so much I shall probably major in this in college. Mr. Reid has inspired and encouraged me."

One of my classmates in Mr. Reid's class was a boisterous roughneck named Stanley Thompson. Stanley was the kind of guy who would tackle you without warning and start a wrestling match. But under the spell of Mr. Reid, he became as serious about chemistry as I did. We often studied together, and, good friends that we became, I never would have guessed then the long-term influence he would have in my life. At the end of the year, Stan finished at the top of the class.

My grades had been nearly perfect until the second semester, when we reached organic chemistry, a discipline that to my mind involved little more than memorizing an endless number of formulas of similar compounds. I loved physical chemistry because we learned principles that we applied to solving problems, but the order in which all those CH's and OH's and CHOOH's fit together didn't interest me in the least. I figured that I'd done well enough in the rest of the work to maintain an A without wasting my time memorizing all those formulas, but the B that Mr. Reid doled out to me for the second semester proved that he thought otherwise.

My independent attitude of choosing what was appropriate for my education might have kept me from graduating, if one physical education teacher had had his way. I could generally finish my assignments in study halls and other odd times at school so homework wouldn't interfere with my free time. In my senior year, a physical education class came at the end of the day. I enjoyed sports and physical activity, but this teacher's regimen—having us stand in rows, jump up and down, and do knee bends—struck me as a waste of time. So when I discovered the teacher wasn't taking the roll, I decided to convert that class into a study hall in the library. The semester was almost over by the time he noticed my absence, and it infuriated him so much that he told other teachers he planned to flunk me. A teacher had to serve you with a notice before giving you an F, and in this case the vice-principal tipped me off and advised me to avoid the coach. In order to pass, I skipped the few remaining classes and escaped with a D.

My debt to Mr. Reid went beyond his teaching—his strong encouragement gave Stanley Thompson and me the confidence to go on to college.

Given my family's finances, the nearby University of California at Los Angeles was my only possible choice because it was tuition-free and I could commute from home. The equivalent of class valedictorian of our forty-five-member high school class, I had the academic qualifications, but managing just the incidental expenses would be a challenge. That spring I even lost my part-time job as a janitor when the church leaders decided that the janitor must be a member of the congregation and I declined to join.

After graduation, I stood in line at the Firestone Rubber and Tire Company plant in South Gate for an interview. I was hired as a "band builder" to add layers to the tires as they rolled by on the assembly line. But once inside the factory, I stole upstairs and found the laboratory. I barged into the assistant chief chemist's office and made my credentials of a year of high school chemistry sound as impressive as possible. I did not hesitate for a moment when he asked if I could work a slide rule, although my experience with one had consisted of only a couple of classes in night school. I was sure that I could learn to use one quickly if the job depended on it. And so my career as a chemist began, working as a laboratory assistant in Firestone's quality control department for thirty-five cents an hour. After two weeks' training, I was put on the graveyard shift. A main duty consisted of cleaning up after the day-shift chemists who caked tar onto glassware as they experimented to improve the rubber formulas. I cleaned the glassware with solvents and prepared compounds for the chemists to continue their experiments. But my most important duty was quality control testing. As each batch of rubber came off the line, I'd poke it with a probe to test its hardness and check its specific gravity to see if it met specifications before it was put into tires. If it didn't, I'd take a "hold" slip down to the factory floor to stop production on that batch.

I'd been on the night shift for just two weeks when a batch came through that didn't meet the specifications, so I gave a foreman a hold slip. The next batch failed as well, and so did the next, until the whole plant was shut down. The plant foreman glowered at this high school kid who was stopping production and asked was I sure I knew what I was doing. Then he became hard to find, to avoid being handed a hold slip, and I felt I was running the gantlet delivering them. The test results were clear, but was I doing something incorrectly to get them? As I walked home in the morning, I worried because I couldn't be sure, and I barely slept that day, wondering whether I'd still have a job when I returned. When I got back to work I learned that the plant had been in an uproar all day trying to figure out what had gone wrong with all that rubber and how to correct it. It turned out I'd saved the plant from making countless defective tires.

When it came time to go to school in the fall, the chief chemist tried to persuade me to stay on, offering me a raise and a spot on the swing shift, but I told him I was determined to continue my education. I'd saved just enough money over the summer to afford the forty dollars needed for incidental fees and to buy my books at UCLA.

# THREE

# A FREE EDUCATION

On a sunny morning in September 1929, I walked across the bridge that served as the east entrance to UCLA's Westwood campus. It was thrilling to gaze into the deep ravine below and consider the prospect of starting college.

The Westwood campus, which had just opened that year, consisted of four buildings facing each other around a stark quadrangle. The still incomplete structures rose from bare earth unadorned by lawns or shrubs, and winter rains soon turned the dusty walks to goo. Lumber and sacks of cement for further construction were stacked everywhere. School supplies were sold in a wooden shack off to the side.

On that morning, Professor William C. Morgan strode into a packed lecture hall, a formidable man standing six and a half feet tall. He glowered at Chemistry 1A's three hundred students for several minutes before commanding in a stentorian voice, "Look at the student on your right." When we'd done so, he told us, "Look at the student on your left." Then he bellowed, "One of you three will not be here at Thanksgiving time."

UCLA was my only chance, and I resolved to do whatever it took to succeed there. My friends and I were the first Jordan High graduates to attend UCLA. Five of us commuted the twenty miles to campus in Jim Merino's Buick coupe, paying him twenty-five cents a day. Stanley Thompson and I shared the rumble seat, donning goggles to keep the wind out of our eyes so we could spend the hour-long trip studying.

I planned from the first day to major in chemistry. During my senior year in high school, Mr. Reid had taught physics with his customary enthusiasm, and the subject had caught my interest even more than chemistry. However, I believed that the only jobs available to physicists were in teaching, and university faculties had few openings. Chemists seemed to have more opportunities in both academia and industry, and I had to be practical about my future.

Professor Morgan's disheartening odds served as a powerful motivator to work hard: Since the lab periods were too short to perform the assigned experiments to our satisfaction, Stan Thompson and I set up a rudimentary lab in his garage when we took qualitative analysis as freshmen. We'd be given an "unknown" to identify, and we'd put in extra hours in our own lab until we were dead certain we'd solved the problem correctly. I also made sure that when I took a test, I had covered the subject thoroughly in my studying.

Stan and I became great study partners and companions, for we had much in common, including our attitude toward the compulsory Reserve Officers' Training Corps program. Part of the price of our public education was that we had to show our appreciation for the country's largesse by demonstrating our patriotism; the state legislature encouraged us in this by making ROTC compulsory for the male students. And we were all equal in the eyes of the officers—everybody got a C. Those of us who worried about grade point averages had to do that much better in our other courses. It was never clear to me what we reserve officer trainees were being trained for. We had to be able to clean a rifle and march with eyes left and then right.

Stan and I decided to join the ROTC band when we noticed that it practiced sitting inside instead of marching around in the southern California sun. I'd learned to play a few notes on the trombone in a church band in high school. Stan took up the same instrument, figuring he could simply move his slide in time with mine. His ruse worked surprisingly well for six weeks, but eventually the suspicious bandleader asked him to play a few notes on his own. Stan was sent back to the drill field, but my minimal competence was enough to keep me in the band.

I found I could make the grades, but arranging the finances to stay in school became a worrisome problem. The Great Depression had swept the country, and after my freshman year I walked the streets of Los Angeles for days looking for summer work. There was nothing at Firestone, or anywhere else. After two weeks of this futility, three of us headed north in Stanley's Ford touring car. In the Central Valley, the apricot orchards were hiring at thirty-five cents an hour. We slept in the orchards, swam in the irrigation ditches, and ate almost nothing but apricots—except for the day Stanley accidentally ran over a chicken. Two weeks' work put a twenty-dollar profit in my pocket, but there was still no work back home.

Then another high school friend helped out. Clayton Sheldon was a big, strong mesomorph who had played halfback on our sandlot football team. One day during high school, a bully had picked me out of the crowd and said that he didn't like my looks and wanted to fight me after school. I always stood a head taller than the rest of my class, but I was test-tube thin and not the fighting kind. So I was aghast when Clayton took it upon himself to reply, "Okay, we accept." I had all day to worry about what Clayton had gotten me into. When I showed up after school at the appointed "ring," Clayton was there waiting. Without a word, he put his muscular body between me and the bully, fists raised in a boxer's crouch. There was no way our adversary could back out without losing face. Every punch Clayton threw knocked the other boy to the ground, and it didn't take many punches for the bully to admit defeat. Clayton never said a word about this, but I never forgot it. Now he arranged for me to fill in for him in his work as a Linotype mechanic while he went on a brief vacation, so I made another forty dollars.

My family's fortunes took a turn for the worse when the Depression claimed my father's job. He went to work one morning, and was sent home at noon unemployed. It would be three years until he found regular employment, when Franklin Roosevelt's jobs programs began in 1933. Our family barely scraped by. My parents had bought some land where they'd hoped to start a chicken farm one day. They'd never raised the capital to start the farm, and now they sold the land to raise money; it was almost as if they'd put the money for the land in a bank. For a while, my mother and sister found factory jobs making neckties. Some nights my mother just made a big bowl of soup for dinner; other nights potatoes from our garden were the main course. We ran a tab at the grocery store. It was embarrassing to go get food and not be able to pay for it, but we had no choice. Neither did the grocer; he had to trust that we'd pay him eventually.

Those times were tough psychologically as well. My father had never made a lot of money, but he was a skilled machinist who was good at what he did. It was devastating to him to go for three years without regular work. When he finally got a job on a WPA labor crew in the San Gabriel Mountains, his whole demeanor changed overnight. He regained the self-respect that his long period of unemployment had undermined.

I have little memory of my political beliefs, if I'd developed any, prior to the Depression. But I became an enthusiastic fan of Franklin Roosevelt. Herbert Hoover's Republican approach was to keep on saying that prosperity was just around the corner and to do nothing while the country sank deeper and deeper into the Depression. But FDR provided leadership to combat the effects of the Depression on working people like my family. His programs put food on our table—and ever since, I've been a Democrat and a believer that government can be a tool for addressing people's problems.

That fall of 1930, my sophomore year, the university offered me a fifty-dollar scholarship and Stanley lent me some money, but our finances were so precarious I still wasn't sure I'd be able to continue. Financial salvation came in the form of a 99 percent score I made on the final examination in quantitative analysis that semester: the score caught Professor William R. Crowell's attention, and he offered me a job working two afternoons a week—one afternoon as his laboratory assistant in a quantitative analysis course and one afternoon in the stockroom checking out chemicals and equipment for the freshman chemistry laboratory. Those six hours a week at the magnificent pay of fifty cents an hour were enough to keep me in school.

The job Crowell gave me illustrates the extraordinary opportunity that UCLA's undergraduate chemistry program offered. The campus was too young to have a graduate school, yet that was a great advantage for serious undergrads: my lab-assistant position would normally have gone to a graduate student, but out of necessity, undergraduates replaced the graduate students whom professors normally would have hired to help in their research.

Stan Thompson and I volunteered to work in Crowell's laboratory the next summer, another great opportunity, researching ways to improve the experiments in his course. We mixed chemicals endlessly and loved it, happy to be spending our time productively, especially since there was no chance of finding paying work. We learned more in six weeks than a year of lab courses would have taught us, and learned it on a practical level that was impossible to duplicate in classes.

My association with Crowell continued in my junior year, when I was his assistant instructor. The additional duties—preparing laboratory samples, correcting problem sets and quizzes, and helping out in the laboratory sections—kept me busy almost one hundred hours a month at fifty cents an hour, which was enough for a measure of financial stability for the rest of my days at UCLA. One semester, he split the quantitative analysis class in two and had me lecture the better students while he taught the C students.

Chemistry came naturally to me, and I received A's in all my courses except my old nemesis, organic synthesis. But the grades I like to brag about were in two courses I took in introductory psychology. I enrolled because I had to meet general requirements, but thought that as long as I had to take them, I might as well do my best. When I looked up the course's old multiple-choice exams, I thought they were filled with ambiguous questions. So I spent as much time studying the professor and the section leader as I did the assigned reading. I listened carefully to learn the professor's prejudices. I doggedly quizzed the section leader to sort out the answers to those ambiguous questions. By knowing what the professor wanted, I was able to score first among four hundred students in both psychology courses. I guess I learned the subject—after all, I'd used psychology to succeed. Whether I learned more about psychology or about the art of getting grades is a matter of conjecture, but both are useful.

By the time my senior year rolled around, I'd decided that an academic career would suit me perfectly: research was fulfilling, the intellectual stimulation was continual, and the teaching was enjoyable. Before I'd started college, I'd had little idea of what a master's or doctoral degree was. Now I'd learned that to continue in academic life, I'd need one or both of these higher degrees.

I purposely finished my fourth year a few units short of graduation, hoping that UCLA would institute a graduate program. That summer I took a trip to Berkeley and dropped in on the president of the University of California without an appointment to press on him the need for more graduate studies at the southern California campus. Robert Gordon Sproul had just begun what turned out to be a thirty-year reign in which he built UC into the greatest public university in the world. He was cordial but noncommittal to this brash student telling him how to run his university. Nearly a year later, I ran into him when he visited the UCLA campus. To my astonishment, he greeted me by name—Sproul could remember a prodigious number of faces and names, a quality that served him well in a job that required a politician's skills.

Los Angeles was home, and I was comfortable and successful at UCLA, so it seemed the right place to continue my studies. But the courses I took that year changed my mind completely. In atomic physics I learned about exciting new discoveries in nuclear science and, in particular, the ones being worked on at the growing laboratory at Berkeley. There Ernest Lawrence had invented the cyclotron, the "atom smasher" that provided an entirely new way of studying the nucleus. Nuclear studies were on the cutting edge of both chemistry and physics, and Berkeley was on the cutting edge of nuclear science. The chemistry faculty there was top-notch as well. All this immediately captured my imagination, and I set my sights on Berkeley as the place to pursue a degree.

I had an ally in one of my professors, J. B. Ramsay. Some of his students said the J.B. stood for "Justify Briefly," the standard instructions on his frequent quizzes. Almost every class, Ramsay would require us to derive a fundamental chemical equation and use it to solve a problem. His demanding approach was a tremendous influence on my intellectual development. I'd never met anyone who demanded such rigorous logic, and the principles he instilled could be applied in any endeavor.

Ramsay had received his Ph.D. from Berkeley and thus had contacts there, and he encouraged me to apply. I pointed out that simply being admitted would not be enough; I'd also need a paying job as a teaching assistant. He assured me that Berkeley would grant both these wishes. I relied on his advice and took the rather presumptuous step of not bothering to apply elsewhere. To my lingering disbelief, Ramsay was right. I was on my way to Berkeley.

# FOUR

# GRADUATE SCHOOL

# WONDERLAND

On an August evening in 1934, I took the night train from Los Angeles to Oakland. I ate breakfast at a diner near campus where they gave me my change in silver dollars—almost a sign of how magical this place was, because for me Berkeley was Wonderland. And it was a wonderful time in the field of nuclear science.

The physicist Hans Bethe has called the era before 1932 the "prehistory of nuclear physics" because that was the year that James Chadwick discovered the neutron, a particle that filled out the triad of the atom's main constituents. Unlike the positive proton and the negative electron, the neutron carries no electrical charge. Neither attracted to nor repelled by the protons or electrons, the neutron is ideal for penetrating the atom, a direct tool for affecting and studying the nucleus. Previously, a nuclear scientist's task was akin to that of a marine biologist trying to study the deep sea from a surface ship. The neutron was our equivalent of a marine biologist's submarine.

Now, two years after its discovery, scientists around the world were reporting exciting results. In France, Frédéric and Irène Joliot-Curie had used bombardment with neutrons to alter the nuclei of various elements and make them radioactive, the first time physicists had induced such a change. The Italian physicist Enrico Fermi had bombarded the heaviest natural elements with neutrons and reported new, synthetic elements. Fermi's discoveries meant scientists could actually add new elements to those found on the planet. The age-old alchemist's goal of transmuting worthless substances into gold now seemed more than a dream.

These people were exploring the fundamental building blocks of our world, the most basic manifestations of nature. Nuclear physics and nuclear chemistry were on the most exciting leading edge of knowledge; there were no limits to what we might discover. The mood of the scientific world was one of great excitement, and of all the places in that world, Berkeley had the most potential—the chemistry department was the best in the United States, and the physics department had the country's most advanced laboratory.

Also in 1932, Ernest Lawrence had unveiled the cyclotron, a machine that could accelerate the charged subatomic particles to such speeds that they could penetrate the nucleus. The particles smashing into the nucleus altered atomic structures in previously impossible ways (hence the popular name atom smasher). The cyclotron could also be used to generate a steady stream of neutrons that was much more useful than the trickles from natural sources. Lawrence's invention would earn him a Nobel Prize by the end of the decade, but he was also busy carving out an even more important place in history by building one of the greatest laboratories in the world. Displaying talents in organization and salesmanship that exceeded even his ability in science, Lawrence introduced the big-machine approach that revolutionized physics.

The texts I'd studied at UCLA had been written by Berkeley faculty members—these men were my heroes, much more than any sports or movie stars could ever be. The legendary G. N. Lewis, the greatest physical chemist of the day, had been lured west from MIT two decades before. He had brought along a well-chosen trio of professors and a smattering of graduate students, and methodically turned what many East Coast academics considered a western backwater into a powerhouse that helped make Berkeley a world-class university. Lewis put his personal stamp on the department, training chemists to his own high standards and hiring the best of them as faculty members—from 1914 to 1937, every chemistry faculty member hired had received his doctorate at Berkeley. As the university's reputation spread, it attracted top students, and Lewis had an unerring nose for talent: of the five chemistry faculty members hired in the 1930s, three would win Nobel Prizes.

Lewis' educational program relied on seminars and hands-on research; Berkeley offered no graduate courses per se. I was thrilled to sit at the same table with these great men. The intellectual stimulation was continual. It's hard to convey the excitement of just being around these people, but for months I walked about almost in a trance.

The seminars were ongoing and open to anyone. Three weekly seminars held me in thrall; they were held in the evening or late afternoon, which left the day free for research, classes, and other matters.

The week started with the Monday evening physics journal club. Ernest Lawrence presided, and he never announced in advance the topic to be discussed. You had to show up to find out whether the presentation that week would be by a world authority or by a graduate student. This approach spurred attendance and added to the anticipation, as did the extraordinary nature of the physics department.

Physicists differentiate between experimentalists and theoreticians. Few scientists manage to bridge this gap, but the Berkeley physics department had an extraordinary complementarity.

The work of Lawrence's crew at the Radiation Laboratory, centered on the cyclotron, focused almost exclusively on experiment. Their machines compiled the physical data around which theories could be built and tested the predictions of theory. In contrast, a theoretician like Albert Einstein did his work with a pencil; he worked out his theory of relativity based on knowledge, intuition, and mathematics. Einstein's theory made predictions that he left to others to verify through experiment, in some cases years later.

At Berkeley, J. Robert Oppenheimer led the theorists. Early in the twentieth century, the main action in physics had been in Europe, and Oppie had studied there with the leading physicists of the day. He was now building what would become known as the American school of physics. The charismatic personality that would bring him mainstream fame for his leadership of the Los Alamos laboratory during World War II was readily apparent. He attracted outstanding graduate students; their devotion to him was so complete that some of them actually imitated his flat-footed walk and mannerisms. For about half the year, they would follow him south to Caltech, where he held a dual appointment with Berkeley. By World War II, helped by the exodus of top scientists fleeing Hitler, the locus of theoretical physics had shifted from Europe to California.

Oppenheimer's work on the bomb overshadowed his scientific achievements, but during the 1930s he proposed some ideas so far ahead of his time that it was thirty years before they could be verified experimentally. This work was of Nobel Prize caliber, but he was not awarded this honor because the verification of the theories came after his death. Had he lived a few years longer, I believe he would have been recognized.

His mind worked almost too fast. When I needed his advice on an experiment or a question of theory, I would ponder in advance about how to present the question. Oppie had a tendency to begin answering your question before you'd finished stating it. I consciously tried to phrase my questions to get the subject out in the first few words, in hopes of getting an answer to the question I sought instead of the one Oppie assumed I was asking or the one he wanted to answer.

When Lawrence's experimentalists ran into roadblocks and conundrums, they would bring their problems to Oppie and his theorists at the seminars. There was perhaps no other institution with such a confluence of experimentalists and theorists, and their Monday evening exchanges were fascinating.

On Tuesday afternoons, G. N. Lewis presided over the chemistry research conference. Faculty members took their places around a table; graduate students, postdocs, and others sat in chairs set at two levels at the sides and back of the room.

A graduate student would open with a detailed report on a topic from the literature. Then a faculty member, research fellow, or advanced graduate student would report on the research he was conducting. There were so many discoveries being made at Berkeley that you felt you could learn as much from the seminar reports as you could from reading the journals.

But what everyone who ever attended the chemistry conference remembered was the way that G. N. Lewis dominated the room through the sheer power of his intellect, no matter what the topic. Lewis always sat in the same spot, in the first chair on the right side, facing the speaker and the blackboard. At ten minutes after four, he gruffly announced, "Shall we begin?" He chain-smoked cigars, lighting the next one off the stub of the last. His suit pocket was lined with them at the start of the hour-and-a-half meeting and empty by its end. Anyone was free to ask questions or speak, but any comments had better be well informed, because Lewis did not suffer fools gladly. We would watch in awe as he punched holes in a speaker's arguments. And anyone who tried bluff or bluster would only encourage him to redouble his attack.

Wednesday evenings, the nuclear chemistry seminar drew Lewis and the other heavy hitters of the department. Run by a young professor named Willard Libby (who would win the Nobel Prize in 1960 for his development of radioactive carbon dating), this seminar was particularly important because it focused on the field I planned to concentrate on.

In Berkeley's heady atmosphere, I couldn't get over the feeling that I'd been plucked from the minor leagues and put on a major league all-star team. The world is filled with talented prospects who can't hit the curveball—would I turn out to be one of them? Though I'd led my class at UCLA, I wondered whether a poor kid from a high school in Watts belonged among this constellation of brilliant scientists. As I had at UCLA, I resolved to work as hard as necessary to keep up; any failures would not be traced to a lack of effort. And that has proved to be the secret of whatever success I've had, if you can call such a pedestrian notion as hard work a secret. Looking back, I can say that my whole life I've been surrounded by people who are brighter than I am, and I've done my best to take advantage of having them to work with.

That fall, I took some undergraduate courses that UCLA hadn't offered and earned the price of my fellowship by teaching an introductory chemistry lab two days a week. But my first order of business was to find a faculty adviser to guide me in the research that would be the heart of my degree program.

My choices were limited to the only two chemistry professors working in the nuclear field. One's pomposity turned me off from the moment I met him, and I'd been warned away from the other one because he all but ignored his students. This warning actually attracted me to George Gibson as my adviser. I had never liked being told what to do, and I would be happy to avoid some professor's constant interference. Though the intellects at the seminars intimidated me, I felt confident in the laboratory after all those hours in the lab at UCLA. I also noticed that Gibson had one of the most impressive lists of graduate students,

students who went on to formidable accomplishments. The best students, the self-starters with ideas of their own, sought out an adviser who left them to pursue their own ideas without interference.

It was quickly evident that George Gibson was as easygoing as a professor could be. When one of his students was offered a fellowship before he'd finished his thesis research, Gibson's solution was simple: "Just write up what you have; I'm sure it will be all right." But the flip side of this easy nature was an absentminded and impractical streak that could prove ruinous to the unwary student. Gibson would periodically burst into the lab in a state of exhilaration brought on by a sudden idea. He'd want us to build a new machine that would be the next cyclotron, say. But a review of his calculations would reveal that he had left out a critical step or forgotten some factor that would change the results by an order of magnitude. Likewise, most of his suggestions for his students' research were so impractical that you could only make progress by ignoring them. Fortunately, Gibson seldom noticed when you did so. And fortunately, Gibson had a competent instructor working with him named Robert D. Fowler, who became as much my adviser as Gibson was.

The chemistry department had a single small room in Lawrence's Radiation Laboratory. Housed in an old wooden frame building, the Rad Lab was a picturesque place. The centerpiece was the 27-inch cyclotron—called 27-inch for the size of the poles of its 80-ton electromagnet. That electromagnet was the dominant feature, twice as high as a human, perhaps twelve feet long in its semicircular arch. Inside the arch was what looked like a giant wrist barbell—the kind with just enough space between the weights for your hand—or a metal spool set on its side to form a table. From the narrow neck of the spool a web of wires and cables spread out. It was in this portion that the particles were accelerated and targets set. The cyclotron ran twenty-four hours a day, with the staff serving in shifts to keep it running. The building was so full of radio waves that you could light up an electric bulb by touching it to any metal surface.

Our knowledge of nuclear science was still in its formative stages. The cyclotron ran for the first few years with no protective measures against potential radiation. In 1935, Ernest Lawrence's physician brother

John joined the Radiation Lab staff and demonstrated the penetrating and tissue-destroying power of neutrons. He insisted that the cyclotron controls be moved into another room to protect the operators, and he had the cyclotron surrounded by tanks of neutron-absorbing water.

The Rad Lab also housed two linear accelerators and several rooms in which lab benches were covered with amplifiers, ionization chambers, electroscopes, and other measurement devices. One room was crowded to overflowing with cages of mice and rats for use in biomedical experiments. Their stench could be overpowering. In a courtyard outside were the transformers and other electrical equipment required to power the cyclotron.

Amidst this chaos, Gibson and Fowler had a small proton accelerator in the chemistry department's room. I spent many hours in this little room during my first year at Berkeley, attempting to build a machine they wanted that would generate neutrons, but succeeding in building little more than experience. The main benefit of that work was the excuse it gave me to hang around the Rad Lab and get to know the researchers.

I spent an inordinate portion of that year run down with persistent colds. Apparently, my body had been too successful in adjusting from northern Michigan to southern California. Believing that my problems were caused by the change in climate from sunny Los Angeles to chilly, damp Berkeley by the Bay, I gave myself a prescription of fresh air and exercise during the summer. I worked for two months as a hand at the Pahrump Valley Ranch, an 11,000-acre dude ranch in the Nevada desert on a line between Death Valley and Las Vegas. In exchange for baling and stacking hay, the ranch gave one room and board. I returned to Berkeley feeling stronger and healthier, and determined to add regular exercise to my curriculum. I made a point of signing up for a physical education class each semester—including a turn at tap dancing. It would not be the last time I resorted to the healing power of fresh air and exercise.

Soon after the start of my second graduate school year, I struck up a partnership with a fellow student named David Grahame. Newly arrived from the University of Minnesota, Dave was extremely bright and much more skilled than I at electronics. With the same day free of classes, it was natural for us to work together, and we forged a close friendship.

In those days, our field was too new for any manufacturers to be involved; you couldn't go out and buy the equipment you required. We needed two major instruments: a source of subatomic particles to perform bombardments and a counter to measure the radiation (to trace the reactions the bombardments had caused). We would have to construct our own, and even the technical literature offered little guidance for either.

Under Fowler's able guidance, we tried many theories and configurations in our attempts to build a neutron-emitting source. When he left to take a position at Johns Hopkins, Grahame and I slowly constructed a balky instrument on our own.

We also worked on building Geiger counters, and here we faced unexpected obstacles. "We are becoming frustrated with our electronic ineptness," I wrote in my diary after six months of work. Then, later: "Electronics is a field more akin to witchcraft than to science." We were not alone in finding the work mysterious. According to my colleague Luis Alvarez, Oppenheimer maintained there were two schools of thought on the correct construction method: one school maintained that the final step before sealing off the Geiger tube was to wave a banana peel over it three times to the left; the other school held that you should wave it twice to the left, then once to the right.

We worked largely through trial and error, and in one model accidentally introduced water vapor into a vacuum tube. Water vapor is corrosive, so you would normally avoid it, but we found that it improved the counter's performance. Many other researchers must have shared our experience, because it's now a standard ingredient. Grahame and I reached version fourteen before attaining anything we considered close to usable.

In the midst of this frustration, a chance encounter put me on a fruitful new trajectory with long-term implications for my career. One April day as I was walking between the physics and chemistry buildings, Jack Livingood stopped me to ask for help with an experiment. A physicist on the Radiation Lab staff, Jack was bedeviled by the difficulty of interpreting the results of some experiments he was performing using the cyclotron. He was bombarding a target just then and asked if I would perform a chemical separation for him when it was done.

This was opportunity knocking. As I have said, the cyclotron ran twenty-four hours a day, and it couldn't come close to keeping up with all the experiments the Rad Lab researchers wanted to run. A graduate student like me couldn't have dreamed of gaining access for an experiment on his own.

The cyclotron was so revolutionary because it made it possible to study in an entirely new way reactions involving the atom's nucleus—the nuclear reaction. The history of chemistry until very recently had been almost exclusively the study of chemical reactions. Chemical reactions are not directly related to the nucleus, but are driven by the movement and sharing of electrons among atoms.

An intact atom has the same number of protons as electrons. The number and configuration of electrons affects the atom's tendency to react with other atoms. Electrons circle the nucleus in orbits called shells— and atoms that contain certain specific numbers of electrons are more stable because the electrons form a full, or "closed," shell. Atoms can join together into molecules in order to share electrons to achieve this closed-shell stability. For example, helium, element number two, is the first to have a closed shell. That's why you never encounter helium in a compound. Whereas hydrogen, element number one, is one electron shy of having a closed shell, so it is reactive. Two hydrogen atoms, each with an electron to share, can combine with an oxygen atom, two electrons shy of having a closed shell, to form one molecule of water, one of the most stable compounds known. Or sodium, with a closed shell plus one "extra" electron, combines with chlorine, short one electron, to form a closed shell in a combination we call salt.

The reactions we encounter in everyday life are chemical: salt dissolving in a glass of water and fire turning a log into smoke are the results of the atoms in molecules rearranging their electrons to form new molecular alliances. Take, for example, the combustion of methane gas (composed of carbon and hydrogen). The carbon and hydrogen in the methane combine with oxygen to form (primarily) carbon dioxide (carbon and oxygen) and water vapor (hydrogen and oxygen). Chemical reactions are driven by the rearrangement of electrons: different molecules form, but within the molecules the elements themselves don't change. In the combustion of methane, the reaction gives off energy (heat) and forms new molecules, but the molecules still contain carbon, hydrogen, and oxygen.

A nuclear reaction is fundamentally different. Rather than involving the electrons that circle the atom's nucleus, it involves the protons and neutrons of the nucleus itself. The number of protons an atom contains determines which element it is, so a change in the nucleus can change the element itself. Adding a proton to the nucleus transmutes it into the next element up in the periodic table, which changes its properties—such as its melting point, what other elements it will react with, even whether it exists mostly as a solid or a gas. (An atom without its proper complement of electrons remains the same element. For example, if you dissolve salt in water, the sodium's "extra" electron stays with the chlorine, its extra negative charge forming a negative ion, while the sodium, minus an electron, forms a positive ion.)

The number of neutrons in an atom does not affect an element's chemical properties, but it does affect the nuclear properties. If you change the number of protons in the nucleus, the identity of the element changes, but if you change the number of neutrons, the element remains the same. The same element can exist with differing numbers of neutrons in its nucleus; these variations of the same element have different atomic weights from one another and are called isotopes. For most elements, there are only one or two isotopes that are stable. The unstable nuclei emit particles and energy in various forms to move toward stability, emissions we call radioactivity; each isotope follows a characteristic radioactive decay pattern—that is, the kinds of particles and energy it emits and the time frame in which they are emitted form a kind of signature.

Before the advent of the cyclotron, a researcher might induce a nuclear reaction by exposing a target to bombardment by naturally radioactive materials. But that could be a very slow, hit-or-miss process. The cyclotron induced nuclear reactions on a scale never before possible. It accelerated positively charged subatomic particles to such great speeds that they could penetrate the nucleus. These particles—protons, deuterons (a proton and a neutron), and alpha particles (two protons and two neutrons)—smashed into the nucleus of a "target."

For many purposes, neutrons would be more effective for bombarding a target, and the cyclotron improved this process as well. You can cause certain elements to emit a steady stream of neutrons by bombarding them in the cyclotron, with these emitted neutrons in turn bombarding another target. You could filter these neutrons through paraffin wax, which would slow them down; rather than hitting a nucleus with great force, bouncing off or chipping off a part of it, a slow neutron might be absorbed into the nucleus, and once inside it, the neutron could transmute into a proton by emitting an electron, changing the nucleus to that of a different element.

Our knowledge of the nucleus was so rudimentary at this point that many experiments consisted simply of bombarding an element to study what kinds of nuclear reactions would take place and what kinds of new isotopes might be formed. This was great adventure as well as science for us. As Jack Livingood later said of this period: "It was a wonderful time. Radioactive elements fell in our laps as though we were shaking apples off a tree."

On the morning he stopped me, that's exactly the sort of experiment he was conducting: bombarding a tin target with the proton-neutron combination called a deuteron. The bombardment would be finished in about three hours, and he needed a chemical separation performed within an hour of its completion to start studying the radioactive patterns.

I thought out what I would need to do. Experience had shown that this bombardment was likely to create a radioactive form (or forms) of the tin, along with smaller portions of elements on each side of tin on the periodic table. So Jack's bombardment would form mostly radioactive tin, element 50, along with smaller portions of tin's neighbors on the periodic table—indium (element 49) and antimony (element 51). Jack needed the help of a chemist because these three products had been mixed together in a soup, from which he could not sort out meaningful results. I needed to separate the three products so he could study each element separately.

Jack gave me the target and led me to his "lab," a spartan corner room in the physics building that contained a sink, a primitive fume hood, and a workbench. I bootlegged the chemicals and equipment I'd need from the chemistry department.

The separation was straightforward. I dissolved the target in acid, then used "carriers" to separate each element expected to be present. A carrier was simply a compound that would combine with a specific element to form a solid precipitate that would drop out of the solution. I'd add the carrier for tin, then filter the solution, which would isolate the tin precipitate on the filter paper; I'd then repeat the process for indium and for antimony.

These were all simple chemical reactions, if you knew which carriers would work for tin, which for indium, and which for antimony. It was the basic qualitative chemistry that I'd spent all those hours learning at UCLA, studying and teaching with Dr. Crowell, experimenting on my own in the laboratory. Easy for a chemist, but for most physicists an unfamiliar world.

Jack then mounted the three samples on cardboard, covered them with cellophane, and studied the radiation pattern of each. From them we would deduce the new forms of the elements the bombardment had produced.

My first collaboration with Jack led to no greater discovery than some new radioactive isotopes of tin with unremarkable properties, but its personal importance was immeasurable because it opened the road to my future. Jack graciously offered to include me as co-author of an article on the experiment. "Deuteron-Induced Radioactivity in Tin," in *The Physical Review*, was my first publication. (The article was nothing to brag about. My hurried chemical separation had resulted in errors that we had to correct later.) More important, Jack's satisfaction with my work on the separation led to an informal partnership. Jack would bombard targets in the cyclotron, and I would separate them chemically; he would then follow the targets' radioactive decay using his electroscope, discovering new radioisotopes, as they are called, by discovering new radioactive decay patterns. Our collaboration lasted five years, until World War II put an end to it.

It was classic basic research, aimed simply at adding new scientific knowledge. Most of our discoveries consisted of new radioisotopes. We never knew what we would find or whether what we found would have any practical use, but sometimes we did have a specific application in mind. One of Ernest Lawrence's tactics in obtaining money to turn his lab into a world leader was to demonstrate that the results could be beneficial. And the radioactivity of the isotopes we were creating made some of them powerful tools. Isotopes of the same element behave similarly in chemical reactions, but the radioactive signals they emit give us a means of tracing them through reactions. Biomedical pioneers had already discovered how to use this characteristic to track a chemical's movement through the body. For example, if you feed someone a pill containing radioactive calcium, you can follow the calcium through the body to see whether, where, and how fast it is taken up in the bones. The technique is so powerful that you can track one hundred-millionth of an ounce of a radioactive material through the body of a thousand-pound cow.

For our second collaboration, we followed up on some work Jack had been doing with a visiting English chemist who was hoping for a longer-lived radioisotope of iron to help track hemoglobin in studies of human blood. Jack bombarded iron in the cyclotron, and in my determination to make an extremely clean separation of the iron fraction from the other products, I worked all night making repeated precipitations. I handed the samples to Jack when he came to work early in the morning, just as the sun was rising. Jack identified the isotope iron 59, which was used in experiments that opened a new era in our understanding of iron metabolism and blood formation.

One day, I ran into Joe Hamilton, one of the pioneers of nuclear medicine. Joe was using a radioisotope of iodine to study thyroid function. Nearly all the iodine the body absorbs is taken up by the thyroid, where it is critical to making the growth-regulating hormone thyroxine. He complained that the radioisotope he was using was too short-lived to be of use. It had a half-life of only 25 minutes,* not nearly long enough for it to progress through the body. When I asked Joe what half-life he would prefer, he replied, "About a week." I promised to see if such an isotope could be found.

We had no control over what we would find. You can't "design" an

---

*Each radioisotope decays in a characteristic time period, which is called a half-life. A half-life is the time it takes for half the substance to decay into something else. Say element A has a half-life of 25 minutes and you have 200 atoms of element A. After 25 minutes, there will be 100 atoms of element A left; after another 25 minutes, there will be 50 atoms; and so on.

isotope; you can only perform bombardments and see what creations natural laws allow. When I mentioned my conversation with Joe Hamilton to Jack, he was intrigued. Because iodine is element 53, he prepared targets of tellurium (element 52) and bombarded some with deuterons and some with neutrons to see what we would find. We were delighted when our separations revealed iodine 131 (the 131 refers to its atomic weight), which has a half-life of eight days.

Over time, iodine 131 turned into a workhorse of nuclear medicine. If a patient drinks a cocktail of radioactive sodium iodide, the radioactivity allows one to measure the rate at which the thyroid absorbs the iodine. This rate of uptake can reveal whether the gland is overactive, underactive, or normal. Iodine 131 can be used to locate metastatic thyroid tumors. Some of these tumors retain the thyroid's ability to synthesize thyroxine, so they take up the radioactive iodine, after which they can be found with a Geiger counter. The radioisotope can be used in similar fashion to locate some brain tumors by incorporating it into the protein serum albumin, which concentrates to a greater degree in brain tumors than in surrounding tissue.

Iodine 131 can be used in treatment as well. The diagnostic tests use infinitesimal amounts, so the patient's exposure to radiation is minimal. But amounts hundreds of times larger can be used for treatment. Because iodine naturally concentrates in the thyroid, its radiation can treat hyperthyroidism, certain goiters, and some thyroid cancers. Even in cases where the cancer has metastasized, the radioiodine can "seek out" these tumors and treat them. Iodine 131 has also been used to diagnose kidney and liver disease, to screen for pulmonary emboli, and to determine blood volume and cardiac output.

And for me, it has a very personal meaning. Doctors used it to save my own mother's life when she contracted hyperthyroidism, a disease similar to the one that killed her sister in the 1930s.

Another example of an important radioisotope Jack and I discovered is cobalt 60. Because of its radioactive properties, cobalt 60 has become a critical medical radioisotope. It emits an exceptionally intense gamma-ray radiation that focuses directly on a cancer to destroy it with little damage to surrounding tissue. Hundreds of thousands of Americans have had their cancers treated by cobalt-60 irradiation, and it is also used to sterilize medical products and equipment.

My collaboration with Jack gave me my first taste of original research, a source of great excitement and fulfillment. The experience in performing the separations turned me into something of an expert in this area of radiochemistry, to which few researchers had access. Even before I received my doctorate, our discoveries led to a steady stream of publications. But the work was always extracurricular to my teaching and degree-related research as a graduate student, and this research was proceeding much less productively.

During my third year at Berkeley, Grahame and I both had fellowships that freed us from teaching to do research full-time. Because we planned to work so closely together, I moved into the rooming house where he lived. The streets around the Berkeley campus were dotted with boardinghouses in those days. It was a respectable business for a widow raising a family and an ideal living arrangement for a bachelor like me who loved mixing ingredients in the lab but had no interest in doing so in the kitchen. For the past year and a half I'd lived three blocks from campus in the Elliott boardinghouse. A shared room with the bath down the hall and three meals a day cost me half my teaching assistantship's fifty dollars a month. Mrs. Elliott and her mother served about twenty-five boarders; the presence of her eight-year-old son and four-year-old daughter made it feel like a home. The boarders ate family style, enjoying each other's company and becoming friends. I even dated one of my fellow boarders at the Elliott boardinghouse. The rooms were spare, with a simple bed and a small desk, but most of my time was spent on campus. My roommates were all amiable, except for one fresh-air fiend who insisted on the windows being open: it didn't take many nights of shivering in the damp Berkeley chill before I found a more compatible partner.

Dave Grahame's rooming house was just across the street from campus. It had no boarding plan, but eating our meals in restaurants turned out for the best because our schedule soon took an unexpected turn. We continued to work on our neutron-emitting machine through the fall. The design required a supply of liquid air, which we were at the mercy of the machine shop to obtain. Its head, George Boies, was notoriously uncooperative with graduate students. We did whatever we could to get our machine working, including attending a Christmas-music program that George invited us to at his church. I noted in my diary: "George

Boies was obviously very pleased to see us there. We may have solved our liquid air problem."

But just when we had achieved a workable machine, a much better prospect presented itself. Professor Lewis had rented a radium-beryllium neutron source to try his hand at some nuclear experiments. The source emitted neutrons twenty-four hours a day whether used or stored, so we asked if we could use it after hours. Lewis said we could pick it up in the late afternoon, as long as we had it back in his apparatus in the morning. Working at night was a small price to pay to avoid fiddling with our own balky instrument.

In searching for thesis topics, Grahame and I noticed a paper by a Japanese scientist named Seishi Kikuchi. Kikuchi had reported an interesting effect when bombarding lead with neutrons: some of the neutrons rebounded softly off the lead, with almost all their energy dissipated, while the lead shot out energetic electrons. Kikuchi hypothesized that the phenomenon was caused by collisions between neutrons and electrons; the neutrons were hitting the lead's electrons and sending them spinning off into space. Now, a neutron colliding with an electron is equivalent to a steamroller running into a marble. Kikuchi was proposing that the steamroller bounced slowly off the marble, transferring almost all its energy to the marble. A marble that flew off faster than a bullet would still not contain nearly so much energy as the steamroller. Kikuchi's explanation was inconceivable to us, so we decided to replicate his experiment.

Lewis had rented a 200-milligram lump of radium mixed with beryllium. The radioactive radium rammed alpha particles into the beryllium, which knocked free a steady stream of neutrons. We simply placed lead and other metals close enough to this source to be bombarded by neutrons under a variety of conditions, then measured the radiation the bombardment caused.

We began our experiments in the chemistry department's small room in the Radiation Laboratory, but all the stray neutrons from the other experiments and apparatus there made accurate measurements impossible. Even in a room in the Chemistry Annex, the natural scattering of neutrons from the walls interfered with our measurements. We built a frame to hold our counter outside a window, but that setup proved impractical. Eventually, we found the cavernous auditorium of East Hall, an abandoned building where we could operate far from any interfering walls.

Our research consisted of long bombardments followed by painstaking measurements on our counters. We brought in a cot and often worked all night, taking turns napping or walking around the corner to the White Tavern, where we could get a snack of Boston baked beans and brown bread for fifteen cents or coffee and doughnuts for a nickel. On Friday evenings, I'd even take a date to the movies, then return for a night of work at the laboratory.

The lead we bombarded gave off the same electron radiation that Kikuchi described, but we came up with a very different explanation for it. The neutrons were colliding not with electrons but with the *nucleus*, and this transferred energy to the nucleus and excited the atom to a higher energy level; the atom returned to its normal energy state through the act of shooting out an electron. The discovery was beyond theoretical explanation at the time.

Some time after we'd published our results, Kikuchi sent us a charming letter acknowledging his mistake that began, "We are so ashamed of us." (Kikuchi went on to head the Japanese Atomic Energy Commission.) Many years later, a member of his research team told me he'd known that Kikuchi had to be wrong, but a Japanese student simply did not challenge a teacher. That ethos is, I believe, the antithesis of science, where progress requires that the issue be not "who's right" but "what's right," and was in stark contrast to an experience I had that spring.

I was walking past Professor Lewis' laboratory one afternoon when he called me in to ask my opinion of some surprising results he was getting in experiments using that radium-beryllium source. He thought he was focusing the neutrons, that the paraffin wax he was using to slow the neutrons was acting as a lens. Everyone used paraffin, and nobody had found that it focused neutrons, so his interpretation didn't make sense. I had to summon my courage, literally swallow hard, and tell him I thought he was mistaken. I suggested that the same stray neutrons from the surroundings that had caused so much trouble for Dave Grahame and me were causing spurious results in his experiments, that he was in fact being affected by neutrons scattering rather than focusing. As Grahame and I had done, Lewis later repeated his experiment outside. Away from the neutrons scattering from the walls and ceilings, he could not replicate his results.

It took me only a couple of weekends to write my thesis, "The Interaction of Fast Neutrons with Lead." Its nineteen pages would amount to little more than a long footnote in today's theses of two to four hundred pages. Today you have to search long and hard to find a manageable problem, small enough to solve, on increasingly specialized topics with increasingly extensive literature reviews. Life was easier when the field was so new that there was little literature to review. And no one on my review committee was so crass as to point out that my thesis had nothing to do with chemistry; the subject was entirely within the domain of physics. But Berkeley was unconcerned about such crossovers, and it presented me with a doctorate in chemistry in May 1937.

A month later my fellowship and sole means of support expired. I had no idea what I would do next, my only plans a vague hope of landing a position at Berkeley, though none had been offered or appeared forthcoming. I wanted desperately to stay on, and I continued to come to the lab every day as if my fellowship hadn't expired. Dave Grahame and I continued our neutron studies. Jack Livingood and I had bombarded seven additional elements while I was completing my thesis research, and we looked forward to more.

The research was so absorbing that I didn't dwell on worries about the future. I just wanted to continue there as long as I could. Stanley Thompson, my friend from high school and UCLA, was now living in the Bay Area, working as a control chemist at Standard Oil. Just as he had at UCLA, Stan came to my rescue again with another small loan. I certainly hadn't saved money on my fellowship income, and how long I could continue without finding a job was a question I didn't want to think about.

# FIVE

# APPRENTICE TO

# A MASTER CHEMIST

G. N. Lewis, the "Chief," the cigar-chomping dean of the College of Chemistry, was Berkeley's main gatekeeper for chemistry positions. Any schools hoping to recruit a promising chemistry graduate for a faculty opening would contact Lewis. Lewis had not recommended me for any such jobs, and I didn't know whether that was a very bad sign, that he thought I didn't make the grade, or a very good sign, that he was considering keeping me at Berkeley. Lewis had been on my thesis committee, so he probably knew me better than he did the average graduate student.

Two weeks after my fellowship expired, Lewis had still not said a word to me about my future. Then one day he summoned me to his office, and to my complete surprise asked me to be his personal research assistant. Lewis was unique in having such a full-time assistant. Caught completely off guard, I asked if he really thought I could handle the job. With a smile, he replied that he wouldn't have offered it if he had any doubts.

I never knew why the Chief singled me out for this honor, but I suspect that the advice I'd given on his neutron experiments influenced him, whether because my assessment had been correct or because I'd had the courage to disagree with his interpretation. The two-year appointment would be a detour from my goal of working in the nuclear field, but it was an incredible opportunity to work with the greatest physical chemist in the world.

Lewis has never received the recognition he deserves, even in the scientific community; he is perhaps the greatest scientist ever snubbed by the Nobel committee. Lewis' contributions to chemistry were remarkably wide-ranging. He developed the theory of the importance to chemical reactions of valence electrons—the electrons in the outer shell of an atom—and how atoms join to form molecules when these valence electrons pair together in what are called covalent bonds. He invented an elegantly simple notation, still in common use, of representing valence electrons as dots around the chemical symbol of an element, which shows at a glance what electrons are available to react and thus what kinds of reactions are likely for this element. His text on thermodynamics showed how this entire discipline, once the exclusive domain of physicists, applied theoretically and practically to chemistry. And, as I'll relate in this chapter, he changed and expanded our understanding of acids and bases.

Lewis came to Berkeley when it was still a raw, unrecognized university, and was content to stay there, an ocean and a continent away from the luminaries of Europe. He preferred the quiet of his laboratory to the traveling, giving visiting lectures, and networking at conferences that bring a scientist's name regularly before the establishment elite. Although there is a popular notion that scientists can campaign to win a Nobel Prize, such campaigns have little hope of success unless based on genuine research achievements. Just the same, the committee must choose from an entire world of successful researchers. Participation in the activities of the larger scientific community brings you to their attention.

A network of friendly colleagues can advance recognition of your work, and in this respect, Lewis' approach was the opposite of productive. His fame was such that others sought him out at Berkeley, but he could be a most ungracious host. Even when eminent visitors were invited to present their latest theories, Lewis would not attenuate his customary domination of the Tuesday research conferences. He was relentless in his quest fully to understand an issue, and his questions could resemble a lawyer's cross-examination. If he detected any hot air, he would poke whatever holes it took to release it. Lewis would sniff out any attempt to filibuster like a dog scenting fear, and hold on to his quarry with the tenacity of a bulldog. His barbed questions and fast retorts could reduce even the brightest visitors to an embarrassed, even humiliated, state.

The Lewis treatment alienated more than a few influential scientists. In those days, the Nobel committee sent telegrams to prominent people to test the names of nominees, and there must have been too many dissensions from Lewis' victims.

Some people were afraid even to speak at the research conference. Only a handful of professors showed no fear or hesitation in taking Lewis on, such as the future dean, Wendell Latimer, who played a great role in my career. Lewis never held it against anyone who argued with him, but the very fact that so many hesitated illustrates his power.

I was a twenty-five-year-old newly minted Ph.D., and I worried about my ability. Having witnessed Lewis' refusal to suffer fools, I wondered how miserable he would make my life if I didn't measure up as his assistant. His dominating presence at the seminars had made me tremendously nervous whenever my turn came to make a presentation. For my first talk I studied the subject as intensely as I could. Thorough preparation was my trademark, but for this I redoubled my efforts. I sat quietly, asked myself every question I could conceive of, and ran over the answers until I figured I'd covered every imaginable issue. I made my presentation, then turned to Lewis for his traditional opening question. To my chagrin, he came up with one I couldn't come close to answering. Rather than try to bluff my way through, I simply admitted the fact, a response Lewis had no problem accepting.

To my astonishment, Lewis' aggressive seminar tone never once appeared in our work together. I don't recall a single harsh word during our two-year association, even when I might have deserved it. One morning, after an evening's overindulgence in alcohol, I needed to steady my right hand with my left when turning a stopcock on our vacuum line. When Lewis noticed my difficulty, he suggested with a wry grin that I go back to my room to "rest" a while. When I returned that afternoon, we resumed work without a word of censure. Lewis treated me as if he valued my opinions and had confidence in my ability, which did a great deal to build my self-esteem.

The Chief was a colorful character, amiably gruff, with an ironic wit. He had been strikingly handsome as a young man, and was a good-looking sixty-two when I worked for him, his head topped with a shock of white hair set off by a full white mustache. An Alhambra Casino cigar was his constant companion. I noted in my journal that it was "rather amusing to see him eat [breakfast at the Faculty Club] as he places his ever present lighted cigar down beside his plate." A rumor held that the manufacturer threatened to discontinue that cigar model unless he increased his order, which he agreed to double. When he was preparing once to travel to Philadelphia to lecture and demonstrate some experiments, I was happy to see that he brought two large suitcases to the laboratory—there would be ample room for me to pack the glassware and chemicals he'd need. But then he filled one suitcase and part of the other with boxes of cigars. It took all my ingenuity to fit the equipment into the space he left.

As his assistant, I took advantage of my eligibility to move into the Men's Faculty Club. Our workdays soon began to follow a regular pattern. Lewis would arrive each morning between ten and eleven. When I saw his green Dodge appear on the road between the chemistry building and the Faculty Club I would go down to join him in the lab. We'd work together until noon or one, when he'd head for the Faculty Club to play cards, usually his favorite game of hearts, while I ate lunch. We'd then work together until the late afternoon. At times he gave me assignments to assemble materials and prepare solutions during the noon hour, overnight, or when he left town for a day or two. He regularly underestimated the time these tasks required, and I had to scramble to meet his deadlines. Sometimes we'd work during the evening after dinner, often on Saturday morning, and occasionally on Sunday. (When we needed equipment from the machine shop, I was amused to see how cooperative its head had suddenly become.) This schedule left me free to continue my other research in the early morning, at lunch, in the evening, and during the breaks Lewis took from research. I took every opportunity to continue working with Dave Grahame and Jack Livingood; I believe Lewis expected as much.

I've often been asked which scientist among the many I've known was the greatest, and I can say without hesitation that Lewis was one of the two. (The other was Enrico Fermi, but he comes later in the story.) From his brilliance in the seminars to his research contributions, I've never met anyone quite like him.

Across the street from the chemistry building where Lewis and I worked, Ernest Lawrence had his Radiation Laboratory, where he was pioneering the style that would become known as Big Science. Lawrence's research depended on complex instruments, machines too large to be built and handled by a single researcher, and interdisciplinary teams. Lewis eschewed such complexity. He concentrated on elegant, uncomplicated experiments that he could perform with a single assistant. From his simple experiments he would deduce growing cascades of information.

Most of our experiments consisted of mixing together relatively common chemicals to observe how their colors changed, what precipitates they formed, how they acted when heated—experiments simple enough to be performed in any college chemistry lab with test tubes, beakers, and a Bunsen burner. But from such rudimentary materials Lewis redefined our conception of what constituted acids and bases. The development of a new generalized theory of acids and bases was his primary interest during my tenure with him. At that time, in order to be considered an acid a substance had to contain hydrogen, while a base contained a hydroxide (OH) molecule. Lewis greatly broadened the definitions.

A typical series of our experiments went something like this. We used acetone as our solvent, a medium in which we would dissolve other chemicals to see how they reacted. We first dissolved in the acetone an indicator dye such as thymol blue; a color change would indicate that an acid or base had been added. When we dissolved a chloride of tin, the dye's color changed to red, indicating the presence of an acid. But we obtained an identical red color when, instead of the chloride of tin, we dissolved boron trichloride, sulfur dioxide, or silver perchlorate, none of which contained any hydrogen and so could not meet the then current definition of an acid. And when we added chemicals such as pyridine or triethylamine to the acetone and dye, the color changed to yellow, indicative of bases, though neither fit the then current definition of a base.

Lewis demonstrated that the compounds that acted like acids had something in common with hydrogen—they could "accept" and share an electron or electrons to fill out their outer electron shells—and the bases shared the common trait of having "excess" electrons to donate. The more restrictive definition of an acid had required the presence of hydrogen, which is an electron acceptor. But Lewis showed that the basis of the reactions we were getting in our experiments was the property that hydrogen had in common with other elements: that of accepting a shared electron. He similarly expanded the definition of a base to include any molecule that could donate an electron to be shared.

This theory was yet another application of Lewis' earlier concept of the importance of electrons as the source of molecular bonding: certain numbers of electrons make for stability, and by sharing electrons to fill out electron shells, atoms can form stable molecules. Lewis' theory still holds today, and the class of chemicals he identified and defined are called Lewis acids and bases.

Of course, we did many other experiments, but they were not much more complicated. Sometimes we added an acid to the acetone-dye mixture, then a base, to see how the two reacted. Sometimes we used a stopwatch to measure the rates of reaction, as shown by color changes. We might repeat the experiment over a wide range of temperatures to see what effects that had. Lewis used the data to extend his theory to a new concept, that of primary and secondary acids and bases. Primary acids and bases reacted on their own with no heat added; secondary acids and bases had similar properties, but required the addition of heat to the system to get a reaction going.

For me, working with Lewis was like receiving an additional degree in the craft of research from a master. I marveled at the way he could plan the next logical step toward our goal. His systematic approach taught me how to break a huge problem down into solvable parts, a lesson very valuable in my later work on the Manhattan Project.

From these simple experiments he made powerful deductions, such as how the electrons rearranged among the molecules, which led to successively more sophisticated conclusions upon which he built his generalized theory on acids and bases, a theory still valid and useful today.

We wrote up the findings in several papers, a process he liked to reserve for the quiet of Sunday afternoons. He would pace back and forth from one end of the laboratory to the other, smoking his ever-present cigar and methodically dictating to me while I took it all down in longhand. Lewis composed carefully in his head, with a beautiful control of language. Each sentence emerged clearly and carefully framed, part of an articulate whole that scarcely required editing.

Periodically I would inject editorial comments, and he frequently interrupted the writing to discuss how to make a particular point, which evidence was best to use to back up an assertion, and other matters. The act of formulating his thoughts in order to set them down on paper brought to mind many small experiments that might confirm his hypotheses, and then we would suspend the writing and get out the test tubes. So the process of composition was long and laborious.

We had completed two papers in this fashion when Lewis said he was tired of the procedure and asked me to write the abstract for the second paper. I worked hard at this, and Lewis accepted what I wrote without change and with scarcely a glance at it. This signal of confidence made a lasting impression; it gave me a significant boost to think that I was holding my own with the greatest physical chemist in the world.

The papers I wrote with Lewis were so far from my later life's work that chemists who come across them sometimes ask me if there was another Seaborg who did research in acids and bases.

In addition to his research program, Lewis shouldered heavy administrative burdens as dean of the College of Chemistry and chairman of the chemistry department. He managed to discharge his duties—making teaching assignments, hiring, budgeting, and everything else involved in running a college—almost entirely from his laboratory, often in the middle of one of our experiments. His efficient secretary, Mabel Kittredge, undoubtedly deserved much of the credit for the smoothness of the operation. She would come into the laboratory, stand poised with her notebook, and when she had his attention concisely describe the issue that required his decision. He would either answer immediately or ask her to come back after he had given the matter some thought.

Running a department from a laboratory would be unheard of today. And even in those less bureaucratized times, only an administrator as brilliant as Lewis could manage it. The demonstrated effectiveness of decisiveness and of delegation was one more meaningful lesson I learned from my two years with Lewis.

Shortly before my research assistantship expired, in early June 1939, Lewis told me he was putting me on the chemistry department faculty as an instructor starting July 1. He gave me full faculty credit for my work with him and started me at the salary of a third-year instructor. His offer was not framed as a question or an invitation—he assumed it was what I wanted. The Chief said it was time for me to move on because, as he put it in his wry way, he had been "taking up too much" of my time. The assistantship was supposed to be a full-time job, but I had four research partnerships going in my spare moments.

Dave Grahame and I continued studying the scattering of neutrons until he left Berkeley in the fall of 1939 for a job teaching chemistry at Amherst College, in Massachusetts. Dave shifted from nuclear to traditional chemistry because he feared that the nuclear field's requirement of expensive equipment meant jobs that were fewer and harder to find. With my passion for radiochemistry, such a fear was no deterrent.

Jack Livingood had taken a job at Harvard in the fall of 1938, but we continued to collaborate. We would correspond to agree on an experiment, then I would have the bombardment made, separate the samples, and mail them to Jack. In those days, I could simply put the radioactive samples in an envelope and drop them in the mailbox. Even during his move, Jack didn't miss a measurement on his electroscope. Today, that electroscope is one of my most treasured possessions.

About the time that Livingood departed, a graduate student named Joe Kennedy appeared. Joe had come to me at a loss—George Gibson, his professor, had assigned him one of those quixotic Gibsonian tasks that wouldn't work under the current laws of physics: to build an accelerator all by himself. A desperate Joe asked me for guidance. I suggested he sort out a vexing conundrum that Jack Livingood and I had encountered concerning the isotopes of the element tellurium. Joe solved the problem brilliantly, but when it came time to write it up as a thesis, he wondered: How would he tell Gibson he had done this research in place of the project assigned to him? "Don't tell him anything," I counseled. "Just write it up and present it to him. He'll probably think he thought of the project himself." Sure enough, Gibson complimented Joe's work and accepted it unquestioningly.

In the summer of 1938, Emilio Segrè had joined the Radiation Lab as a research fellow. Segrè already had quite a résumé. He'd been on the brilliant Enrico Fermi's research team, where he and a colleague had discovered element 43, technetium, filling one of only two holes in the periodic table below uranium. Segrè had actually made the discovery from material Ernest Lawrence had sent him from the Rad Lab after an earlier visit Segrè had made. Lawrence had mailed Segrè some copper and molybdenum that had been part of the cyclotron, thus indiscriminately bombarded with neutrons for long periods. In this material, Segrè discovered element 43, the result of the transmutation of molybdenum, element 42. It was typical of Lawrence to be generous in spreading the benefits of his invention instead of reserving the analysis and discovery for his own laboratory.

Segrè arrived for this second temporary appointment around the time that Mussolini began promulgating anti-Semitic laws. A Jew, Segrè sent for his wife and son to join him and to build a new life in America. He was familiar with my publications with Livingood, and we agreed to collaborate on some research into the isotopes of element 43. We found an isotope that had an interesting radioactive decay pattern, emitting intense, short-lived gamma rays.

Gamma rays are an extremely penetrating radiation form. Rather than consisting of particles, like alpha and beta radiation, they are electromagnetic photons, like light. We identified this isotope as technetium 99, which eventually became a mainstay of nuclear medicine because of its intense radiation and came into widespread use for diagnostic imaging involving thyroid, bone, liver, spleen, lung, brain, kidney, and cardiovascular disorders. Most hospitals now have in-house machines that bombard molybdenum to generate technetium 99.

But the medical uses did not come into play until twenty-five years after our discovery. At the time, the isotope greatly intrigued us because of its unusual decay pattern and other properties. Gamma rays originate from a transition in energy levels in the nucleus, such as occurs after emission of an alpha or beta particle, and we identified technetium 99's radiation as caused by a hitherto unknown phenomenon involving these energy state transitions.

Ernest Lawrence showed our paper to Robert Oppenheimer, who declared we must be mistaken. Our interpretation deviated too far from accepted theory; we must have made an error in our measurements or interpretation. Lawrence told us to delay our paper's publication until we could make additional measurements. Segrè and I had already submitted the article to *The Physical Review*, so I sent a telegram requesting that it be withdrawn from publication. Within a couple of weeks, *The Physical Review* ran a paper by a former Segrè colleague in Italy, Bruno Pontecorvo, that described the same phenomenon in a different isotope. Lawrence then agreed that we could resubmit our own findings, but we had missed out on credit for the discovery.

I relate the story here because it illustrates many points—from Oppenheimer's cocksure confidence to the workings of the Radiation Laboratory, beginning with the relationship between Lawrence and Oppenheimer.

The two had been fast friends since the day Oppenheimer had joined the faculty, though they appeared an odd, contrasting couple. Oppie in those days had wild, curly dark hair and a nervous slenderness even to his thin beak of a nose. He was an Easterner who had benefited from the educational opportunities of growing up in a well-to-do Jewish family. He'd had a well-rounded education that led to interests to match and had done his graduate work overseas. Trust-fund money enabled him to live in a fashion that made him seem rich to the rest of us on academic salaries. Lawrence was the solid, clean-cut, middle-class Midwesterner, with his hair neatly swept back from his forehead and always in place, rimless glasses framing a fair, Scandinavian, youthful face. His education and interests focused closely on science. Whatever their contrasts, the two greatly enjoyed each other's company.

And they complemented each other perfectly, with separate hegemonies in the physics department, Lawrence leading the experimentalists and Oppie the theorists. There was no need for the rivalry that often complicates such relationships at universities and research laboratories; it was in everyone's interest to work together.

By the late 1930s, Lawrence had largely turned from being a hands-on physicist to being a hands-on administrator. After designing the cyclotron, most of his energy went to maximizing the value of his invention and subsequent refinements and variations. He excelled at running the lab, and he contributed as much to physics in this role as he did as a researcher.

Lawrence pioneered the team research that is the rule today. There had been a tradition, almost a pride, that an academic scientist used only the tools he could make himself. Lawrence's introduction of engineering and technology into the basic science laboratory and the new problems being tackled necessitated a different approach. The cyclotron demanded a large team; Lawrence even introduced shift work to keep it running constantly. At the Rad Lab, researchers specialized to the extent of developing expertise in their own favorite types of radiation counters. (The specialization arrived with perfect timing for me, because I could always work with an expert who could make up for my weak point of instrumentation.)

Teamwork had the additional benefit of being enormously stimulating intellectually. The different strengths, ideas, and approaches of each member gave the team a synergistic power. And Lawrence's approach brought together teams concerned not only with solving particular problems but with crossing disciplines to apply discoveries. His laboratory brought together physicists, chemists, biologists, physicians, engineers, and agricultural scientists. We might discover a radioisotope with nothing more in mind than its intrinsic interest, but the physician might be able to put it to use. In time, the laboratory's achievements affected a large number of disciplines. Lawrence's approach from the beginning was that the laboratory would need to show some practical applications of its work for him to get the funding the laboratory needed.

In Lawrence's Big Science, the cyclotrons were growing ever larger and more powerful, the first steps toward even more sophisticated machines that required what were then astronomical sums for science, especially for an esoteric field such as physics. He was responsible for raising this money, and he was uniquely qualified for this responsibility because he was an incredible salesman. His enthusiasm for physics discoveries and for his lab was contagious, and foundations and men of wealth found him hard to resist. He could work a room like the best politician. The only person I've met who could be more persuasive in a small-group, face-to-face conversation was Lyndon Johnson. And, like Johnson, Lawrence was a poor speaker in front of a large audience. His voice rose an octave; he fidgeted and lost his train of thought.

His sales ability grew naturally out of an inexhaustible energy and boundless enthusiasm that astounded all who worked with him. Discoveries made by others in his laboratory made him as joyful as if he'd made them himself, perhaps a reflection of the belief he'd once put forward: "There is no greater work than research, and no finer title than professor of physics." His overflowing enthusiasm and skillful direction of the laboratory made him a natural leader. His faith in himself and the people around him was inspirational.

Lawrence took full advantage of his opportunities. As his fame grew and other universities tried to lure him away, he used their offers as leverage with the University of California to increase support for the Rad Lab. That was quite a feat during the Depression, when budgets were stretched so thin. Even then, the budget couldn't always cover all the staff positions, but such was the loyalty and enthusiasm he inspired that some Radiation Lab staff members of more independent means worked for long periods without compensation.

The Nobel Prize that Lawrence won in 1939 was doubly important because the scientific significance of the cyclotron had been questioned by some leading scientists, who saw it as all sizzle and no steak. Lawrence quickly leveraged the Nobel fame into one and a half million dollars in grants to build a new, larger cyclotron. Just the same, some of that criticism was justified; the laboratory had not attained its scientific potential. The biggest scientific discoveries of the 1930s were of artificial radioactivity and fission; although Rad Lab scientists were in perhaps the best position of anyone in the world to notice the evidence for them, they had misinterpreted it, an almost scandalous failure.

Several staff members later wrote of their frustrations with the regime of that time. They thought the focus seemed to be more on the act of keeping the cyclotron running than on the reason for keeping it running. A tremendous amount of staff time was spent on mechanical aspects, even at the expense of conceiving and executing the experiments the machine was built to run. Lawrence kept a tight rein over the research projects, running the laboratory with an iron hand. Some scientists left because of his heavy-handedness, or because the emphasis on the machine kept them from doing physics. But most of us recognized that it was Lawrence, his invention, and his skill as an administrator that enabled us to do the work we loved. No one else could have combined his physics with his salesmanship. He earned his leadership position and was easy to follow. And we respected his fairness.

So when Lawrence questioned the results of our experiments with technetium 99, Segrè and I accepted it, even though we were confident that our measurements and conclusions were correct. It was harder on Segrè than it was on me. He'd been a professor in charge of his own team in Italy and was unaccustomed to being told what to do. But he was not recognized as a top-flight physicist, like his colleague Fermi. He was trying to make his mark in a new country, and a new discovery would help to establish his reputation and make him marketable. Segrè protested to the limits he thought wise, given that he was also dependent on Lawrence as a patron.

I was unhappy because this could have turned out to be the only discovery of consequence of my career. But there was nothing to be gained by arguing. For a postdoc without portfolio in Lawrence's lab, the wisest course was to go along and to stay in Lawrence's good graces; loyalty was something Lawrence valued highly.

As it turned out, Segrè and I would both soon be in the thick of making discoveries that would make this one look small.

# SIX

# THE ATOM SPLITS

✦ The Faculty Club offered a wonderfully convenient and stimulating environment. A large collection of bachelors on the staffs of
the Rad Lab and the chemistry department lived there: Don Cooksey,
Ernest Lawrence's second-in-command; Ernest's brother John; and
Melvin Calvin, who would win the 1961 Nobel Prize in chemistry for his
work using carbon 14 to elucidate the chemical pathways of photosynthesis. We often congregated for lunch at the Radiation Laboratory table,
joined by Ernest Lawrence and others. The arrangement gave us plenty
of time to discuss research projects and share problems and solutions.

Many of us were close friends as well as colleagues. Joe Kennedy, the
rangy, engaging Texan whom I'd helped with his thesis problem, was
hired as an instructor at about the same time I was, and we became inseparable. On most Saturday nights, Joe and I would descend on Melvin
Calvin's room before dinner for a couple of highballs, then repair to the
dining room in a happy mood, the alcohol giving me enough courage to
flirt with the student waitresses. I envied Melvin for asking some of the
more attractive ones out on dates, which I never had the courage to do.

Joe was a contrarian who loved argument, so much so that it amused
him to take the opposite side of any proposition you might put forward,
from politics to science. After I grew accustomed to this quirk, I would
often avoid an argument when I opened a subject by propounding the
opposite of what I really thought. When Joe argued against me, I would
concede, "Gee, I guess you're right."

After an evening in the lab, Joe and I spent many late nights shooting the breeze in the Varsity, a coffee shop. A favorite topic was the surprising new discoveries in our field. Many of these discoveries didn't add up, and we could talk for hours trying to make sense of them. At the center of our discussions were the new elements that had been discovered, elements called "transuranium" because they were heavier than uranium, the heaviest element found in nature. Enrico Fermi's team in Italy had bombarded uranium with neutrons, and Geiger counters revealed that the uranium then emitted electrons. Where did these electrons come from? Fermi's obvious conclusion was that the uranium nuclei were capturing neutrons, and these neutrons were transmuting to protons by emitting electrons. That process would change uranium, element 92, to a heretofore unknown element 93. When he tested his suspected element for characteristics such as half-life and pattern of radioactive decay, it seemed to form a unique signature.

Fermi's next step was to perform chemical tests on his target. When Jack Livingood and I had bombarded tin, element 50, we'd expected to form isotopes of elements 49, 50, and 51. It would be very unusual and unexpected to find anything farther away on the periodic table. Fermi took this same approach: he used chemical separations to prove that the material produced in the bombardment was not an element near uranium on the periodic table, such as elements 90, 89, or 88; after these tests were successful, Fermi deduced that the newly synthesized material must be element 93. He found other transuranic elements in similar fashion.

I recall only one paper that challenged Fermi's conclusions, written by the German chemist Ida Noddack. Noddack suggested that it wasn't enough to separate the element from its neighbors on the periodic table. Before claiming he'd found a new element, Fermi should separate it from *all* the other elements on the periodic table. She was technically right, but as a practical matter no one thought it was necessary to do this. Noddack suggested Fermi needed to check if his element 93 was a much *lighter* element, for the uranium might have split in two—and no one could take that suggestion seriously. We all knew it was impossible for uranium atoms to break apart in such a manner.

The largest pieces that had ever been split off from a nucleus were alpha particles, which were the size of a helium nucleus (two protons and two neutrons); knocking them loose required great energy. If you hit a car-size boulder with a pick, you may chip off a piece, but you won't split the boulder into two halves. A neutron breaking a nucleus in two would be like a thrown rock breaking a boulder. And at the time that Fermi did this work, our model of the nucleus was that it was like a single particle.

In addition, we were much more likely to take Fermi's word over Noddack's. Noddack's record was mixed. Though she'd done some very good work, she'd also made some bad mistakes. In contrast, Enrico Fermi was already marked for greatness, with several significant discoveries under his belt.

Still, Fermi's work on the transuranics did not sit well. In addition to the question of chemical separations, the other avenue of studying nuclear reactions was to track the radioactive decay pattern of each isotope formed. Each isotope decays in its own characteristic fashion. For example, iodine 131 has a half-life of eight days; its radioactivity is manifested in the form of gamma rays and electrons with a maximum energy of 0.9 million electron volts (MeV). You won't run into iodine 131 with a half-life of eleven days or twenty-nine days, and you won't find iodine 131 emitting alpha particles.

But Fermi found more than one radioactive pattern associated with each isotope he discovered. Some isotopes, called isomers, do have more than one decay pattern, but they are extremely rare. Before Fermi began discovering transuranics, there were only two or three isomers among the 92 known elements. However, for Fermi's scheme of transuranium elements to work he had to keep adding isomers. And when others replicated his work bombarding uranium, again the number of half-lives and patterns seemed to multiply dazzlingly.

In addition, the way these transuranics decayed was topsy-turvy. A radioactive nucleus normally decays toward more stability; that's the point of the decay. In heavy elements, a neutron may change to a proton, thereby moving one step up the periodic table. But Fermi's new elements were decaying two and three steps up the table, and in ways that made them less, rather than more, stable.

There's always resistance to a new paradigm. The drive to make experimental results fit accepted theory was so strong that some of the best scientists in the world twisted their interpretations in ways that in retrospect look ridiculous. Irène and Frédéric Joliot-Curie, a Nobel Prize on their shelf for their discovery of artificially induced radioactivity, bombarded uranium with neutrons and separated out a substance that had all the chemical characteristics of lanthanum, element 57. The substance was so similar to lanthanum that they couldn't separate the two. By any normal definition, that meant that the substance was lanthanum. But they were so certain bombarding uranium couldn't result in an element twenty-five spaces down the periodic table that they announced that they'd found another transuranium element with the same chemical characteristics as lanthanum.

These puzzles were fodder for Kennedy and me to chew on late into the night. I made myself a minor expert on these transuranium elements. I had reread and studied every article even tangentially related to the subject. As early as 1936, I'd presented a talk at the chemistry research conference covering the work of Otto Hahn, Lise Meitner, and Fritz Strassmann. Hahn was the undisputed world leader in radiochemistry; his book *Applied Radiochemistry* was my bible. My talk covered their work on the elements 93, 94, 95, and 96, which they'd studied after bombarding uranium.

Although Fermi had made several other contributions that would have qualified him, the Nobel committee recognized him for his work on transuranium elements in December 1938. The timing was not simple happenstance. War was looming in Europe; Mussolini was doing Hitler's anti-Semitic bidding; and Fermi's wife was Jewish. The quip around the Rad Lab was "Now we'll see if he deserved the prize—let's see how smart he really is," meaning "Would he find a way out of Italy?" He did. He already had a "temporary" seven-month appointment at Columbia University arranged. What a coincidence that a stay of more than six months in the United States required an immigrant rather than a tourist visa; Fermi could bypass the quotas to qualify for an immigrant visa as an academic. He and his family went to Stockholm to collect the prize and then sailed directly for America.

Just a month later, at the weekly physics journal club meeting, I heard the startling news that would turn our field upside down. The German chemists Hahn and Strassmann had revisited this transuranium work, once again bombarding uranium and performing extremely careful chemical separations. Their separations indicated the presence of elements far down the periodic table, including the lanthanum the Joliot-Curies had found, as well as barium (element 56) and iodine. They were torn between the results they had obtained as chemists and the impossibility of what these results implied about the nucleus breaking into pieces. Their paper contained this disclaimer: "As nuclear chemists, being in some respects close to physics, we have not yet been able to take this leap, which contradicts all previous experiences in nuclear physics."

The physicist who had worked with Hahn and Strassmann for years, Lise Meitner, was another Jew who had been hounded out of Germany. From asylum in Sweden, she and her nephew, Otto Frisch, came up with a remarkable explanation of what was happening in the nucleus.

Protons are positively charged, and like charges repel, so protons should repel. But when packed as tightly as they are in a nucleus, an attractive force called the nuclear strong force comes into play. The nuclear strong force closely binds the protons and neutrons. In our experience, the nuclear strong force could not be broken, except in cases such as when a particle accelerated in a cyclotron gave the nucleus a huge jolt of energy.

But we'd all overlooked another factor: the nuclear strong force operates over extremely short distances, even relative to the tiny scale of the atom. As the nucleus gets bigger, with more and more protons, the protons are farther apart, and the repulsive strength grows in comparison with the nuclear strong force. At some point, the two forces could equalize. No one had realized that this might be why we had found no elements in nature with more protons than uranium's 92.

In the years after Fermi's first work with neutrons on uranium, our understanding of the nucleus had changed from the single-particle model to the liquid-drop model, which described the nucleus as analogous to a drop of water. The mutual attraction of water molecules pulls them together, creating the surface tension that holds together a raindrop. Each molecule is attracted to a matrix of surrounding molecules, just as each nucleon (a term that encompasses both protons and neutrons) is attracted to the surrounding nucleons, creating complexly interconnected forces of attachment that are difficult to rend. A nucleus would be no more likely to tear in two than a piece of putty dropped from a roof or shot with a bullet.

But there's a limit to the size of a water drop. And if you disturb a drop of water—add energy to it by shaking it or add more water to it—it might start to oscillate; as it jiggles, two ends that look like the ends of a barbell may form and, as the attractions within the new droplets intensify, the droplets pull apart into two new drops. This process was essentially what was happening to the uranium nucleus. A neutron colliding with the nucleus gave it energy, in some cases just enough to tip the balance in favor of the repulsive forces and split the nucleus. Frisch borrowed a term from biology for the process—fission, for its resemblance to the way a living cell splits to reproduce itself.

Our first inkling of this astounding new discovery was in a brief article in the San Francisco *Chronicle*. The physicist Luis Alvarez came across it while leafing through the paper in a barber's chair. The news was so exciting that he left the barber's chair in mid-snip and took off at a dead run for the Radiation Laboratory. He ran up to the cyclotron, where uranium was being bombarded with neutrons, grabbed a counter, and measured the fission's energy "kicks," corralling anyone who came by to show them off.

I heard the news at the physics journal club. Some attendees greeted the news with strong skepticism, but after hearing the details of Hahn and Strassmann's experiments, I immediately accepted their interpretation. After the meeting on that mild January night, I walked the streets of Berkeley for hours with the news whirling around my head. My mood alternated between exhilaration at the exciting discovery and consternation that I'd been studying this field for years and had completely overlooked the possibility of this phenomenon—and missed a chance for an astounding discovery.

I was in good company in this failure. Many people, such as the Joliot-Curies with their misinterpreted lanthanum, had blown golden opportunities. At the Rad Lab, researchers who'd encountered the huge energy kicks given off by fissioning uranium assumed they'd made a mistake in their method. They took the crazily vigorous reactions of their counters to mean that the instruments were acting up; they put up shielding to keep out whatever particles were causing this interference with their experiments.

My head swam as I tried to fit the news into our understanding of the nucleus. What knowledge would stay and what must be jettisoned? The table of isotopes would be completely rearranged. If Fermi's discoveries weren't new elements, what were they? Fermi's many isomers would be explained by the fact that uranium can fission in many ways, into many combinations of elements. All those former "transuranics" needed to be identified and classified. Of course, there was the possibility of "real" transuranium elements to be discovered. And then, fission itself offered a new frontier to study.

The neutron had been discovered only seven years earlier. Then, our model of the nucleus had changed to the liquid drop. And now fission. What an exciting specialty I'd chosen; truly the cutting edge. What great fortune to be in a field with so much work to be done.

While I don't recall thinking of it as I walked the streets of Berkeley (some scientists did immediately), one implication of this discovery came to overshadow all others: fission gives off a tremendous amount of energy. A free proton or neutron has a greater mass than a proton or neutron bound into a nucleus. When protons and neutrons join together in a nucleus, each loses some of its mass; this mass is released as energy, called the nuclear binding energy. The amount of lost mass, and the binding energy, varies. Smaller nuclei are more stable; they have a greater binding energy. Larger nuclei like uranium's are less stable, with less binding energy per nucleon.

When you bombard uranium with neutrons, a neutron that joins the uranium nucleus gives the nucleus a jolt of energy—just enough energy to cause fission in some atoms. When a uranium nucleus splits, each of these two smaller elements has a nucleus more stable than uranium's; each new nucleus has more binding energy. This binding energy, this nuclear stability, comes from the nucleons giving up some of their mass into energy.

The amount of energy involved is described by Albert Einstein's famous equation: $E = mc^2$, energy equals mass times the speed of light squared. Now, the speed of light is a very large number; the speed of light squared is a ridiculously large number. So a very small amount of mass converts to a relatively large amount of energy. In his excellent book *The Making of the Atomic Bomb*, Richard Rhodes writes that the energy released when a single uranium atom fissions is "sufficient to make a visible grain of sand visibly jump. In each mere gram of uranium there are about $2.5 \times 10$ to the 21st atoms, an absurdly large number, 25 followed by twenty zeros: 2,500,000,000,000,000,000,000." A kilogram of the right isotope of uranium contains the energy equivalent of 3,000 tons of coal, enough to keep a 100-watt bulb burning for 3,000 years. If you can release that all at once, you have the explosive power of an atomic bomb. And, what I believe will still be of more importance to the world, if you control the release, you have the ability to generate power for human endeavors.

That September, Germany invaded Poland, precipitating World War II. The United States did not enter the war for more than two years. Roosevelt did all he could to nudge the country toward readiness, but the attitude of many citizens was that the war was a European, not an American, concern. For many scientists, however, and particularly physicists, war research soon became an important, then dominant, theme.

After I finished my stint with G. N. Lewis, I was assigned a pair of freshman chemistry laboratory classes, which left plenty of time for research. I was tremendously fortunate in my first two graduate students. Arthur Wahl came to Berkeley with an undergraduate degree from Iowa State. After our work together, Art went on to be a group leader at Los Alamos, then to Washington University in St. Louis. Gerhart Friedlander, a native of Germany, had just received his bachelor's degree at Berkeley. His nationality presented some problems in the war research, but after those issues were sorted out he served as a group leader at Los Alamos, then spent most of his career at Brookhaven National Laboratory. He is editor of the excellent magazine *Science Spectra*.

I assigned Gerhart a project that involved working with tellurium isotopes. I was walking toward the laboratory where he was working one day when I smelled a terrifically offensive odor, instantly recognizable as caused by an infamous chemical, tellurium hydride. I practically ran past the open lab door and went straight to the Faculty Club, where I showered and changed, but I still couldn't rid myself of the smell before teaching class that afternoon. If just passing the door affected me, you can imagine the fate of poor Gerhart, who came down with a full-blown case of "tellurium breath." A small amount of one of the tellurium compounds had somehow escaped from his vacuum system. The stuff so pervades your system that no amount of washing gets rid of it; you just have to wait until it dissipates. Gerhart's case was so bad that for days I could tell which books he'd been handling at the library. A week after the accident, I noted in my journal that he still "manifested strong evidence of 'tellurium breath.' " After another two weeks: "Friedlander's breath is still a problem although there has been much improvement." It could take months for tellurium breath to disappear.

The same day that Gerhart had his tellurium accident, a telegram arrived from Stockholm informing Ernest Lawrence that he'd been awarded the 1939 Nobel Prize for his invention of the cyclotron. Lawrence was off playing tennis; his secretary had difficulty convincing the people at the Berkeley Tennis Club that the message was worth calling him off the court to receive.

Lawrence was not only the first Nobel winner at the University of California but also the first from any state university in the United States. Major breakthroughs in science had traditionally come in Europe, especially Germany and England. When American scientists emerged, Harvard practically held a monopoly. It was one of the first steps in proving that we were building a public university that could compete with the best of the private institutions. But with the war on, there was no question of a trip to Europe. He was presented his medal by the San Francisco–based Swedish consul general at a ceremony in an auditorium on campus.

Fission and uranium research were the rage, and Joe Kennedy and I looked for a way to get involved. Uranium occurs in two main natural isotopes, U-238 and U-235. U-235 makes up less than 1 percent of the uranium in a typical ore sample, but it is the isotope that undergoes fission. We thought we'd try our hand at separating the isotopes of uranium and concentrating the fissionable (or fissile) fraction.

Separating an element's isotopes from each other is a difficult challenge. Elements can be separated because you can always find some chemical reactions that will differentiate them, such as a carrier that will combine with one element but not the other. But isotopes act the same chemically. We'd read about a new process called thermal diffusion, based on the difference in weight between the isotopes. If you could put each isotope in gaseous form, the U-238 would be slightly heavier than the U-235, and this difference in weight could be exploited to separate the isotopes.

We built a large apparatus of gas columns and a machine to generate gaseous uranium hexafluoride. One day as Joe, Arthur Wahl, and I were operating the generator to produce the gas, an explosion demolished the trap where the uranium hexafluoride collected. We scrambled out of the room as the gas escaped.

The next day, Joe felt ill, and his urine was cloudy. I noted in my diary, "We have read . . . that uranium is an extremely powerful, slow-acting poison, so we are concerned that his illness may be caused by having ingested uranium hexafluoride in yesterday's explosion. If this is true, Wahl and I may soon develop symptoms."

Joe's condition worsened over the next few days, although Art and I felt fine. About ten days after the explosion, a doctor diagnosed Joe's illness as mononucleosis. That diagnosis was a considerable relief, but the episode soured our enthusiasm for gaseous diffusion work. We soon decided that the process was beyond our capabilities, and turned to other projects. (Thermal diffusion eventually was used successfully in the Manhattan Project, and it did prove to be an enormous undertaking.)

Concerned that the growing threat of war might soon preclude extended travel, Joe and I took a train trip east in the summer of 1940, visiting a number of universities and laboratories to see their facilities, examine the equipment and methods they were developing, and cultivate contacts with colleagues. In Washington, we visited the physicist Merle Tuve at the Bureau of Terrestrial Magnetism of the Carnegie Institution. Remarkably, Merle and Ernest Lawrence had grown up as boyhood friends in the same South Dakota town. Merle described for us the preparations for wartime research and development. President Roosevelt had appointed Vannevar Bush, president of the Carnegie Institution, to head the Scientific Division of the Committee for Defense, and Bush and his staff were busy organizing scientists into sections for research on various projects. He asked me to send him names of chemists and physicists who might fit into the effort. One of the Carnegie Institution's leading players in this project was Philip Abelson. I knew Phil well because he'd just received his Ph.D. in nuclear physics from Berkeley. He was about to make an important discovery.

I expected to be involved in some kind of war research when the

United States went to war, but I would never have guessed the events of the next few months. Given my eventual role, the contacts we made during this trip would be put to good use.

Upon our return, I received an unexpected offer to join the faculty of UCLA as an assistant professor, a tenure-track appointment that would be an important promotion. I could hardly turn down such a professional opportunity, and southern California still felt like home. But Berkeley, with its cyclotron and outstanding faculty, was the perfect place for my interests. It took me two weeks to work up the courage to tell Professor Lewis of UCLA's offer. Worried that he would simply congratulate me and wish me luck, I tried to convey the impression that I would be happy to receive an equivalent offer from Berkeley. I could see that my message put him to thinking, so when he asked when I intended to give UCLA an answer, to give him time I said I planned to call after seven, when the phone rates went down.

I would have to make such a call from the main lounge at the Faculty Club, and my heart was pounding as I made my way slowly toward the phone. Lewis was there, long after he usually departed. He motioned me over and said that, although he couldn't guarantee that the university president would approve it, he would recommend me for an appointment as an assistant professor after one more year as an instructor. Lewis then asked if I still intended to call UCLA.

"Yes," I replied. "To tell them that I have decided to accept your offer." I was ecstatic to be staying at Berkeley, and by the end of that summer had begun the research that would change the course of my life.

# SEVEN

# PLUTONIUM:

# A SECRET DISCOVERY

On one of his trips east, Ernest Lawrence had been impressed by a Princeton Ph.D. named Edwin McMillan. Ernest had charmed him into moving to California, where Ed became a charter member of the Radiation Laboratory. His knack with instruments greatly improved the performance of the cyclotron, and his expertise was critical in the design of larger versions. Also, Ed's ties with Ernest were especially close—they married sisters.

Intrigued by the discovery of fission, Ed McMillan set out to study how far the fission products are propelled by the reaction's energy. He noticed in particular one "activity." (In our shorthand jargon, we referred to a substance with a particular radioactivity signature as an "activity.") What was remarkable about this activity was that it remained close to the uranium target instead of being scattered off like a regular fission product. The substance had a half-life of 2.3 days, which didn't fit any of the known isotopes of uranium. The lack of mobility implied that it might not be a fission product; it wasn't moving as if it had been subjected to fission energy. Ed speculated that some uranium nuclei were absorbing neutrons instead of undergoing fission when hit by them. If such an absorbed neutron then transmuted to a proton, the 2.3-day activity would be element 93.

There is a logic behind the way the periodic table of elements is arranged: certain characteristics of elements tend to recur periodically—hence the name. For example, the elements in the column farthest to the left all have one electron to donate. Lithium, sodium, and potassium, all with this "extra" electron, can form salts. If you move from left to right across a row, you are adding an electron at a time, thus tracing the filling of the outer electron shell. If you read down a column, you are following a grouping of elements with the same number of valence (outer) electrons, which largely determines their chemical characteristics. So these elements tend to be alike chemically, so much so that if you know the behavior of one element, you can predict with some confidence the behavior of the element in the row below it.

In the 1930s, there was one break in the table, between element 57, lanthanum, and element 72, hafnium. The fourteen elements in this sequence were so much alike that they were grouped together below the regular body of the periodic table. These elements all bore a striking resemblance to lanthanum and to each other. Their added electrons, instead of being valence electrons added to the outer shell, were filling an inner shell. That was the reason they were so alike, and so difficult to separate chemically from one another. They were sometimes called the lanthanides (after lanthanum) and sometimes the rare earths (in the mistaken belief that they were all rare). This peculiarity in the periodic table came to play an important role in our drama.

According to this system, element 93 was expected to fall in the same column as, and thus be chemically similar to, technetium and rhenium. Emilio Segrè had discovered technetium and knew as much about the chemistries of technetium and rhenium as anyone. So Ed McMillan enlisted Segrè to do the chemical separation of his 2.3-day activity. Segrè did enough chemistry to show that this unknown entity did not act like rhenium but, rather, like a rare earth. That was enough for him; he published a paper called "An Unsuccessful Search for Transuranic Elements."

Segrè had been a member of Fermi's group that had mistakenly reported the discovery of transuranic elements, a mistake caused by their failure to separate their unknowns from all known elements. Had they continued their separations, they would have found that the "transuranics" were actually known elements, fission fragments, and so would have discovered fission. Apparently not learning from that experience, once again Segrè saw no need to follow up with careful chemistry. Earlier, he'd identified fission fragments as transuranics. This time, he called the unknown activity a fission fragment.

Segrè's work left Ed with nagging doubts. If the 2.3-day activity was a fission product, why didn't it act like one? Why didn't it shoot off like the other ones? Ed was still thinking about this problem several months later when Phil Abelson, the recent doctoral graduate who was now working in Washington, came back to Berkeley on vacation. He and Ed discovered a mutual fascination with this problem, and Phil agreed to work on it. With a doctorate in physics and a bachelor's in chemistry, Phil was ideally qualified to investigate it.

The task of proving that an unknown acts like no known element is not quite so tedious as it sounds. The chemistries of many elements are so similar that you can rule out a whole category with a single test. Phil required only a day or two to demonstrate that the 2.3-day activity's chemistry was different from all other known elements. The transmutation of a neutron to a proton had occurred just as Ed suspected, and they had discovered element 93, the first element heavier than uranium. Soon it was named neptunium.

Abelson returned to his job in Washington, and during the summer of 1940, Ed continued on alone, now looking for element 94. Element 93 was unstable, decaying after a half-life of only 2.3 days. Perhaps it decayed to element 94?

Ed was another denizen of the Faculty Club, and anytime I ran into him I quizzed him on all the details of his fascinating transuranium research, even discussing it in the shower room.

The periodic table predicted that element 93 should be a homolog of rhenium, but its chemistry was instead similar to that of uranium. Ed reasoned that element 93 resembled uranium because there was another group of elements with similar properties, like the lanthanides. If this group started with uranium, it would be called the uranides, by analogy to the lanthanide name.

Element 94 would therefore also be similar to uranium, and that gave Ed a starting point to look for it. Uranium decays by emitting alpha particles (two protons and two neutrons), so Ed looked for an alpha emitter among the decay products of uranium and element 93. Each element emits particles with a characteristic energy and a characteristic range of travel, another aspect of an isotope's radioactive signature, so he could distinguish these alpha particles from those emitted by uranium by the distance they traveled (their range). Ed found an alpha emitter and began isolating it. He showed it was not element 91, 92, or 93.

Then Ed disappeared without a word. I soon learned that he'd gone to MIT to work on radar, one of the first big research projects of the war and a top priority. (The scientific community geared up for the war more than a year before the rest of the United States did; these disappearances increased in frequency as the war approached.) I wrote to Ed at the end of November and suggested that since he couldn't continue his transuranium work, Joe Kennedy, my graduate student Arthur Wahl, and I would be glad to carry on with it as his collaborators. I noted that Art Wahl had already begun exploring the chemical properties of element 93, perfecting the technique for isolating very pure samples of it. Ed wrote back immediately to say he had no idea when he would return to Berkeley and expected a long absence, so he would be happy for us to continue the research on elements 93 and 94.

The simple timing of these events influenced my career to an extraordinary degree. Had Segrè not misidentified element 93, Ed would have had time to find element 94. Had Ed departed for MIT just a few months later, he certainly would have found it. As it was, I was at the right place at the right time, for the discovery we were about to make opened all the other doors for me, changing my career to the fascinating adventure it became.

I had no inkling of any of this at the time, but we were aware early on that element 94 could be a big prize. The prospect of synthesizing new elements was exhilarating from a scientific standpoint, but our search held even greater potential consequences. Element 93 was too short-lived to have many practical applications, but if element 93 were decaying into element 94 in the way we suspected, then 94 could be very interesting.

The isotope uranium 235 is usefully fissile, whereas uranium 238 is not, because U-235 has an odd number of nucleons. (The numbers 235 and 238 refer to the atomic weights of these isotopes. The weight roughly translates to the number of nucleons in the isotope. Thus, because an element always has the same number of protons, uranium 238 contains three more neutrons than uranium 235.) Each neutron has a "spin"—think of them as being either "plus" or "minus." Neutrons are more stable when paired off with a partner of opposite spin. So when U-235 captures a neutron, the captured neutron pairs with the available neutron; the paired-up neutrons excite the nucleus, give it a little jolt of energy—again, like the jiggling of a drop of water. That little jolt of energy, combined with the energy from the neutron colliding with it, is just enough to take the nucleus over the threshold and to result in its splitting—and giving off the great energy of fission.

The addition of a neutron to U-238 seemed to be affecting the stability of its nucleus in a completely different way. Apparently, it was changing U-238 into the odd-numbered U-239—an unstable configuration—so a neutron was transmuting to a proton, the element transmuting to 93-239. If 93-239 then transmuted to 94-239, the latter would be similar to U-235 in its proton-neutron relationship. Therefore, it would likely be similarly fissile.

Moreover, a fissile 94 might be more useful than U-235 for two reasons. First, element 94 could be separated chemically from uranium, while we knew of no reliable way to separate isotopes of the same element from each other (and therefore U-235 would be very hard to separate from U-238). Second, U-235 is rare, making up less than 1 percent of uranium. The rest is U-238. So less than 1 percent of the uranium stock, which seemed to be an exceedingly rare element, was usable. If we could transform U-238 into a fissionable material, we could increase the amount of usable material a hundredfold. But that's getting ahead of the story.

In the fall of 1940, we had several cyclotron bombardments performed to study element 93. We bombarded beryllium with deuterons (a proton and a neutron) in the cyclotron, and the beryllium emitted neutrons. Our target, the uranium compound uranyl nitrate hexahydrate, was placed in the path of the neutrons outside the cyclotron. The uranium nuclei would absorb some of the neutrons, which would transmute to protons and form element 93. Of course, the neutrons would also cause some of the uranium to fission, so the target would be full of radioactive fission products as well as element 93.

We performed half a dozen such bombardments, enough so Wahl could perfect the technique for separating out element 93 and study its chemistry. Despite his success in isolating element 93, our new alpha emitter proved elusive. One problem was that it appeared very long-lived. Ironically, an unstable, short-lived isotope can be easier to identify than one with a longer life: A shorter-lived isotope's radiation is more intense and energetic, and thus more easily measured. An isotope with a one-day half-life is decaying at twice the rate of an isotope with a two-day half-life, emitting radiation at twice the rate. An isotope with a half-life of several thousand years will let loose few particles, and when you consider that we were dealing with small numbers of atoms, there might be a click on the counter every few minutes or hours.

We thought we might circumvent this problem if we could create a different isotope. So far, the transuranics had been created through neutron bombardment of uranium. So, in mid-December, we placed the uranium inside the cyclotron and bombarded it with deuterons, which appeared to accomplish our desired effect of creating another isotope of 93.

The same separation techniques that we'd used to isolate the known isotope of 93 worked with this new isotope, which indicated we were dealing with another form of element 93. This isotope had a 2.1-day half-life, similar to the other 93 isotope, and it was also a vigorous beta emitter, meaning that it decayed by emitting an electron—a neutron was transmuting to a proton, thereby forming element 94. Sure enough, the decay product—or "daughter," in the parlance of the nuclear lab—was an alpha emitter.

It was fairly easy to create samples of this daughter because we could isolate rather pure samples of the 93 isotope. We isolated the 93 and waited for it to decay. After two days, half of it would have turned into the alpha emitter. We could use our knowledge of 93's chemistry to separate the 93 from its daughter, which left a relatively pure sample of our alpha emitter. Then we'd wait for more 93 to decay, and do another separation, and so forth, a process we called milking the alpha emitter from the 93.

Preliminary chemistry tests showed that our new alpha emitter was not element 93.

Next we tried an oxidation test: using certain reagents, you can add electrons to or subtract electrons from the element you are working with. Subtracting electrons is called oxidizing (or raising the oxidation state). The oxidation states of an element are among its defining characteristics.

Our unknown resisted oxidation by a powerful agent, a property shared by a limited number of elements, narrowing the possibilities to thorium, actinium, one of the fourteen "rare earth" elements, or a brand-new element. Those tests had taken only two weeks, but then six weeks went by without a breakthrough.

Wahl tried without success as many ways as he could think of to oxidize our alpha emitter to a state that would differentiate it from these elements. We sought the advice of Wendell Latimer, the second-in-command in the College of Chemistry (he would soon succeed Lewis as dean), who suggested that we try the strongest oxidizing agent he knew, peroxydisulfate ion. Working past midnight on a Sunday, Wahl dissolved the sample in acid and found that his manipulations with peroxydisulfate and a fluoride solution were successful—the alpha emitter had been oxidized to a higher state than could be accomplished with any of these other elements. We weren't yet certain that it was not an isotope of thorium, so we conceived a final definitive experiment. Wahl was up past midnight again the next night demonstrating that our unknown would not precipitate out of a fluoride solution under conditions in which thorium did.

I greeted the news in matter-of-fact fashion in my journal: "With this final separation from thorium, it has been demonstrated that our alpha activity can be separated from all known elements and thus it is now clear that our alpha activity is due to the new element with the atomic number 94." We felt like shouting our discovery from the rooftop. Under normal circumstances, we would have rushed to publication to establish our claim to the discovery of a new element. But the war had changed everything. When McMillan and Abelson had published their discovery of element 93 in *The Physical Review* in June 1940, the British government had lodged an official protest, upset that Americans would reveal potential military secrets, even though element 93 was not likely to have military significance. But we were aware from the beginning that its daughter element 94 could be very important.

We immediately filed a report with the Uranium Committee, a secret body of the U.S. government that was exploring the potential wartime uses of uranium. To establish a record of discovery, we also sent a brief report to the editor of *The Physical Review*, requesting that he withhold publication because of security concerns. The report listed the discoverers as Seaborg, McMillan, Kennedy, and Wahl. (Throughout our investigations, I kept up a correspondence with McMillan, as a collaborator.) The world would not learn of the discovery for more than four years, and the announcement then came in the most dramatic form possible.

At first we gave the new element no name, simply referring to it as 94. But even that revealed too much for casual conversations around the Faculty Club or the lab, so we adopted the code name of "copper" for element 94 and "silver" for element 93. This code worked well enough through 1941, until some experiments required the use of some real copper, which we then referred to as "honest-to-God copper."

A year after its discovery we finally named our new element. It was so difficult to make, from such rare materials, that we thought it would certainly be the heaviest element ever formed. So we considered names like extremium and ultimium. Fortunately, we were spared the inevitable embarrassment that one courts when proclaiming a discovery to be the ultimate in any field by deciding to follow the nomenclatural precedents of the two prior elements.

A new planet had been discovered in 1781 and, like the rest of the planets, named for a Greek or Roman deity—Uranus. A scientist who discovered a heavy new element eight years later named it after the planet: uranium. The planet Neptune was discovered in 1846, so Ed McMillan followed this precedent and named element 93 neptunium. Conveniently for us, the final planet, Pluto, had been discovered in 1930. We briefly considered the form plutium, but plutonium seemed more euphonious. Each element has a one- or two-letter abbreviation. Following the standard rules, this symbol should be Pl, but we chose Pu instead. We thought our little joke might come under criticism, but it was hardly noticed.

In *The Making of the Atomic Bomb*, Richard Rhodes writes of the symbolism that we "would name element 94 for Pluto, the ninth planet outward from the sun, discovered in 1930 and named for the Greek god of the underworld, a god of the earth's fertility but also the god of the dead." Any such symbolic meaning, however, was entirely coincidental; I was unfamiliar with the god or why the planet was named for him. We were simply following the planetary precedent.

Even before Art had finished his experiments proving that our alpha emitter was element 94, we were so confident of the outcome that we began a new phase of experiments to see if we could find an isotope that would be usefully fissile. (Element 93's half-life was so short that we never even tested its fissionability.) Realizing the importance of the work we were doing, Ernest Lawrence wanted more involvement by the Rad Lab staff, so he assigned Emilio Segrè to the project. We had no need for a physicist, and Segrè had already proven his lack of affinity for chemistry, but he became my main partner in this next step.

Segrè's status as a recent Italian immigrant, an "enemy alien," left me in an awkward position. The Uranium Committee, which reviewed such matters, wouldn't give Segrè a full clearance. Although I had no formal ties or commitments to the committee at the time, there was no question about following its guidelines as much as was practical. But I did not hesitate to use my own judgment either; science can't work if it's straitjacketed by secrecy. For example, Lewis and Latimer were not officially cleared, mainly because, with their tangential involvement, there was no reason for them to go through the clearance process. Nonetheless, I kept them apprised of our progress and sought their advice, confident of their discretion. Latimer's suggestion of an oxidizing agent for element 94 was a key to its discovery. We worked as much as we could within the rules, but results were more important than rules.

Segrè was a different case entirely. It was one thing to consult experts not officially cleared, quite another to deal with a person whom the Uranium Committee had refused our request to clear. I was not allowed to reveal to him all the information about our project, but there was no explicit guidance on where to draw the line. He was apparently allowed to know about the fissionability of element 94 but not about its chemistry, which led to some absurd situations. I would gather the chemicals for our procedures, then give him instructions on what to do without telling him what chemicals he was using.

Of course, had Emilio been bent on spying, it would have been simple enough for him to abscond with enough chemicals to figure out what we were doing. These precautions seem especially ridiculous in retrospect, considering that Segrè eventually worked in the innermost circles at Los Alamos, the most secret of laboratories.

One advantage of working with Segrè was that he had access to uranium through his friendship with his former colleague Fermi (another "enemy alien," by now engaged in uranium research at Columbia University). Uranium, then a rare commodity, had few industrial uses, so there was little reason to mine it, and the known reserves were almost exclusively in what was then the Belgian Congo. Fermi had five kilograms of a uranium compound shipped to us.

For this work of testing fission properties, we would need the longer-lived isotope of 94, which we hoped to isolate using our knowledge of the chemistry of the shorter-lived one. So we returned to neutron bombardment—placing a beryllium target in the cyclotron and using the neutrons it emitted to bombard our uranium. We'd built a wooden box filled with paraffin wax, which was the best material for slowing the neutrons to the right speed for being absorbed into the nucleus instead of smashing into it. We drilled holes in the paraffin, and slid in glass tubes containing the uranium.

Our previous uranium bombardments had been in the range of 5 to 6 grams. In January 1941, we bombarded larger samples, 10 grams, then 575 grams, to test refinements in the method for separating the element 93 formed in the bombardment. These experiments confirmed that the bombardments would provide a good yield of 93-239. If we could isolate enough of this isotope of element 93, we could simply wait for it to decay into what we hoped would be 94-239.

We calculated that we'd need to bombard 1.2 kilograms of uranium to produce and isolate about a microgram—a millionth of a gram—of 93. The same night that Wahl first oxidized a sample of element 94, Segrè and I put our 1.2 kilograms of uranium next to the cyclotron, where it remained on and off for about a week.

Compared with the 6-gram bombardments we'd been performing, this one was huge, some two hundred times greater. The quantities that Art Wahl had been working with were so small that the radioactivity involved was negligible. Segrè and I would have to shield ourselves from the exposure to the much larger amounts of material we'd be dealing with. The kilogram of uranium would contain not only our microgram of 93 but would be laced throughout with radioactive fission products from the bombardment.

On a Monday morning in March, Segrè and I carried our now highly radioactive uranium sample out of the Rad Lab, across the street, and up two flights of stairs in the Chemistry Building. Our shielding methods were jury-rigged and unsophisticated. The irradiated sample went into a lead bucket that we carried precariously on a long pole. We wore lead-impregnated gloves and goggles. The room where we worked opened onto a large outdoor porch where we could carry out evaporations in the open air, exposing ourselves to a minimum of fumes.

The physics department glass blower had made us a special extraction apparatus that we could operate by remote control. We dissolved our target in two liters of ether, and poured the mixture into the extraction apparatus, where most of the uranium compound dropped out, leaving the element 93, any 94 that formed, and fission products in the solution.

We heated this to reduce the volume by evaporating off some of the liquid. We added carriers that would combine with the element 93—a technique similar to the one I used in isolating Jack Livingood's isotopes. Our room contained no centrifuge, so we poured this suspension into a centrifuge tube, placed the tube in a lead beaker, put the beaker in a wooden box with long poles for handles, and carried it to the Crocker Laboratory, where the chemistry department had a room with a large centrifuge. We spun the sample in the centrifuge, which separated the constituents by density, the fission products being lighter than element 93. We washed our sample in acid and spun it again. Then we put the sample in its lead-beaker carrier and walked back to our workroom. We put the precipitate into a nickel-plated platinum dish, dissolved it in acid, oxidized it, and added carriers again. Then it was back to the centrifuge at Crocker Laboratory, then back to our room, all the while carrying our sample in its special box. We called it a night at 10 p.m., but were back in the morning to repeat the process, six cycles of reprecipitations and centrifugations over the next three days, all the while taking care to avoid exposure to the radiation. The hours flew by quickly, the otherwise tedious work made thrilling by the anticipation of discovery.

On Thursday, we poured the precipitate into a specially constructed circular platinum dish about the size of a dime and evaporated off any liquid. We covered the sample with a thin layer of Duco cement to hold it to the dish, glued the dish to a cardboard backing, and labeled it Sample A. Now we merely needed to leave our precious nugget of 93 to decay on its own, as, atom by atom, a neutron transmuted to a proton and formed 94-239. We would monitor this process by tracing its radioactive footprints.

Joe Kennedy joined us now, full of brilliant ideas on detection instruments, and quick to put together whatever we might need next. Joe built counters tailored to an isotope's characteristic decay pattern—varying amounts of alpha, beta, or gamma radiation, at slower or faster rates. Alpha particles travel only a few centimeters, so in our search for alpha-emitting element 94, Joe used mica to make an extremely thin-walled counting window, which the alpha particles could penetrate. He built another special counter for the measurements on Sample A. As element 93's neutrons transmuted to protons, they would give off electrons—high-energy, penetrating beta radiation that would mask the less penetrating alpha radiation of the slowly growing element 94. Joe put together an ionization chamber with a magnetic field that would bend out the negatively charged electrons of the beta radiation and admit the positive alpha particles, and with this we watched the activity of the 94 fraction grow.

After three weeks, the instruments indicated that the decay of element 93 was essentially complete; by our estimations Sample A contained a quarter microgram of element 94 (that estimate turned out to be low).

The moment of truth came on March 28 with an experiment with potentially momentous implications, not only for us personally but for the world. Was this new element fissile—and therefore a potential source of immense power?

We put Sample A in paraffin and placed it in the path of the cyclotron's neutrons, and had our answer almost immediately. Joe had constructed another instrument, a portable ionization chamber for detecting fission pulses. He put the sample up against the counter's window; the counter registered the unmistakable kicks indicating fission in Sample A.

We put a sample of uranium in front of the cyclotron to check its fission rate as a standard for comparison. The uranium's fission rate was well above the one we observed for Sample A, but we knew the count for

Sample A was below its true rate because of its thickness. The Duco cement and impurities in the sample were absorbing many of the fission fragments and alpha particles; we had no idea what proportion made it out to our ionization chamber to be counted.

The experiment had demonstrated that plutonium would fission, a result that encouraged us to move on to the next step—to test the fission *rate*. For this we needed a thinner, purer sample. The carrier material in Sample A was several times the weight of the element 94; we needed to separate some of it out. Wahl went to work immediately on investigating the chemistry of element 94.

In the midst of this excitement, I flew to the East Coast for a job interview. It was my first plane flight—at a time when a coast-to-coast flight lasted so long you could book a "sleeper" similar to a train's. I visited American Cyanamid, a large chemical company, because I was excited by the thought of advancing the use of radioactive tracer techniques in industry. In the end, even a job at the princely salary of $6,000, almost three times what I was making as an instructor, did not tempt me to forsake the academic life for which I sensed I was fit. I only mention the incident here as a gauge of my commitment to my research, which I thought might be as important as any in the country I could be doing. (American Cyanamid next turned to Joe Kennedy, who accepted their offer. Within a few weeks of moving east, Joe confided his unhappiness with his situation. We greatly missed his expertise, and when I presented his dilemma to the powers at the chemistry department, they arranged for his return in September.)

Wahl's work on the chemistry of element 94 was streamlined by the acquisition of a large new centrifuge, a signal of Professor Lewis' endorsement of the importance of our investigation at a time when research funds were scarce. By early May 1941, Wahl had worked out a purification process for plutonium similar to the one for neptunium, involving various precipitations and centrifugations. Wahl performed this operation on Sample A, forming a very thin sample we labeled Sample B and placed in a centrifuge tube.

From the test on this sample, we calculated a fission rate almost 1.7 times that of U-235, the fissionable natural isotope of uranium. (The modern value is 1.24 times, not as high as we thought but still significantly better than uranium.) We could also take a stab at estimating the half-life of 94-239, which we pegged at around 30,000 years (reasonably close to the true value of 24,000 years). Our calculations were based on a sample of about half a microgram; I would be proud of the ultimate precision of our calculations, but in retrospect, that precision can only be explained by the fact that the great number of errors we made somehow, conveniently, canceled each other out.

This fission rate was momentous news—element 94 would in fact be better than uranium. And that half-life was certainly long enough for it to be used in nuclear power, a bomb, or other applications. We'd shown we could make a fissionable isotope from the common uranium isotope, U-238. That increased the potential material available for a bomb by a hundredfold. And the new material might even be better than U-235.

These findings lit a spark in Ernest Lawrence. He had recently joined a National Academy of Sciences panel evaluating American efforts in nuclear science. Lawrence was perhaps the first in the high-echelon scientific establishment who really pushed to put resources into developing an atomic bomb. He immediately called the chairman of the committee, his fellow Nobel laureate Arthur H. Compton. Compton and Lawrence had become friends when Lawrence was a graduate student at the University of Chicago, where Compton was chairman of the physics department and a dean. Lawrence conveyed his contagious enthusiasm to Compton, but the Uranium Committee in Washington remained skeptical. We soon mailed a report of our results to Dr. Lyman Briggs, its chairman.

Up to this time, our research on elements 93 and 94 was done entirely on our own time, as part of our university research and teaching duties, and Wahl's thesis research. But now the government took notice. Soon there were contracts to perform a search for elements 93 and 94 in nature (to see if they could be obtained without the need for the cyclotron), to pay for the cyclotron operations to produce more of element 94, and to work on various other projects.

I took another trip east, personally reporting on our findings to the Uranium Committee. I visited several companies to see about obtaining uranium ores to use in the search for elements 93 and 94 in nature—an interesting process, since I couldn't tell them why I wanted the ore.

The best part of the trip, however, was my return, when the flight landed in Oakland. Melvin Calvin had agreed to give me a ride home from the airport, and he'd brought along Helen Griggs, Ernest Lawrence's attractive secretary. I'd first met Helen almost three years before, when Lawrence had asked Segrè and me to rescind the article on technetium's isomerism we'd submitted to *The Physical Review*—I'd dictated the telegram to her. She was then working part-time for Lawrence while pursuing her undergraduate degree in English. I'd been taken with her immediately, but I was going steady with a woman I'd met at the Elliott boardinghouse. That friendship had ended the previous winter. One night when we were working late on the discovery of plutonium, I'd completely forgotten a date with her. She'd taken that a sign of my priorities, which I guess it was.

Helen began working full-time for Lawrence after getting her degree. Like a schoolboy with a crush, in the past few months I'd taken to making up excuses to drop by the office just to chat with her. However, I'd only had the courage to ask her out once, but on that occasion she had a previous engagement with the assistant lab director, Don Cooksey, whom she seemed to be seeing regularly. Now, Melvin had evidently had enough of hearing me pine over her without doing anything about it and had taken the matter into his own hands.

Melvin was that kind of friend to me. We had an arrangement in which I paid the insurance on his Oldsmobile convertible in exchange for the right to use it frequently, and now we dropped Melvin at home and I took Helen on a drive through the golden hills east of Berkeley. Helen was cleared for any information on the project—she typed our reports—so I could speak freely with her about the trip I'd just completed.

Helen had moved from the Midwest to southern California at about the same age I had. We began seeing each other regularly almost immediately, and soon I was completely, head over heels in love. I'd never had this feeling for anyone else, before or since. Coming simultaneously with the thrilling work we were doing on element 94, these months seemed then to me the most exciting time of my life.


That summer, as our research progressed on several fronts, our team expanded with the addition of a couple of postdocs. Segrè and I did further studies of 94's fission properties; Wahl refined the chemical separations of element 94; we found evidence of naturally occurring elements 93 and

94 in uranium ores; we studied the half-lives of isotopes of element 94; we discovered a new isotope of uranium, uranium 233, and confirmed that it was fissile. All our findings reinforced the evidence of element 94's suitability as a nuclear explosive.

I was promoted to assistant professor. In the fall of 1941 I taught two lab sections of Chem 1A and was graduate student adviser for the chemistry department. But my "uranium" research took up most of my attention.

A National Academy of Sciences committee made a report to President Roosevelt on November 27 that summarized the work around the country and addressed the question: Should the work on an atomic bomb continue? On December 6, Roosevelt established a committee charged with the task of doing everything possible to find out whether nuclear weapons could be made. The committee, which became known as Section S-1, included Ernest Lawrence, Lyman Briggs (head of the National Bureau of Standards), James Bryant Conant (a chemist and president of Harvard University), Vannevar Bush (president of the Carnegie Institution), and Arthur Compton. The members split up their responsibilities, with Compton in charge of the design of the bomb.

In his book about the Manhattan Project, Compton tells a story about going to lunch after that fateful December 6 meeting with James Conant and Vannevar Bush. Conant's path to the presidency of Harvard had run through its chemistry department. Bush would soon lead the nation's entire broad scientific war effort as head of the Office of Scientific Research and Development. (It has been said that nearly two-thirds of all American physicists were working under him during the war.)

The report that the National Academy committee had submitted to Roosevelt had focused entirely on a uranium bomb. Compton had purposely omitted any mention of the newcomer plutonium because he did not want to make a complex subject even more confusing by adding another wild card. But he was convinced of the necessity of following up every reasonable possibility, so at lunch Compton took the opportunity to advocate the potential of plutonium as a possible explosive. Both Bush and Conant saw mainly drawbacks and obstacles. Bush said that it was not known if plutonium could be made in large quantities, Compton reported.

Conant added that, even if we could produce plutonium, we knew almost nothing of its chemistry. Even when we had this knowledge, the task of extracting plutonium from the uranium would be greatly complicated by the intense radioactivity. It would take years to get the chemical extraction process in operation. This was Conant, the expert chemist, speaking from experience.

"Seaborg tells me that within six months from the time the plutonium is formed he can have it available for use in the bomb," was my comment.*

"Glenn Seaborg is a very competent young chemist, but he isn't that good," said Conant.

But as a result of this meeting, Compton was given the authority to investigate the possibilities of plutonium. Compton's foresight was indeed prescient, and it was fortunate he was the one who would make the decision on whether to pursue element 94 as a possibility.

The day after those scientific leaders met on December 6, the world as we knew it came to an end. I was in my room at the Faculty Club listening to a radio broadcast of a football game that was interrupted by the electrifying announcement that the Japanese had bombed Pearl Harbor. Our team had been working hard in anticipation of the war, but "the day that shall live in infamy," as Roosevelt called it, made work on anything

---

*Whether this conversation—which I knew nothing about at the time—actually took place when Compton says it did is doubtful to me; at least it contradicts my records of meetings. I can find no record of being in Chicago to meet with Compton in the fall of 1941. My journal records my trip to Chicago as occurring in February 1942, when I made this journal entry: "When Compton asked me if I thought I could devise very soon a chemical process for separating 94 from . . . uranium and fission products—a process that could be successfully scaled up for actual use in a chemical extraction process—I indicated that I could, but I must confess to some misgivings." Of course, whether the conversation took place in December or two months later is of little consequence. My rather hasty expression of confidence, delivered by a young man not likely to admit to probable failure, who was too ignorant to realize the ultimate magnitude of the project or even his inexperience about the intricacies of large-scale production, may have had a more important effect on events than I imagined when I uttered it.

not aimed at victory seem irrelevant. Before, we'd been jogging toward our goal; now we would hit a dead run. The feeling was palpable that results could be a matter of survival.

The next evening I had dinner with some friends across the bay in San Francisco. The city was completely blacked out. After hearing a radio report of an air-raid alarm, we sought refuge in the basement of their apartment building. Huddling in a basement while straining to hear the hum of incoming bombers was a frightening experience that brought the reality of war home in dramatic fashion. This country has never experienced anything since like World War II.

Within days, I was relieved of all teaching duties to concentrate full-time on plutonium research. The university was given a $400,000 contract for related research, administered by Ernest Lawrence. Yet many scientific leaders saw scant reason to expend resources on little-known plutonium, compared with uranium. (Given the secrecy we'd observed, many had never even heard of it.) I believed our work in the past year had proven its potential, but why would any objective observer take the word of a twenty-nine-year-old with every reason to be overly optimistic? Thanks to the support of Lawrence and Compton, however, my group was expanded; it was up to us to find proof of plutonium's usefulness.

Under Section S-1's parceling out of duties, Compton's responsibility for the design of the bomb turned out to be something of a catchall. Until the War Department took control with the Manhattan Project in the fall of 1942, Compton was the de facto leader. He soon decided to consolidate as much of the work as possible at the University of Chicago. The decision made sense. He was in a powerful position there, and the school's administration had pledged unqualified support, which would be important—it would have to empty entire buildings to provide space for the researchers. Chicago's location in the middle of the country made it less vulnerable to foreign attack than the coasts and was a compromise relocation position for people on both coasts.

Enrico Fermi moved to Chicago from Columbia to continue his work on a chain reaction. Ernest Lawrence continued to work in Berkeley—moving his machine-dependent laboratory was impractical. But the main chemical work on plutonium was to be carried out in Chicago.

I visited Chicago in early February for meetings on the status of the plutonium research. In these early days of flight, the trip required me to fly from San Francisco to Los Angeles first to make a connection. My flight arrived late, so I had to stay there overnight. The next flight east did not depart until the next evening, and bad weather diverted it to Kansas City. At least I could take the train from Kansas City, but I arrived in Chicago around 10 p.m., almost two days late. After that adventure, I traveled by train for the rest of the war.

The meetings impressed me with the magnitude of the planned plutonium project. I realized that Chicago would be the heart of the project, and I wanted to be where the action was. When Compton's assistant, Norman Hilberry, came to Berkeley in March, I told him of my willingness to relocate to Chicago with several colleagues, and he agreed immediately.

That evening I took Helen out for a fried chicken dinner at Tiny's Waffle Shop, a favorite diner in Oakland. Back at her apartment, I told her of my impending move to Chicago and shyly beat around the bush about my deep feelings for her, looking for signs of encouragement that I wouldn't be rejected, and finally managed to tell her, "I'm sitting here trying to think of a way to ask you to marry me." She accepted despite my poor effort at a proposal. We made plans for me to go to Chicago while she wrapped up her affairs.

When Helen asked Ernest Lawrence whom she should train to replace her, Lawrence immediately offered her a raise to stay on. "But don't you think I should get married?" she asked.

Lawrence grinned and replied, "Why, of course. Who's the lucky man?" Evidently, our dating had been so discreet that scarcely anyone had noticed. Helen enjoyed such an impeccable reputation at the lab that some spread the rumor that I only proposed because I needed a good secretary in Chicago.

The story of our wedding is worth telling. I moved to Chicago in April 1942 but returned to Berkeley in June to pick up my bride-to-be. We took the train to Los Angeles, so Helen could meet my family. Then we caught another train east, planning to stop for our wedding in Nevada, the fast-marriage state. We noticed Caliente on the map, so we got off the train there, thinking it would be easy to get married and continue east on the next train.

The small station had no checkroom, but the stationmaster said we could leave our bags with him. Caliente was about two blocks of stores overshadowed by the dry, brown Nevada hills. We shyly strolled around the town, but found nothing that looked like a city hall. We went into the town telephone office and asked the operator where we could get a marriage license. "Why, from Evans Edwards," she replied in a tone that indicated we must be terribly stupid to be ignorant of such an obvious fact. Where could we find Mr. Edwards? "Why, down around the corner next to the drugstore," in the same tone that said he was in the same place he'd always been and there must be something the matter with us if we didn't know.

Evans Edwards was leaning back precariously in a swivel chair, staring vacantly into space. He informed us that the closest place to obtain a marriage license was in Pioche, twenty-five miles to the north. Ev went back into his reveries, making it clear that we had already passed the limits of his communicativeness. A woman appeared and told us that we could probably get a ride to Pioche in the mail truck.

Helen went to buy a pair of tennis shoes—the town's pervasive dust found her toeless shoes an attractive resting place—while I set off in search of the mail-truck driver. Perhaps tipped off to the presence of strangers, a deputy sheriff approached. This made me uneasy, given our reception so far.

"Are you a teacher?" he asked.

I was taken aback, embarrassed that such obvious professorial attributes were evidently emanating from me, and nervous that a teacher's unauthorized entry into town and loitering might be an arrestable offense in Caliente. Or perhaps I was about to be detained to make up for a teacher shortage there. The deputy followed up with the even more unsettling: "Do you teach chemistry?"

"Yes," I said. Now I was convinced I was really in for it.

It turned out the young man recognized me because he had just graduated with a chemistry degree from Berkeley. He was back home in Caliente for the summer before taking a job in research laboratories in Washington. How could he help us? He escorted me back to the telephone office to call Pioche to make sure the courthouse would be open (it was Saturday), and then provided an introduction to the mail-truck driver. We drove up the dusty highway, filling mailboxes at ranches.

Thanks to my phone call, the assistant county clerk was waiting for us at the courthouse, though they normally closed at noon on Saturday. She seemed even more nervous than we were when she made out our license. She drove us the mile from the courthouse into town and dropped us at a restaurant to have lunch while she went looking for the minister or judge—there was one of each. We'd passed the point of worrying about which she found; a sorcerer with a wand would do at this point.

She returned while we were eating and said she'd found the judge. He came in a few minutes later to tell us they were waiting for us across the street. I replied that we'd be there as soon as I finished my apple pie, a comment Helen has not forgiven me for more than fifty years later.

They drove us back to the courthouse, where we were married. After the ceremony, the judge made a show of placing the marriage certificate in Helen's hands, saying, "This is for *you*," and telling me that I should keep my hands off it.

Since our ride back to Caliente didn't leave until 4:30, we took a walk into the hills above Pioche and looked out on the expansive desert. The denizens of this town were much friendlier than some of those uncommunicative ones in Caliente. On our way back we were hailed by a man who proudly showed us pictures of the Pioche High School band. They had just won some honor or other, the only honor that had ever been bestowed on Pioche, and they could go on to something else wonderful if they could just raise the money for it, which was difficult in a little town like this, but if we would just buy a picture of the band, he was certain they'd be able to raise the money. How could we refuse? Next, a tipsy man invited us to have a cigarette with him. We gravely thanked him, and told him we were very sorry but we didn't smoke, which caused a look of deep sadness to sweep across his face. He assured us he wasn't angry, however, and said we didn't have to share a smoke with him. We loafed around the street and drank Cokes until it was time for the mail truck to head back to Caliente. There, we checked into the hotel, which occupied the second floor above the railroad station and restaurant. In the morning we caught the train to Chicago.

But that's getting ahead of the story. Let me back up two months.

# EIGHT

# THE MANHATTAN PROJECT

★ I stepped off the *City of San Francisco* and into the Chicago and Northwestern Railroad Station in Chicago on Sunday, April 19, 1942, my thirtieth birthday. The forty-degree temperature contrasted sharply with the early spring weather of Berkeley; the dark, dreary day spawned immediate misgivings about the midwestern climate.

Isadore Perlman had accompanied me on the train. Iz had been a fellow chemistry student at UCLA who'd gone on to receive a doctorate in physiology from Berkeley. I had run into him there toward the end of 1941 and invited him to work with us on "an important war project." He'd immediately shown a wide-ranging ability as an idea man, an experimentalist, and a leader, so I'd asked him to be the first to come with me to Chicago to help set up the group there. Our train trip had taken two days, time that was not in the least wasted because we used it for lively discussions on how to approach the problem we were coming to Chicago to solve—separating element 94 from uranium and fission products. It felt as if there was not a moment to waste.

It's hard for anyone who didn't live through World War II to imagine the desperation and sense of impending doom that we felt, hard to imagine that we believed that Germany and Japan could conquer the world. Looking back from the perspective of superpower America, the United States's advantages of size and industrial capacity seem obvious, but on the day Iz and I got off that train in Chicago, we had little reason to believe America would win. In fact, the evidence pointed the other way.

The United States was not the world power it is today. The bulk of our Pacific fleet lay at the bottom of Pearl Harbor. Almost effortlessly, Japan had overrun the Philippines, the Malay Archipelago, and Burma, and in the process had destroyed another U.S. fleet in the Java Sea. Japanese troops had made it as far as New Guinea and Alaska's Aleutian Islands. The Germans had swept across North Africa, had Leningrad under a viselike siege, and were sweeping through the heart of Russia toward Stalingrad.

These events may have seemed far away, but they were brought home by the total mobilization on the domestic front—gas rationing, food rationing, practice blackouts—which made the idea of the war a dramatic reality.

Even in our corner of the war—work on the bomb—we believed we were behind the Germans and in danger of losing the race. Hahn and Strassmann, the discoverers of fission, had a two-year head start on us. People like Robert Oppenheimer had studied physics in central Europe because it had the leading physics schools. German engineering was the most respected in the world, especially when it came to arms; those Panzers rolling across Europe in the blitzkrieg seemed unstoppable.

I believe that most scientists who worked on the bomb were motivated primarily by the fear of what would happen if the Germans got there first. Politicians and generals, those who thought of strategy and the practicalities of war, were likely to expend the vast resources needed for this because of the offensive capacity they envisioned. But scientists like me thought less about the benefits of having the bomb than about the potentially disastrous consequences of not having it.

Every day, we would follow the war's distant events in the newspapers—German tanks rolling across North Africa, Germans advancing across Russia—events over which we had no control. We could just as easily awaken one day to read the news that Germany had unleashed a powerful new bomb. Every day, every moment, counted.

So, when people pose the common question of whether I had any moral qualms about working on a nuclear weapon, my answer is simple. I didn't have time, couldn't afford to think about such a question. We were fighting for survival, pure and simple, and element 94 might be the one area where we had an edge. We'd kept our discovery secret, and the Germans did not have a cyclotron powerful enough to make it.

Iz and I checked into a hotel, and the next morning walked to the University of Chicago to begin work at a place code-named the "Metallurgical Laboratory," or Met Lab. There I took charge of Section C-1, the group responsible for developing the chemical process for separating element 94 from the uranium and fission products that accompanied its creation. One of our first stops was to see the leader of the Chicago effort, Arthur Compton.

Tall and strikingly handsome in a distinguished way, with a jutting chin, stylish mustache, and winning smile, Compton was chairman of the physics department and dean of the division of physical sciences at the University of Chicago. He was perhaps more conflicted than the rest of us about work on an immensely destructive weapon because of a pacifist upbringing by his Mennonite mother. He had been awarded the 1927 Nobel Prize in physics for his discovery of the Compton effect—the scattering of a photon of light in an interaction with an electron—which was evidence of light's strange duality as both a wave and a particle.

A likable man whose door was always open if I had a problem I wanted to discuss, Compton did an extraordinary job of leading the project. I witnessed his striking power of concentration one wintry night when he slipped on a patch of ice as we were walking down the sidewalk. His limbs went flying in all directions as he spilled head over heels onto the pavement; then he got up, finishing his sentence without a moment's interruption.

Compton told us that our section would work in a laboratory on the fourth floor of the Herbert A. Jones Laboratory. Our space consisted of a big, plain college chemistry lab with the same benches, sinks, and fume hoods as in thousands of labs across the country. Iz and I set up barricades at the entrance to keep any strangers from wandering in.

At first, Iz and I were the only two members of Section C-1. So our immediate task was to assemble a staff. Some of the people we'd been working with for the past few months in Berkeley would join us, but additional recruitment was an interesting challenge. (My two closest collaborators, Joe Kennedy and Art Wahl, continued working in Berkeley;

Glenn Seaborg at about eight months, 1912.

Glenn (four) and his sister Jeanette (two), 1916.

Glenn (thirteen) with his mother, father, and Jeanette at Home Gardens, South Gate, California, 1925.

Glenn (seventeen), with his father, Jeanette, and his mother in South Gate, 1929.

Dwight Logan Reid, the high school teacher who inspired Seaborg to dedicate his life to chemistry.

The small, unfinished UCLA campus in 1929.

Seaborg doing his doctoral research on neutron bombardment of lead in the cavernous East Hall at UC Berkeley, 1937.

Seaborg and Jack Livingood walk past UC Berkeley's Sather Gate on their way to the post office to mail off their history-making manuscript on the discovery of radioactive iodine isotopes, which would find great medical applications.

The old Radiation Laboratory at the University of California at Berkeley, a ramshackle building filled to overflowing with equipment, lab animals, and radio waves.

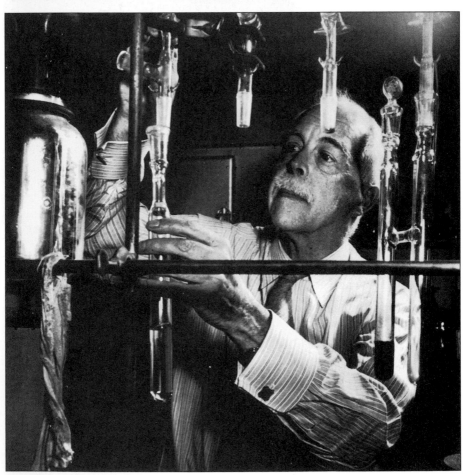

The great chemist G. N. Lewis with the typically simple apparatus he used in experiments from which he deduced amazing amounts of information.

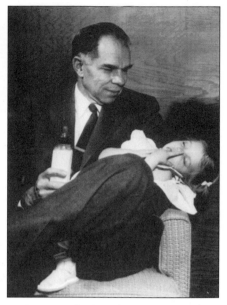

Seaborg and Helen Griggs, who was to become his wife, in San Francisco, Christmas 1941.

Seaborg with his fourteen-month-old daughter Dianne, just after he had been appointed chairman of the Atomic Energy Commission, January 21, 1961.

The Seaborg family playing a game at their new home in Washington, D.C., November 1961. From left: David, Lynne, Glenn (holding Dianne), Helen, Peter, Stephen, and Eric.

Ernest Lawrence, Seaborg, and Robert Oppenheimer at the controls of a cyclotron, 1946. The cyclotron was being converted from its wartime use of producing atomic bomb material to its original purpose as a research tool.

The physicist Stanley Livingston with the cyclotron's inventor, Ernest Lawrence, and an early 27-inch model, 1934.

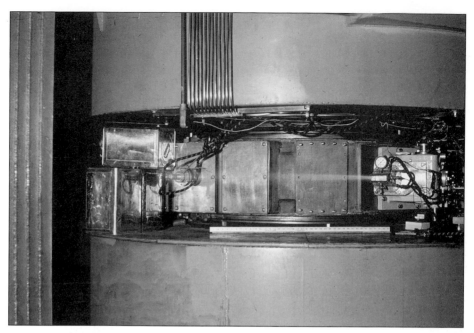

The beam of the 60-inch cyclotron, with deuterons streaming to bombard a target.

Arthur Wahl and Seaborg, co-discoverers of plutonium, with Sample B, which confirmed the favorable fission rate of plutonium 239. The sample was put away in a cigar box and forgotten for years, but now is on display at the Smithsonian.

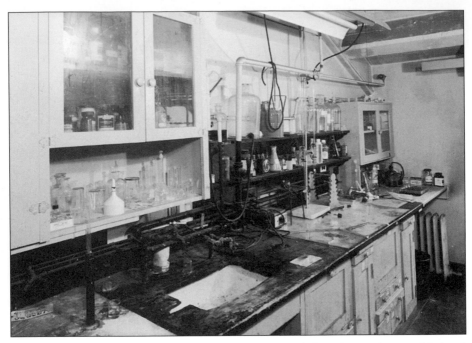

Room 307, Gilman Hall, Berkeley, site of the discovery of plutonium and now a National Historic Landmark.

Arthur Holly Compton, director of Chicago's Metallurgical Laboratory, part of the Manhattan Project.

Seaborg listens for the clicks of a Geiger counter, 1941.

they moved to Los Alamos to lead groups when that laboratory opened.) We were starting very late compared with other war projects, and many scientists were already working on important tasks. (As I've said, Ed McMillan had left Berkeley in the fall of 1940 to do radar research.) I was an unknown young chemist, not a well-known researcher who could attract colleagues by personal reputation or influence; moreover, I couldn't tell a potential recruit the nature of our project. At times I was apprehensive about inviting people to give up secure university positions and gamble on the future of their careers, moving up to two thousand miles away from their homes for a period of unknown duration. To prevent financial competition, we were not allowed to offer any greater incentives than other war projects. But I believed fervently in what we were doing, and noted in my journal: "There is a statement of rather common currency around here and Berkeley that goes something like this: 'No matter what you do with the rest of your life, nothing will be as important to the future of the World as your work on this Project right now.' "

The letter I wrote to my old high school and college friend Stan Thompson, who was languishing as an analytical chemist for an oil company, was typical:

> The work here is extremely important, perhaps the number one war research project in the country, and it is of such a character that it will almost certainly have post-war significance and develop into a large industry. I mention the latter because it shows you there is some possibility that you would find a more agreeable permanent position with this project than your present position with Standard. Unfortunately I cannot divulge to you the nature of the work but, knowing the nature of my activities in the past, you are in a fair position to guess. It is research work of the most interesting type; it is the most interesting problem upon which I have ever worked.

We needed primarily two kinds of skills, those involved with working with radioactive materials (radiochemistry) and those involved with working on a minuscule scale (microchemistry and what we came to call ultramicrochemistry). There were few scientists trained in either discipline in the country.

I wrote to the heads of nuclear chemistry programs at various universities; John Willard joined us from the University of Wisconsin, where he had a radiochemistry program, and he opened the doors to hiring people he knew. I wrote to any classmates I could think of from UCLA and Berkeley. They in turn referred me to their friends. Wendell Latimer, who'd succeeded Lewis as dean at Berkeley, put me in touch with promising students and recent graduates.

A typical example was Dan Koshland, a chemistry graduate who'd been turned down by the Navy because of his eyesight. He accepted a Met Lab job on the basis of Latimer's promise that "this is the most important job in the world." "A couple weeks later I was on my way to Chicago," Dan later wrote, "not knowing on what subject I was going to work, what I was going to be paid, or where I was to be located."

Another recruit kept putting me off week to week, promising, "I'll be there next week." Finally, I sent an urgent telegram saying we needed him by the end of the week, and he showed up. At the end of the war, he came to me with a grin and said, "By the way, what was that project you needed done by the end of the week?"

The few people who turned me down did so because they thought they were already working on more important problems. One friend, who'd been a brilliant student at UCLA and was now on the faculty there, was working on a new antimalarial drug. Besides, his boss heavily discouraged participating in the Met Lab because he suspected we were working on an atomic bomb, which he was certain was a boondoggle that would taint the career of anyone involved with it. Another guessed that we were working on nuclear energy, and responded, "Can't that wait until after? We have a war to win."

Our recruits arrived with amazing rapidity. By June there were twelve of us. By September there were twenty-five and by April 1943, fifty. As recognition of the complexity of our task grew, there were few limitations on hiring to fill our needs. At the peak, my section included one hundred scientists. A new chemistry building was constructed on the edge of the campus.

When a new worker arrived, I took delight in breaking the news about our work. I would usher him into my office and inquire if he knew what we were working on. One said, "I'm a chemist, and you're a chemist, so you must be working with some of the ninety-two elements God created. That must be why you called me here, and that's what I want to work on!" He nearly fell out of his chair when I told him it had nothing to do with the ninety-two elements he'd studied, that we were working with a new element 94. Some stared in disbelief at the news, glassy-eyed and openmouthed; others poured forth a torrent of excited questions.

Considering our hasty, haphazard recruiting, we assembled a remarkable group. Most writers who have described it have remarked on its youthfulness, an average age of perhaps twenty-five. One reason our group's members were young was that they were the ones we could get to uproot themselves on a month's notice. But also, radiochemistry and microchemistry were so new that my college cohort was among the first to have any training in them.

We provided training for those unfamiliar with these fields. Every Tuesday evening we would have a lecture. Notes from the lectures on nuclear chemistry I gave during the summer of 1942 were later given out as a text to new arrivals.

Youthfulness was an advantage in light of the long hours we worked; we usually put in a full day and returned to the lab in the evening after dinner, six days a week. With the war's urgency weighing on everyone, there was little need for pressure from me to get people to work these long hours, although one veteran of the times recalls my complaining about a slacker who did not return in the evenings. He quotes me as saying I was "not opposed to romantic adventures provided the night work did not suffer"!

This intense atmosphere led to a camaraderie akin to that which develops among soldiers. Iz Perlman and I became lifelong friends and collaborators. After the war we were next-door neighbors for years, our families even building and sharing a swimming pool together. We forged friendships with people we scarcely would have known otherwise. Our families and old friends were miles away, and travel for personal affairs was difficult. Helen and I spent the first Christmas of our married life along with Enrico and Laura Fermi as guests at the home of the physicist Walter Zinn and his wife. The presence of the Zinn and Fermi children helped make it really feel like Christmas.

Some of our recruits were fresh from college, too young to have had an opportunity to make a mark. And some seemed to have been caught in unstimulating jobs, as if waiting for the right challenge to come along. At the Met Lab they found their true calling. The core of the research team I worked with for many years first came together at the Met Lab.

My friend Stan Thompson, for example, had been little better than average at UCLA, and he'd worked for years in an undemanding job as a control chemist at Standard Oil's facility near Berkeley. We were golfing partners, and such close friends that I'd been best man at his wedding. I thought I knew him well, so when I invited him to join us in Chicago, I expected a hard worker, reliable and competent but not spectacular. Yet a new Stan Thompson blossomed at the Met Lab. He suddenly displayed an astounding flair for experiment; it was he who conceived and developed the process used for separating plutonium. Stan turned into the best experimental chemist I've ever known. After the war he studied for his doctorate at Berkeley and continued in nuclear research until his early death in 1976.

Albert Ghiorso was another unexpected star. I knew him vaguely at Berkeley because he serviced our radiation counters; Helen knew him well because he'd recently married one of her best friends, another secretary at the lab. When Al asked me to write a letter of recommendation to the Navy for him to do radar work, Helen said, "Al's much too independent for the Navy. He'd be miserable. You should offer him a job here."

According to Al's version of events, he responded to my offer by saying he'd come so long as he wouldn't be assigned the work he was trying to get away from—simply repairing counters and wiring circuits—and that's the work to which we immediately assigned him upon his arrival. He also professes that for the first year he had no clue as to what we were talking about with this enigmatic element. He simply busied himself with the detectors that were his province. He was such an electronics wizard that I eagerly invited him to return to Berkeley after the war as part of our research team, where he designed all the instruments we needed, large and small. He has discovered more elements than anyone, ever. I regularly nominate him for a Nobel Prize, but the same free-spirited nature that makes him such a valuable scientist keeps him from doing the things that would help to get him chosen.

The Met Lab had a central instrument group, but we had better luck relying on our own: when you spent hours setting up an experiment with a short-lived isotope, you couldn't afford to mess with an unreliable counter. Al and Spofford English were so good at this that our instruments were the envy of the other groups, and this even caused some friction: when I insisted that we have priority in the use of our own instruments, they claimed we were unwilling to share.

Our group also displayed an extraordinary esprit. Dan Koshland's attitude was typical. (After the war he became a well-respected biochemist at Brookhaven National Laboratory, then at Berkeley, and served ten years as editor of the prestigious journal *Science*.) He wrote of this time:

> When I was first hired it was explained to me that pluto-nium was extremely lethal, a conclusion based on calcula-tions showing it to be much more dangerous than radium, which had caused many deaths in the radium-dial industry. We were told to take precautions such as wearing gas masks and performing elaborate pipetting procedures to protect ourselves from inhaling the plutonium. Almost unanimously, we young scientists discarded this advice be-cause we believed we were in a necessary war against an evil Hitler bent on global domination. With our friends dy-ing on battlefields, slowing research to be extremely cau-tious about our own lives seemed inappropriate.

When Dan found himself mixing chemicals on the roof, he deduced that he was given such an odd workspace because of the danger of an explosion. There was another young worker on the roof from a different section, and security rules forbade them from telling each other anything about what they were doing, but they worked out signals to warn each other to evacuate in case something went wrong. (Dan was probably working with ether. Ether can explode, but it's more likely he was told to work in the open air to lessen his exposure to the fumes. Segrè and I had often worked on a porch at Berkeley.)

We didn't encourage anyone to ignore the radiation precautions, but Dan's willingness to take some risks was typical of the spirit of the lab. We tried using lead shields, but it was awkward and tiring to hold a beaker at arm's length and the shield in between. Lacking an effective way to measure radiation exposure, we rotated people in and out of the more exposed jobs, and drew blood from them every day. We relied on crude measurements—a drop in the white blood cell count or the cells changing shape indicated that overexposure had already occurred.

Security was a major concern. Soon our makeshift barricades were replaced by the presence of a security guard at the door of the lab. We didn't talk about the project outside it, even at the university cafeteria or faculty club. If you received a phone call from someone claiming to be on the project, you took the number and called back; the lab's phone numbers were easily recognizable. Although we dropped the cumbersome "copper," we still used code to discuss plutonium. We took the final digit of element 94 and the final digit of the weight of its isotope (239) and called it 49; the code could be adapted to other isotopes.

Security rules called for compartmentalization of knowledge based on one's "need to know," a policy we followed as much as possible, but in science you can seldom define what someone "needs to know" to solve a problem. An unexpected, apparently unrelated detail is often a key. We sometimes made our own judgments; I never withheld any information from Fermi, for example.

For our section, however, compartmentalization was relatively simple. The chemistry of plutonium was a particularly important secret, and even small details could be vital. Arthur Compton considered the fact that plutonium fluoride was insoluble to be an especially precious secret, because it was unexpected and a key to its separation.

Our chemists proved to be remarkably closemouthed. At a party celebrating the end of the war, a group of chemists were playing charades with their wives. When the husbands tried to act out the word "plutonium," the wives were mystified; they'd never heard of the stuff. Not one had revealed what he'd been working on for the past three years, not even to his wife. (Compton was so accustomed to confiding in his wife that he had her cleared; fortunately for me, Helen had already been cleared because of her work at the Rad Lab, and already knew about much of what we were doing.)

From the beginning, the atom bomb project focused on two potential bomb-core explosives—uranium and plutonium.

The huge question in the uranium research was how to separate the main fissile isotope of uranium, uranium 235, from the great mass of uranium 238, which made up about 99 percent of natural uranium. That question was being investigated at several laboratories around the country, with the most promising processes being a magnetic separation process that Ernest Lawrence was deeply involved in and an isotope-weight-based gaseous diffusion method being pursued at Columbia University.

The plutonium work was centered at Chicago and focused on two key questions: how to make enough of it to be useful and how to isolate it once it was produced. The first was mainly a question of physics, the second a question of chemistry, which my division was assigned.

Enrico Fermi's team was working on how to produce plutonium. At Berkeley, we'd bombarded a kilogram of uranium for a week to produce less than a millionth of a gram of plutonium. At that rate, a yearlong bombardment might produce fifty micrograms; it would take 20,000 years to make a kilogram. No one knew exactly how much material would be needed for a bomb, but it was estimated to be several kilograms. Cyclotron bombardment was not a practical method for making large amounts of plutonium: it relied on the hit-or-miss process of neutrons from the beryllium target colliding with uranium nuclei and transmuting them an atom at a time.

Theoretically, there was a much more efficient way to produce plutonium, something called a chain reaction. When a uranium nucleus fissions into two elements, the total number of neutrons in these elements is always less than the number in a uranium atom. Thus, extra neutrons are sent flying. If these neutrons collide with other uranium 235 atoms, these atoms might fission as well, giving off more neutrons, which will cause still more uranium 235 nuclei to split. Meanwhile, stray neutrons will also be absorbed by the uranium 238, making it uranium 239, which will then transmute into neptunium 239, then plutonium 239. The chain reaction will last until all the potential "fuel" has been used. If you had uranium 235 at a high enough concentration, an instantaneous, uncontrolled chain reaction in which all the material would fission simultaneously would provide unimaginably large explosive power—the bomb. But by interspersing material that would absorb some of these neutrons, we hoped to control the rate of the reaction.

The chain reaction is analogous to the growth of bacteria—one bacterium splits into two, two split into four, four split into eight. They say that a single bacterium reproducing under ideal conditions could cover a football field with a foot-thick layer of descendants in twenty-four hours. Fermi's team of physicists applied themselves to the work of sustaining a controlled nuclear reaction.

The chemistry group's challenge was to come up with a process by which we could separate out the plutonium from all the material in the aftermath of the chain reaction. This process would have to work on a large scale. The plutonium would be present in a concentration of about 250 parts per million. That meant that there would be about half a pound of plutonium in each ton of irradiated uranium. The uranium would also contain a large selection of intensely radioactive fission products. So our challenge was to find a way to separate relatively small amounts of plutonium from tons of material so intensely radioactive that no one could come near; the separation would have to be performed by remote control behind several feet of concrete. There could be no breakdowns requiring repairs because the radioactivity would keep anyone from approaching the apparatus once it started operating.

We would have to develop this process for an element that now existed in such minute amounts that no one had ever even seen it. All our knowledge of it was based on the secondary evidence of tracer chemistry—measurements of radioactivity and deduced reactions. Tracer chemistry was itself relatively new; deductions based on it were often subject to doubt.

The first question was how to have any plutonium to work on in a meaningful way. I thought we might be able to work with even the minuscule amounts that could be generated through cyclotron bombardment. Even micrograms could be useful if we adopted the techniques of microchemistry.

The project commandeered the cyclotron at Washington University in St. Louis, which bombarded the uranium nonstop, twenty-four hours a day, for a year. (We obtained smaller amounts from a Berkeley cyclotron.) For our first year and a half, these cyclotrons were our only source of plutonium, supplying a total of 2,000 micrograms (two milligrams). From an amount equal in size to a grain of salt, we tried to devise a process to separate pounds of plutonium from tons of uranium.

The scale-up of this process would be unprecedented—on the order of a billion times. A billion is a hard-to-conceive number: if you took a ball an eighth of an inch in diameter and increased its diameter a billion times, it would be close to the size of the moon.

No one had ever tried such a thing, and I had no experience in taking a process from laboratory to industrial scale. My experience with industrial processes consisted of little more than my summer at the tire plant. I did know that processes that work in the lab often do not work in industry because the relative concentrations change as the process is scaled up. Chemical reactions change when you alter the concentrations of the reactants; a reaction that occurs in a 10 percent solution may not occur in a 20 percent solution. For example, in our small-scale studies, we might have been able to use twice as much acid in the laboratory as would have been practical in the scale-up. It would be easy to use misleading concentrations—you need to dissolve a product in some reaction matrix to get it to react, and the tendency is to use a matrix that makes your life easier.

But I thought we could try to replicate the projected conditions of the separation process by using the same concentrations. This would mean working on a scale invisible to the naked eye, a scale much smaller than even standard microchemistry, which led Paul Kirk, one of our leading practitioners, to coin the term "ultramicrochemistry."

Our ultramicrochemists would work under the microscope with micrograms per microliter, which is the same proportion as grams per liter, the concentration that would be used in the scaled-up separation. If you used a microliter of this and two microliters of that in the lab process, you would scale up directly to a liter of this and two liters of that in the large-scale process, just as if you used one egg for a single loaf of bread, you would need a thousand eggs to make the dough for a thousand loaves of bread.

Perhaps the first laboratory task Iz Perlman and I performed was to build a balance for weighing materials; our group had to construct whole new sets of instruments for these fantastically small requirements. A typical balance consisted of a thin quartz fiber—the fibers ranged in size from four times the diameter of a human hair down to a thinness invisible to the unaided eye—with a tiny holder at one end for the sample, perhaps a pan of platinum foil. An object's weight was determined by measuring the amount that the quartz fiber arm bent when you had the object in the holder. Some of our researchers referred to this as weighing "invisible material with an invisible balance."

By using minuscule amounts of solutions, even microgram quantities of plutonium and associated fission products could be used in relatively high concentrations. We handled the infinitesimal volumes of solutions, ranging from 0.1 to 0.00001 milliliter, using specially constructed capillary containers, pipetters, and micromanipulators. Our "test tubes" and "beakers" were made of finely calibrated capillary tubing with an inside diameter of from 0.1 to 1 millimeter. Measurements could be made using air pressure to govern the movement of the liquid. The solids in the reagents and precipitates weighed from 0.1 to 100 micrograms. The components were all so small that researchers could mix and measure reagents on the stage of a microscope, with everything contained within the field of view. (I didn't quite believe that some of these tiny amounts could be measured, until one of the microchemists gave me a demonstration.)

On the morning of July 27, a truck pulled up to the laboratory with our first 300-pound shipment of neutron-irradiated uranium from St. Louis. Two of our researchers were detailed the unenviable task of carrying the shipment up to our fourth-floor laboratory. The uranium had been shipped surrounded by a layer of lead bricks and packaged in Masonite and plywood boxes made in various odd sizes designed to fit in the nooks and crannies around the cyclotron target. Some of the seams of the boxes had cracked open, spilling radioactive cargo, and we could not get hold of an instrument to measure the radioactivity. The best advice I could give our workers was to wear rubber gloves and lab coats, and to stay as far away from the boxes as practical.

We waited a week or so for the "hot" material to cool down enough for us to work with it, and then began the laborious process of dissolving it in liters and liters of ether so as to reduce greatly the amount of overall material we would deal with. We had crews constantly on the roof stirring the tanks of ether for this extraction.

Meanwhile, two microchemists, Burris Cunningham and Louis Werner, worked with a small sample created at the Berkeley cyclotron. Using techniques similar to those we'd developed with Arthur Wahl, they were trying to isolate some plutonium. On August 20, I wrote in my journal: "Perhaps today was the most thrilling day I have experienced since coming to the Met Lab. Our microchemists isolated pure element 94 for the first time! It is the first time that element 94 (or any synthetic element, for that matter) has been beheld by the eye of man. I'm sure my feelings were akin to those of a new father who has been engrossed in the development of his offspring since conception."

One of our workers brought in floodlamps and his camera and photographed everything in sight for the historic occasion. We watched as this small precipitate of a plutonium salt (plutonium fluoride) slowly took on a pinkish hue. I felt like passing out cigars when I announced our success at a research meeting that evening.

A few days later, on September 10, Cunningham and Werner weighed a pure plutonium compound for the first time, setting 2.77 micrograms of plutonium oxide on one of their scales. (For comparison, a dime weighs about 2.5 grams, about a million times as much.)

When we were making these breakthroughs, excited researchers from other sections often stopped in for a peek at the first visible artificial element. But every bit of material was so precious that at times we couldn't spare any to put on a viewing stage. At one point, we colored some aluminum hydroxide with ink and put it on a stage for handy viewing. Not wanting to sacrifice our scientific allegiance to the truth, we presented it with the careful remark: "This represents a sample of plutonium hydroxide." It was not our fault if the viewer believed it to be a pure plutonium hydroxide sample.

Not everyone was impressed with our achievements. In September, the army was given control of the atom-bomb project, code-named Manhattan Engineer District, under the command of General Leslie Groves. General Groves was on an introductory tour of the laboratory when we invited him to view one of our precious new samples. A researcher carefully lined up the sample under the microscope with great pride, only to hear Groves's gruff "I don't see anything!" followed by the equally deflating "I'll be interested when you can show me a few pounds of the stuff!"

That reaction was typical of the hard-driving Groves, who was almost consciously unpleasant and abrasive, in stark contrast to the collegial tone we were accustomed to. But the way he ran the Manhattan Project was nothing short of spectacular, with all the parts, including huge industrial projects, up and running successfully in time to go on to the next step that depended on them. His personnel choices—such as putting Robert Oppenheimer in charge of the Los Alamos laboratory—were always on the mark. (Much has been written about Groves picking Oppenheimer out of relative obscurity, and this when Oppenheimer had no administrative experience. But such comments neglect the fact that Compton had already brought Oppie into the project as leader of the theoretical physics studies. I knew of no better choice for the position.)

As limited quantities of plutonium from the cyclotron-bombarded uranium became available, we carefully apportioned them among our many tasks, decisions that required me to apply the lessons I'd learned from Lewis about how to break a problem down into its parts. If we'd been performing academic research, we might have tested the most likely approach until we ruled it in or out, then gone steadily step by step, ruling out one avenue at a time, perhaps being distracted to pursue items of interest encountered along the way. But lacking time for that, we attacked on as many fronts as possible simultaneously, emphasizing practical results over theory, single-minded in keeping to our goal and timetable.

A group parallel to ours was assigned research into the fission byproducts produced along with plutonium during the bombardments. Their results would be critical to us—we needed to know what isotopes would be in the mix in order to separate them out.

Frustrated by this group's plodding approach, Iz Perlman and a partner spent a couple of weeks on a brief survey elucidating the broad points critical to the separation chemistry. One day, in the midst of this work, Iz placed a beaker filled with his sample on a shelf before going home for the night. Someone came along behind him and, evidently worried about radiation, clumsily surrounded the beaker with lead bricks. One of these bricks fell on and broke the beaker. Iz came in the next morning to be greeted by the sight of perhaps a quarter of the world's supply of plutonium 239 soaked into the Sunday edition of the Chicago *Tribune*. Quick-witted Iz placed the soggy newspaper in the largest evaporating dish he could find, and over several days reclaimed the sample by dissolving the newspaper in acid.

When Iz "published" his fission-product results in the Met Lab's internal publication, the leader of the other group complained bitterly that we had skimmed the cream off from his research area. He demanded a meeting with our supervisors to confront us—an ugly scene—but we responded that we were simply pursuing information critical to our assignment. One supervisor spent the meeting reading his newspaper and grumbling that "if Seaborg minded his own business" such disagreeable incidents wouldn't happen. I thought it was better to endure a few such confrontations and meet our assignments. We weren't looking for academic laurels when we published; we had a job to do.


That fall, I uncovered a disturbing phenomenon that almost derailed the plutonium portion of the Manhattan Project. Plutonium was an alpha emitter; that made it a desirable bomb explosive—its alpha emissions would not cause reactions with other plutonium atoms (as neutrons would). But it would be impossible to achieve 100 percent purity; there would always be some other fission products present. What if the plutonium's alpha particles collided with the fission products and caused them to give off neutrons? Could these neutrons cause plutonium atoms to fission, giving off even more neutrons? My calculations indicated that even a very small amount of these "impurities" could cause premature fissioning in enough of the plutonium to cause the bomb to fizzle.

When a couple of physicists in Fermi's group confirmed my calculations, I wrote to Robert Oppenheimer and Arthur Compton to inform them. I believed that plutonium was still practical and we could find a way to purify it to the required level, provided that we be allowed to hire substantially more chemists and metallurgists to do the necessary research. Those letters sparked the appointment of a high-level special committee to reexamine whether plutonium might be practical bomb material after all.

While the special committee was debating the future of the plutonium project, Fermi's team spent several weeks preparing to attempt a chain reaction. The final experiment lasted less than a day, but the preparation involved piling up six tons of uranium metal, fifty tons of uranium oxide, and four hundred tons of graphite. Fermi called this unwieldy apparatus a "pile," a term that enjoyed currency for years in the nuclear lexicon but that has been superseded in modern usage by the term "reactor."

The relatively pure uranium's normal radioactive decay would start the chain reaction. The graphite was interspersed with the uranium as a "moderator" that would absorb neutrons. By taking neutrons from the fission out of circulation, it would slow down the reaction. Graphite control rods could be withdrawn to start the reaction or slid back in to slow or stop it.

Yet no one could know for certain what would happen when the control rods were withdrawn—whether the chain reaction would start and whether it could be stopped once it did. Because of the impossible-to-rule-out possibility that the chain reaction might run away uncontrollably, the first test was to be held on the outskirts of Chicago at what is now the Argonnne National Laboratory; however, labor difficulties had delayed the construction of the buildings needed there. Fermi was ahead of schedule, and rather than wait for the buildings, he made the case that it would be safe to conduct the test in a squash court under the stands at the football stadium at the University of Chicago. Compton made the courageous decision to do so. Some say his decision to go ahead with the experiment in town was based on a desire to show substantive progress in the plutonium project, which was then under review. If that is so, it is perhaps evidence of the political as well as scientific instincts of this remarkable man.

Late in the afternoon of December 2, 1942, I ran into one of the members of the committee evaluating the plutonium project. I described the encounter in my journal: "As he approached me, I could see from his demeanor he was bursting with good news. The aura of cheerfulness and excitement that he carried with him and the way he held out his hand in greeting told me that this signified more than just taking pleasure in seeing me again. Then when I heard him say he had just come from the West Stands, I understood the reason for his jubilation. Fermi has produced a chain reaction—the pile is a success! Of course, we have no way of knowing if this is the first time a sustained chain reaction has been achieved. The Germans may have beaten us to it."

Boosted by Fermi's exciting demonstration that we had a way of creating plutonium 239, the committee backed the continuation of the project. My plea for more help was heeded, and I was given carte blanche to expand the staff to work on separation to an unprecedented level of purity.

Handling a staff of more than fifty scientists was quite a challenge. More than one of the staff members commented later on one aspect of my management style. If a researcher was not producing, I didn't think that berating him or speaking to him harshly would do much good. (I say "him" because we had virtually no women researchers.) But soon he would notice that another researcher at a neighboring bench had been assigned the same problem. Almost everyone to whom this happened quickly got the message and picked up the level of his work. Word would get out when this occurred, and no one wanted to be a victim of it.

# NINE

# SCALING UP A BILLION TIMES

✸ Just two months after he joined the project, Stan Thompson made a key breakthrough in the chemical separation puzzle. We knew that plutonium had at least two oxidation states, in which it held different numbers of electrons and would therefore have differing chemical properties. The different properties of the two states could be exploited as a way to effect the separation.

Uranium and the related element thorium can both be induced to rise to the plus-four (IV) oxidation state, in which they form phosphate compounds that are insoluble in moderately acidic solutions. That is, if they are oxidized and mixed with phosphates, they will form solids that precipitate out of the moderate acid. We expected plutonium to share many of uranium's properties, and this property could be a useful one. Stan took on the task of testing whether the phosphates known to be insoluble in acid solutions would "carry" plutonium out of the solution. He had little luck until he got to bismuth phosphate—an unlikely candidate, based on our knowledge of its chemistry. His preliminary tests were not successful, but in December 1942 Stan had one of those hunches that made him such an outstanding experimentalist.

Established practice in working with carriers was to use the carriers at low concentrations. Stan decided to try using a quite high concentration of bismuth phosphate. His results were so positive that he immediately interrupted Cunningham and Werner and asked them to do an ultramicrochemistry test of the process. Their test, at the concentrations expected in the industrial plant, found that bismuth phosphate carried the plutonium at the tremendously encouraging rate of 98 percent.

The process Stan eventually developed works as follows. Neutron-irradiated uranium is dissolved in nitric acid and sulfuric acid. The high acidity prevents the uranium from precipitating when the bismuth phosphate is added; however, the plutonium does form a precipitate with the bismuth phosphate. This precipitate is then recovered and dissolved in less acidic nitric acid. An oxidation agent is added that oxidizes the plutonium from level IV to level VI. The bismuth phosphate does not carry the plutonium (VI), and the bismuth phosphate precipitates out, leaving a relatively pure plutonium still in solution. A reduction agent (which counteracts the oxidation agent) is then added to return the plutonium to the (IV) form, so the cycle can be repeated for greater purity.

The process sounds simple in this summary, but the development and optimization took months of intensive work. Stan's discovery was a touch serendipitous, because the process works in inexplicable fashion. Bismuth phosphate's ability to carry plutonium (IV) was totally unexpected; in fact, it conflicted with theory and is still not well explained.

We couldn't be certain the bismuth phosphate process would work, so we spent the early months of 1943 testing and refining several possible separation techniques. In the spring it was time to choose the one process on which the Manhattan Project engineers would base a huge industrial enterprise. In normal times, if you were scaling up a process from the laboratory to an industrial plant, you'd take as much time as you needed to perfect the process on a small scale, then build one or more small-scale pilot plants to test the process for an extended period of time. Only when you knew it worked on the pilot scale would you start design drawings for a production plant.

But the war didn't allow time for normal procedures. All the steps would have to be telescoped to overlap in ways no company would ever dare try. The pilot plant would be built before we'd finished developing the process. The production plant would be built before returns were in from the pilot plant. The separation process had to be chosen by the spring of 1943 so workers could break ground if the plants were to be completed in time to contribute to the war effort.

We'd narrowed the choice to two finalists—the process that used bismuth phosphate as the carrier for the plutonium and a similar process that used lanthanum fluoride as the carrier. We had used lanthanum fluoride to isolate plutonium since our incipient experiments in discovering it. Lanthanum fluoride was a tried, reliable carrier, but it had a huge drawback: it is fiendishly corrosive, especially in large quantities and high concentrations. We knew of no pipe material that lanthanum fluoride wouldn't eat through.

The drawback of the bismuth phosphate approach was that it contradicted theory. Many scientists opposed it vociferously because, according to accepted theory, bismuth phosphate should not carry plutonium in the plus-four oxidation state. James Franck, head of the chemistry division, was a particularly outspoken opponent. A Nobel laureate physicist, Franck insisted it would be irresponsible to count on a process whose mechanism of action couldn't be explained. Perhaps it worked in our test tubes and tiny capillary tubes, but it wouldn't work in the plant. How could we be confident it would work on a scale-up of a billion, a scale-up never before attempted? How could we build huge plants on the basis of a process that we couldn't understand?

I had faith in our empirical evidence that showed the bismuth phosphate process worked. We'd tested it on the microchemical scale at the concentrations that would be present in the separation plant. Some of our microchemists had difficulty with it, but the best of them, Burris Cunningham, assured me that it worked. But how could I be sure, and how could I oppose a man of Franck's reputation?

The pressure was tremendous. What if the Germans beat us to the bomb because we'd picked the wrong process? Not only would the choice lead to a huge industrial commitment, but the entire war might turn on this question.

A decisive meeting was called for June 1. The final decision would be in the hands of Crawford Greenewalt, head of a research division for Du Pont. Du Pont had agreed to build several plants for the Manhattan Project, taking on the assignment, in Greenewalt's words, "with considerable trepidation" only after General Groves convinced their board that their corporation was the best in the country to attempt it. Du Pont's contract with the government provided a corporate profit of one dollar for their entire effort.

Greenewalt went on to serve with distinction as president of the company after the war, an outcome that did not surprise those of us who worked with him. As head of the company's effort on plutonium, he impressed us from the beginning with his quick grasp of the technical concepts involved.

Many scientists on the project, having spent careers in academia, were as suspicious of dealing with a huge corporation as they were concerned with being swallowed by the military. Greenewalt was sensitive to this concern, saying that Du Pont would be a "handmaiden" to the laboratory. The research and development would still be in the hands of the scientists; Du Pont's role would be to take the techniques we developed to an industrial scale.

Greenewalt's background inspired confidence because he'd played a key role in bringing a new product called nylon from the laboratory to an instant marketing sensation. Du Pont researchers had discovered the class of superpolymers that included nylon in 1930; in 1934 they'd learned how to draw it out into fibers. After six years of intensive development and a twenty-million-dollar investment, a large-scale production plant had come on-line in January 1940. While his experience was reassuring, we didn't have anything near the ten years it had taken a product as simple as stockings to go from discovery to market. At one of his first meetings with the Met Lab staff, Greenewalt proved he'd be a take-charge person willing to shoulder responsibility and face unpleasant consequences by saying that the only way we could keep to our ambitious schedule would be to take chances at each step of the way: "There should be no hesitation to spend an extra fifty million dollars to insure reliability and speed."

The June 1 meeting he called was an intense all-day affair. We dissected every aspect of the two potential methods, down to the details of the likelihood that each weld on the stainless-steel vessels would be properly heat-treated to keep from failing.

In many ways, the lanthanum fluoride process was superior. It made more sense chemically; we had more experience with it. It was likely to have a better yield, and some were certain the bismuth phosphate process couldn't work. After hearing all the arguments, Greenewalt said that what concerned him most was not the potential positive aspects of the processes as much as the potential negatives, the dangers. He deftly summarized the worst-case scenario for each process. For bismuth phosphate, the worst case would be inefficiency; the yield would be lower than we hoped. For the lanthanum fluoride process, the worst case would be a failure of the equipment, a complete loss with no yield at all.

Those were the points on which the decision turned: the downside of the lanthanum fluoride process was catastrophe; the downside of the bismuth fluoride process was poor performance. But how bad would the performance be? How bad a performance could we afford?

For me, the climax of the meeting came late in the afternoon, when Greenewalt asked, "Glenn, using the bismuth phosphate process, can you guarantee me a yield of fifty percent?" That was a horrible yield; we would be retrieving only half the plutonium formed in the reactors and letting half go to waste. "Yes," I answered without hesitation, I was certain we could clear a hurdle that low.

Greenewalt picked the bismuth phosphate process, and asked that we have it completely operable by August 1.


In the weeks before the meeting my sleep had been disturbed and restless. When I went to bed, I was so wound up with worry, my mind so alive with the problems and possibilities of the day, that it would not let go; there was no refreshment in what little sleep I found.

Right after the meeting, I felt too fatigued and ill to make it into the lab some days. I had papers sent to our apartment and visitors came by to discuss business. When my condition didn't improve, Helen insisted on calling a doctor. After an examination I was admitted to the hospital with the diagnosis of an upper respiratory ailment and low-grade fever. In retrospect, I would call it stress-induced nervous exhaustion.

Spending ten days in the hospital was more frustrating than helpful. My fever showed no signs of subsiding, and the hospital would not release me until it did. A physician friend on the Met Lab staff who came to visit suggested a way out of this dilemma. When the nurse left the room, I took the thermometer out of my mouth until the temperature returned to normal. That got me released from the hospital, but I was still too weak to return to the lab. Joyce Stearns, the Met Lab personnel director, wrote me a note saying that he had consulted with a physician, who recommended a four-week vacation. Stearns added: "This is not a request—it is an order, one of the very few ever issued by this office."

A few days later, Helen and I caught a train to New Mexico. The desert would be warm and restful, but I was also drawn there by the possibility of visiting old friends who had recently relocated to the new secret laboratory we knew as Site Y. We were never told Los Alamos' exact location, but we had a pretty good idea of where it was when a large number of friends and colleagues suddenly changed their addresses to Post Office Box 1663 in Santa Fe.

My body rested during a week at a ranch in the country, but my mind found too few distractions. A week of sightseeing amidst the bustle of Santa Fe was more relaxing. The La Fonda Hotel was made interesting by the too-well-dressed FBI sorts, conspicuous by their conformity, who populated the lobbies and restaurants. Robert and Kitty Oppenheimer and Joe and Adrienne Kennedy came down from Los Alamos for an enjoyable dinner talking about old times, with any mention of present endeavors strictly off limits. Compartmentalization precluded us from visiting Los Alamos.

The Met Lab had sent a 200-microgram sample of plutonium to Site Y so the scientists there could measure its rate of neutron emissions, an important characteristic for assessing its feasibility as an explosive. That sample was close to our entire supply, and we needed it back as quickly as possible. It had been shipped by courier to Los Alamos, but to save time I planned to carry it back myself. The morning of our departure, the physicist Bob Wilson met us for a predawn breakfast to transfer the sample. For protection, he'd brought along his Winchester hunting rifle. The sample made the bus and train trip back to Chicago tucked in my suitcase.

The trip did little to improve my condition. A week after we returned, I was still spending more time at home than in the lab, when Foster and Ann York invited us to their home for dinner. Foster, the patent attorney for the Met Lab, told me that he'd had a similar problem. He'd found only one way to cure it, and that was playing golf. I replied as politely as I could that that sounded rather far-fetched, but Foster insisted. Golf was the only cure. Since no medical advice had helped, what did I have to lose by trying?

Stan Thompson and I had often played together in Berkeley, and he came with me to the Jackson Park course the next Saturday. It was completely exhausting, taking all my energy to drag myself around the links. But that night I had my first good night's sleep in months. I couldn't believe it at first, but it made such an incredible difference that I was quickly converted to Foster's cure. I played golf as often as possible and, finally able to sleep again, recovered from my malaise.

Once again, my body had told me that neglecting exercise would be costly to my health. I became scrupulous about getting regular exercise for the rest of my life. Golf was my mainstay for many years, until I discovered hiking could be even more beneficial, especially climbing steep hills.

Among my various golfing partners at the Met Lab, perhaps the most unusual was Zene Jasaitis, another UCLA chemistry classmate. Zene's skills as an amateur jeweler were indispensable in our metallurgical studies of plutonium. He also stands out as the most efficient golfer I ever met, carrying only one club—a putter. Why drag around a whole set of clubs when you can hit any shot with a putter?

During my illness, Iz Perlman did a first-class job of running our section. He was bright, personable, easy to work with, well liked, and ready for any assignment. Accordingly, he was selected to head the contingent from our lab that would transfer to Site X, where the plutonium separation and pile reactor pilot plants would be built.

The Army had purchased eighty square miles in an isolated area of Appalachian valleys and ridges, all but empty of people, near Knoxville, Tennessee. It later became better known as the Oak Ridge National Laboratory, named for the town constructed to house our personnel, but we called it Clinton Laboratories then, after a nearby hamlet that predated our arrival.

Met Lab staff began transferring to Clinton by the fall of 1943. Starting in September, I visited every month for a year for meetings and to track the progress. It was an overnight train trip from Chicago, with a change of trains in Cincinnati, and you always had to arrive early enough to save your "confirmed" sleeping berth from being preempted by interlopers on the overloaded wartime conveyances.

Oak Ridge looked like an unfinished movie set, with freshly bulldozed streets and prefab houses, the Tennessee clay permeating everything. During my first visits, I invariably contracted "Clinton fever," nausea and diarrhea brought on by contaminated food in the cafeteria. I learned to avoid it by staying at the home of my friends Vance and Mary Cooper. Mary graciously fed me breakfast and dinner and even sent me off in the morning with sandwiches for lunch.

Following the decision to use the bismuth phosphate process, Du Pont moved with amazing speed to construct the pilot plants. Huge plants for the separation of uranium 235 would also be built at this site. The chain-reacting pile began operation on November 4. Six weeks later the first chain-reacted uranium entered the pilot plant to test the plutonium separation process. Some chemists were still so certain that the bismuth phosphate process was doomed they were betting money against it right up to the moment the plant began to run. From the start, the plant's yield met the lowest-acceptable 50 percent hurdle Crawford Greenewalt had set. In six months the yield was between 80 and 90 percent.

The plant provided vital information on how to improve the separation process. For example, the early yields suffered because the bismuth phosphate–plutonium precipitates often stuck to the walls of the tank. Equipment was installed to wash these precipitates off the tank walls with nitric acid. The researchers also found that they could dissolve the precipitates more readily by changing the order in which reagents were added.

The plants began producing plutonium in milligram and then gram quantities. The plutonium was what we called decontaminated—separated from most of the dangerously radioactive uranium and fission products—but it was still far from pure. Laboratory-scale operations were still needed to isolate or purify it.

Some of this plutonium was shipped to Los Alamos so researchers could study its properties as a pure metal, the form in which it would be used as a bomb ingredient. Some plutonium was also shipped to the Met Lab, where we could scale up our studies, abandoning the glass capillary tubing of ultramicrochemistry for stainless-steel equipment that would test on the scale of liters.

The Met Lab received its first plutonium from the Clinton Laboratories on January 1, 1944: 1,500 micrograms, which almost equaled the total amount of plutonium produced in all previous cyclotron bombardments. Within a month, we expected it to begin arriving in gram quantities, a thousand times larger than this shipment. We'd recently moved our work into a new building constructed for the Manhattan Project, where I was making my rounds when I suddenly realized that when these greater quantities arrived we would have to change our work methods completely.

We still knew very little about radiation poisoning. Looking back in my journals, I am struck by how important the experience of the radium dial-painting industry was. Women who painted radium on the dials of watches to make them glow in the dark habitually had licked their paintbrushes into better points. The effects of their thus ingesting radium gave the first evidence of radiation poisoning.

I was determined that none of my people would be subjected to avoidable dangers from plutonium. Actually plutonium is not penetratingly radioactive. Its alpha particles travel a few centimeters and can be blocked easily by glass. Outside the body, these amounts of plutonium would not be worrisome. But if it finds its way into the body, plutonium is extremely hazardous. Studies would soon show that plutonium is readily assimilated into bone, where it becomes a permanent source of internal radiation.

The Met Lab's otherwise outstanding medical staff had completely overlooked the danger of alpha radiation when the new lab was being planned. I immediately contacted them about taking remedial action. The plutonium began to arrive before any corrective measures had been implemented, and I all but threatened to stop work until they were. My insistence was not popular, considering that the building was new, but soon the lab was revamped with hoods to filter the air and linoleum floors that would be easier to wash.

We had some minor accidents. For example, late one night a test tube containing about 5 milligrams of plutonium broke in one researcher's hands. We recovered about a milligram from the washings from his hands—which meant his hands were contaminated. To avoid ingesting the residue he had to wear gloves whenever he ate or drank until the alpha count on his hands went down.

But no one contracted any acute radiation sickness, and in later years there's been little or no evidence of increased rates of cancer or other radiation-related maladies among the Met Lab staff.

Our main research problem at the Met Lab became that of ensuring that the separation process would work well at the concentrations we now expected in the industrial plants. Our work was largely devoted to testing many oxidizing and reducing agents to select the best ones for each step, working out optimum conditions for each step, improving the removal of fission products and other contaminants, and developing procedures to concentrate and isolate the plutonium after the decontamination process.

We had to make sure that our decontamination process, which we'd developed using uranium bombarded in a cyclotron, would work as well on uranium chain-reacted in a pile. We found that the process did in fact work well, and we pursued further refinements. But soon a huge problem surfaced in the plutonium itself from the reactor-generated material.

One morning in the summer of 1944, a pair of Met Lab leaders stopped in my office to tell me that the ultrapurification program for plutonium—the program started in the fall of 1942 to remove fission products to an extremely high degree of purity—was being canceled because it was no longer needed. When they said that I had been cleared to know the reason but I was not to tell anyone else, I quickly responded that I didn't want to hear any more about it from them. Under the somewhat byzantine rules of compartmentalization, if they told me the reason I would be forbidden to tell anyone else, but if they didn't tell me, I would be free to speculate. Compartmentalization couldn't prevent you from having ideas. The cancellation would result in many people being laid off or reassigned, and I thought it only fair to tell them why.

I was pretty certain I knew why; I'd published a report about the problem more than a year before. All the plutonium we'd dealt with early on had been formed through cyclotron bombardment, which resulted in adding a single neutron to uranium 238 to form plutonium 239. In the reactor, the presence of many more "free" neutrons drove the chain reaction. My report speculated that these neutrons could cause other plutonium isotopes to form in the reactor; one additional neutron could lead to the formation of plutonium 240, an isotope that would be susceptible to spontaneous fission because of its even-numbered atomic weight. Plutonium that underwent spontaneous fission would be compromised as a bomb fuel, since it would emit neutrons causing premature fissioning in the plutonium 239. It was the same trouble impurities could cause and the reason for our ultrapurification program. But if there was a plutonium isotope that would lead to the bomb fizzling instead of exploding, separating out the impurities was irrelevant.

At the time I wrote the report, we had no idea whether plutonium 240 existed. And—perhaps because of compartmentalization, perhaps because of the great amount of research material we were accumulating—the problem I presented never entered the consciousness of the physicists at Los Alamos. But they discovered it immediately in the summer of 1944, when the first reactor-produced, purified plutonium arrived, which they quickly ascertained had an unacceptably high rate of spontaneous fission. And because the 239 and 240 were isotopes of the same element, they could not be separated chemically.

The physicists at Los Alamos would have to come up with a way around the problem, and they eventually did in an ingenious fashion. A nuclear explosion cannot occur unless an adequate amount of fissionable material is present—the so-called critical mass. Our purification of plutonium and uranium was intended to create the several pounds of fissionable material needed to reach the critical mass. With well-behaved fissile material, the mechanism of the bomb itself could be simple. In the case of uranium 235, the relatively uncomplicated bomb mechanism was called the gun design. The uranium was simply divided into two parts. Then one part, the target, would be shot with the other part, the "bullet." When the two parts came together, they would form the critical mass and explode.

But if you put the plutonium in two large lumps, the stray neutrons would cause a premature fizzle before you could bring the parts together. So a gun assembly wouldn't work. The ingenious Los Alamos solution became known as implosion. The plutonium portions were kept apart in an unformed sphere. Exactly timed explosives drove them together at the same instant (imploded them) with such force that they gathered in the critical mass before spontaneous fission could spoil it.

The development of the implosion device was a tremendous physics and engineering achievement.

While we continued our studies of the decontamination and isolation processes, the industrial-scale plant—Site W, in Manhattan Project jargon—began materializing in south-central Washington State. The Hanford Engineer Works was built on a 700-square-mile reservation bounded on three sides by a huge bend in the Columbia River. This odd combination—huge amounts of water flowing through sparsely inhabited desert—made the site ideal. The remote location was chosen because it was far from any population center—to mitigate the effects of an accident such as a radioactive release—and for security. The Columbia River provided the large amounts of water needed for cooling the reactors.

I visited Hanford in the spring of 1944 while it was under construction, and have never seen such an awesome, wild and woolly place. At one time more than 40,000 people were living in trailers and barracks at Hanford, helping to build the complex. With most able-bodied men serving in the armed forces, it was hard to find construction workers, especially ones who were willing to live in a barracks in the desert. To fill all these positions, Du Pont was hiring almost anyone they could find "off the street." I ate lunch in a huge mess hall surrounded by a sea of faces, the workers being fed in shifts. People were talking about a murder that had been committed the night before—a too common occurrence there. The site even had its own jail, filled with a motley aggregation of tough-looking characters. This massive assemblage of workers, spirited off into the desert, had no idea what the enormous buildings they were erecting were for, although one oft-repeated rumor had it that the site would be a home for pregnant Waves. (From its size, it would seem to have room for the entire Navy.)

I first went to Hanford in the company of John Willard, an associate section chief at the Met Lab, who soon transferred there as an area supervisor on chemical separations of plutonium. John and I took the train to Pendleton, Oregon, then a car out into the flat, lonesome country. Our tour guide was Walter Simon, the plant manager and "mayor" of Hanford. Driving us back to town for the night, Walter decided he could save time by leaving the road for a shortcut straight across the wide-open desert. In a particularly desolate spot, loose sand trapped the car's wheels. John and I discovered a water hole nearby; we used the water to pack down the sand to improve the traction and finally free the car.

When I visited Hanford again in December, the construction was essentially complete and the construction-worker encampment evacuated. Huge buildings housed the reactors and chemical extraction plants. One reactor was already processing uranium.

Before the extraction plants went on-line, I attended a step-by-step review of the operating standards of the bismuth phosphate process. We spent three days working through documents specifying the standards and discussing the stages of every step. Then I was asked to sign each document, along with other representatives from the Met Lab and Du Pont, as a final approval.

It was awesome to me that all this enterprise had resulted from our discovery of plutonium, and then from our work developing this process at the Met Lab. It had been less than four years since Arthur Wahl went searching for the strongest oxidation agent he could find, since Emilio Segrè and I had carried ether-filled buckets suspended from poles to test plutonium's fissionability. Who would have guessed that it would come to this gigantic industrial effort?

The uranium came to Hanford by the ton to be irradiated in the three piles (reactors). Each pile could process two hundred tons of uranium, cooking it for about two hundred days. That netted a little more than half a pound of plutonium from each ton of uranium. So tons and tons of material were shipped in to Hanford, but nothing ever seemed to come out.

The chain-reacted "slugs" (our name for the uranium in its casings for the pile) would glow from the heat as they were removed from the piles. This highly radioactive material would be dropped into a deep channel of water and caught in big buckets that carried it into large lead coffins. The slugs would be hauled five or ten miles out into the desert to cool. Then they'd be transported to the chemical extraction plants, some ten miles away from the piles. These enormous concrete structures, some 860 feet long, were a tremendous sight to behold from their operating galleries. Along the length of almost three football fields lay a row of valves, meters, indicators, and controls, separated by several feet of concrete from the cells where the processing actually occurred.

Everything was done by remote control; the Du Pont engineers had done a fantastic job in developing these operations. The insides of the cells where the separations took place could be seen only through a shielded periscope hanging from an overhead crane that ran on rails the length of the building. From a lead-shielded cab, the crane operator could remove a block's fifteen-ton concrete cover, and then, watching through the periscope, operate wrenches and other tools by remote control to repair or replace defective equipment. The plutonium–uranium–fission product mixture would pass through a maze of reaction vessels via thousands of feet of piping with only instruments and an occasional sampling to chart its progress.

Extraction and decontamination, concentration, and isolation of the plutonium product took place in different buildings.

The final process used was indeed bismuth phosphate, with a lanthanum fluoride step included at the end. The lanthanum fluoride turned out to complement the bismuth phosphate by removing some fission products that slipped through the earlier steps. By the final step, enough radioactive fission products had been removed that the material was more approachable; the issue of lanthanum fluoride corroding the pipes was therefore not a major problem. The yields in the first runs, in December 1944 and January 1945, were between 60 and 70 percent. By February, the yields reached 90 percent, and within months were up to 95 percent.

The plutonium was shipped to Los Alamos, where chemists, including my colleagues Arthur Wahl and Joe Kennedy, further purified it for studies of it as a metal.

# TEN

# REFLECTIONS ON THE BOMB

By the spring of 1945, the plants were turning out plutonium at Hanford and bomb-grade uranium at Oak Ridge, and it was clear that the new weapons, an almost impossible dream four years ago, would be ready soon. The energy of the atomic nucleus was about to explode on the world stage—and we knew that afterward the world would never be the same. Arthur Compton appointed six committees at the Met Lab to consider the ramifications of this epochal event and to make recommendations to the government about postwar policy regarding nuclear energy.

I served on the Committee on Social and Political Implications, chaired by James Franck. Franck had been a German war hero in World War I. He'd won a Nobel Prize in physics for work involving the interaction of electrons with atoms. After Hitler came to power in 1933, anti-Semitism had forced him to flee his post as head of a leading German physics institute. Compton and others trusted him so thoroughly that he was given a high position in the Manhattan Project, where Franck hoped to work to end the sickness that had infected his homeland.

The physicist Leo Szilard had the greatest influence on our committee's report. One of a remarkable group of physicists who had fled Hungary in the 1930s, Szilard (and his compatriot Eugene Wigner) had convinced Albert Einstein to write the letter to President Roosevelt that set the Manhattan Project in motion. His role was hard to pin down; he seemed to be in many places at once, full of suggestions on everything, a one-man idea factory. He was an eccentric man who sometimes spent hours in the bathtub because that's where he got his best ideas. When our work was done, Szilard shifted his attention with remarkable facility to visualizing the future. Deeply affected by the development of the bomb, he moved from physics to biology, and spent much of the rest of his life working for arms control and disarmament.

For many Manhattan Project scientists, the defeat of Germany in May 1945 and our progress in the Pacific, which made the defeat of Japan seem to be only a matter of time, changed the moral tenor of the bomb research. The United States no longer had to fear the enemy's obtaining the bomb first. Atomic weapons shifted from being needed for survival to being a unique, world-changing factor in America's offensive arsenal. It was apparent that we could win the war without the bomb, and that the bomb would have vast effects on the future of war, international relations, and many other aspects of the future world. Our committee cautioned that it should not be treated as just another weapon.

Our recommendations, which came to be known as the Franck Report, urged "that the use of nuclear bombs in this war be considered as a problem of long-range national policy rather than of military expediency, and that this policy be directed primarily to the achievement of an agreement permitting an effective international control of the means of nuclear warfare." Such a policy should be guided by two impending developments. First, "nuclear bombs cannot possibly remain a 'secret weapon' at the exclusive disposal of this country for more than a few years. The scientific facts on which their construction is based are well known to scientists of other countries."

Second, "unless an effective international control of nuclear explosives is instituted, a race for nuclear armaments is certain to ensue following the first revelation of our possession of nuclear weapons to the world. Within ten years other countries may have bombs."

The report stated that we should not base our long-term policy on the belief that the United States could maintain a nuclear monopoly. Once our adversaries, or even allies, knew that we possessed this weapon, they would be driven to do everything within their power to overcome our advantage and regain a measure of parity. These two points led us to our conclusion:

We believe that these considerations make the use of nuclear bombs for an early unannounced attack on Japan inadvisable. If the United States were to be the first to release this new means of indiscriminate destruction upon mankind, she would sacrifice public support throughout the world, precipitate the race for armaments, and prejudice the possibility of reaching an international agreement on the future control of weapons.

We urged that rather than being dropped on a military or civilian target, the bomb should be used in a "demonstration in an appropriately selected uninhabited area." If the Japanese could see the intimidating destructive power of the bomb, perhaps they would understand the futility of further opposition to American power.

Franck thought it so critical that these arguments be considered by the higher decision makers that he hand-carried the report to Washington, where Arthur Compton was visiting on other business. Secretary of War Henry Stimson chaired a committee that was planning how to use the atomic bomb, and Compton put the Franck Report in the hands of the deputy chair of this committee. Whether Harry Truman ever saw it is doubtful; and obviously he chose a completely different course, using the bomb without warning in as destructive a fashion as possible.

In hindsight, our points in the Franck Report were actually on the mark, although not necessarily material. It took the Soviet Union only a few years to break the American nuclear monopoly, and the arms race became perhaps the most dangerous development of the years after the end of the war. International control of atomic energy is still the best hope for quelling the arms race and nuclear proliferation, but American use of atomic bombs has often been cited to accuse the United States of a lack of "moral authority" in nuclear policy.

Just the same, it is hard to see how we could have averted the arms race, considering our relations with the Soviet Union after the war. And I understand and do not quarrel with Truman's decision to use the bomb on Hiroshima (though I'm not convinced that the follow-up bombing of Nagasaki was necessary).

Many people whose judgment I respect, and who are in a better position to judge, have said that they can conceive of no demonstration that would have swayed the Japanese militarists from their fanatical course. A panel consisting of Compton, Fermi, Lawrence, and Oppenheimer considered our report, and recommended nonetheless that the bomb be used in order to save American lives. This recommendation is significant, considering how deeply Robert Oppenheimer was affected by his work in the development of the bomb; his passionate advocacy of arms control changed the course of his later career.

Only three bombs were ready in the summer of 1945, and one of them had to be used in a test. It was critical that the other two be used to optimum effect. If the United States had announced its intention to hold the demonstration, the Japanese military might have interfered with it, and an ineffective or failed demonstration would have prolonged the war. And any hint of hesitancy to use the bomb could have been interpreted by the Japanese as faintheartedness, which might have increased their determination to fight on for better terms.

The bombing of Hiroshima was a dramatic demonstration of the bomb's awesome power, and no one could ignore it. Everyone in the world could see the destruction, and this knowledge undoubtedly deterred any further steps toward world war. This demonstration that we were willing and able to use atomic weaponry has probably helped since then to keep us out of situations where we might have to use it again. In the Persian Gulf War, for example, intelligence reports suggest that Saddam Hussein was prepared to use chemical weapons but stayed his hand when he got the message that his country would be obliterated if he did. Even he could understand that having used the bomb once, the United States would use it again; if this restrained him, then we once again saved lives.

I'm often asked about my feelings regarding my work in developing such a destructive weapon. I can honestly say that I have no regrets about it, either in the short-term sense of its relevance in World War II or in the long term since then. It ended World War II, and in doing so, it saved lives on both sides. All of us—scientists, soldiers, and politicians—who witnessed Japan's behavior during the war expected it to fight on to the bitter end. Even after we dropped a single bomb that obliterated an entire city, Japan did not lay down its arms.

To us, Japan was an unnerving enemy. Kamikaze pilots slammed explosive-laden planes into our ships. On Iwo Jima, a Japanese army was pinned down with no hope of rescue or reinforcement, yet in a month of fighting, only 1,000 of 21,000 soldiers surrendered; the rest fought to the death; many hid in caves to try to take an American with them rather than surrender. In the spring of 1945 an Allied invasion of the Japanese homeland seemed certain, and we expected every house to be defended to the death in this same manner. We had no reason to doubt the estimates that such an invasion would cost tens—even hundreds—of thousands of American casualties. These are well-known arguments—I cite them to add one more voice from someone who lived through that time and to stress that we believed them then, and see no reason to disbelieve them now.

We saw no end to the war in sight. On July 15, 1945—just weeks before the bombs ended the war—twenty-five war correspondents on the front lines predicted when they thought the war would end. Their collective guess was June 1946, almost a year away. The Joint Chiefs of Staff forecast that the Pacific war would end eighteen months after the European war, which meant the end of 1946.

The atomic bomb was one more step in an increasingly destructive war. In the battle for Okinawa, more than 100,000 Japanese and 12,000 Americans died. One night's firebombing of Tokyo killed at least 100,000 people (probably tens of thousands more), injured a million people, and left a like number homeless. Fifteen square miles of houses burned. Given this context, the casualty numbers from the atomic bombing of Hiroshima were not as high as you might expect: 140,000 dead by the end of 1945; a total of 200,000 dead five years later.

What if the atomic bomb had not been used and the war had lasted another year, with more Okinawas and more firebombings? Considered in this context, the bomb saved not only American lives but Japanese lives as well.

But those are only numbers. I also had an emotional stake in the outcome. Some of my cousins whom I'd grown up with in South Gate were stationed in the Pacific islands, preparing for the invasion of Japan, which they were certain would be necessary to force Japan's surrender (military planners had it scheduled to begin around November 1). For years after the war, at family reunions they made a point of thanking me for my work—they were convinced that the bomb had saved their lives. That gave our achievement personal meaning; I never regretted it.

In the longer-term context, has the existence of nuclear bombs been good or bad for humanity?

In the first half of this century, two all-out world wars killed millions of men and women. The advent of nuclear weapons has forced wars to be limited in scope. During the forty years of the Cold War, the United States, the Soviet Union, and China fought for hegemony using ideology, economics, surrogates, and limited wars. Without the threat of mutual assured destruction (MAD), is there any doubt that the struggle would have escalated to full-scale war?

In his memoirs, Nikita Khrushchev wrote of a proposal Mao Zedong made in the 1950s. If Russia would supply the weapons, Mao would supply unlimited manpower. Khrushchev wrote:

> "Listen, Comrade Khrushchev," [Mao] said. "All you have to do is provoke the Americans into military action, and I'll give you as many divisions as you need to crush them—a hundred, two hundred, one thousand divisions." I tried to explain to him that one or two missiles could turn all the divisions in China to dust. But he wouldn't even listen to my arguments and obviously regarded me as a coward.

The logic of mutual assured destruction, MAD as it is, has worked. Who can doubt that without it Mao or some similar leader might have launched a war? Now we must ask how long this precarious balance can continue, as more countries obtain a nuclear capability. And crucial questions must be asked about keeping the former Soviet Union's dangerous fissile nuclear material out of the wrong hands, and about the threat of nuclear proliferation to more and more countries. Our best hope continues to be international controls.

Another reason I do not regret this work is that I believe strongly that science is neutral. A scientific discovery cannot be termed good or bad, as the uses to which it is put can. Scientists can do only what is possible. If it can't be done, no scientist can do it. If it can be done, some scientist somewhere someday will. If American scientists hadn't developed the atomic bomb when they did, someone else would have done so, with potentially catastrophic consequences. Germany, the Soviet Union, and Japan all had active atomic bomb research programs during the war. It's a good thing for humanity that the United States was the first to develop the bomb.

Moreover, you can't have all the positive aspects of nuclear research without the negative aspects. And, on balance, I'm quite happy with the uses to which my discoveries and contributions have been put—millions of people annually diagnosed and treated with isotopes I discovered, lives saved through smoke detectors, and electricity generated through nuclear power.

All the same, the experience of working on the atom bomb affected me deeply, as it did many others. The soul-searching among scientists of the Manhattan Project became abundantly clear as time went on—virtually all the major contributors later felt the need to participate in developing public policy with regard to the control of nuclear energy in its military and peaceful uses. They showed a marked willingness to leave the laboratory for public service, sometimes at considerable personal sacrifice. For me, arms control would become a major lifetime goal.

# ELEVEN

# REARRANGING THE TABLE

# OF ELEMENTS

At the Met Lab, once we'd broken the back of the plutonium chemistry problem, our investigations continued into the general chemistry of the transuranium elements. As I've said earlier, when we discovered plutonium we considered the name ultimium because we believed it would be the last element found; it seemed amazing to have this new element two places up the periodic table from the last naturally occurring element, and we thought nothing further was likely. But now we'd had several years' experience with plutonium and found it to be stable, with a very long half-life, and this suggested that even heavier elements were possible, even likely. It made sense to look for them, for at least two reasons: to learn whether they had military potential and to see if they might interfere with our efforts to purify plutonium or interfere with the workings of the bomb.

We'd begun to suspect that such elements were being formed in the reactors as by-products of the process that created plutonium, because we found new radioactivities (radioactive patterns) in the material from the reactors. But there was a plethora of fission products, and our attempts to isolate the unknown radioactivities were fruitless. We needed to have some idea of their chemistry to have a chance at isolating them successfully, but apparently our assumptions about what to look for were wrong.

Our best hope was to predict their chemistry on the basis of their positions on the periodic table in order to deduce the reagents that might combine with them to help us isolate them. But the traditional arrangement of the periodic table where these elements would appear was not working for us, nor was a proposed new arrangement, and it began to dawn on me that our lack of success stemmed from the periodic table itself.

According to the traditional arrangement of the periodic table, elements 89 through 92 (actinium, thorium, proactinium, and uranium) occupied the seventh row from the top. They fit well enough there; for example, uranium fell in the same column as chromium, molybdenum, and tungsten, so was expected to resemble them, which it did acceptably.

But the new elements neptunium and plutonium did not fit comfortably into their assigned columns. This lack of fit was obvious to McMillan and Abelson almost from the moment of their discovery of neptunium. Instead of resembling rhenium, its presumed homolog element immediately above it on the table, neptunium shared many properties with uranium. This resemblance was so marked that McMillan and Abelson speculated that perhaps uranium was the start of a "uranide" series of related elements. The "uranides" would be analogous to the lanthanide group, elements 58 through 71, the "rare earths" that so closely resembled each other that they were broken out into their own grouping, traditionally displayed below the body of the periodic table. In the late nineteenth and early twentieth centuries, when these elements were discovered, they caused conniptions among classifiers because they did not repeat properties in the same periodic fashion as the previously discovered elements.

The key to understanding the lanthanides was the discovery that they contained an inner electron shell. As you moved from element 57 to 58 and so on, adding an electron each time, the additional electrons went to fill an inner orbital shell instead of an outer shell. It's the electrons in the outer shell, where they are available to form chemical bonds with other atoms and thus form molecules, that define an element's chemistry. Because the lanthanides had the same number of electrons in their outer shells, they tended to be very much alike. Instead of having characteristics that recurred "periodically," like other elements, they resembled one another.

The uranide concept had worked adequately when it came to neptunium and plutonium, but the concept was never quite satisfactory. While we'd succeeded in working out a separation process approaching plutonium as if it were similar to uranium, the more we learned about plutonium, the more we saw that our success was largely a matter of luck. This kind of evidence led us to feel that there must be a better theory. And as much as these elements resembled uranium, they resembled the lanthanides even more closely.

I began to believe that it was correct to propose a second lanthanide-style series of elements, but that we erred in our idea of where the series started. I came to believe that it started with element number 89, actinium, the element directly below lanthanum on the periodic table. Perhaps there was another inner electron shell being filled. This would make the series directly analogous to the lanthanides, which would make sense, but it would require a radical change in the periodic table. The uranide concept had affected the placement only of newly discovered elements, but this actinide concept would require moving three elements whose chemistries were fairly well established.

When I broached the idea at upper-level Met Lab meetings, it went over like the proverbial lead balloon. I remember that at one meeting the head of the chemistry division said that even if the concept was correct, he doubted it would be of much use. Latimer told me that such an outlandish proposal would ruin my scientific reputation. Fortunately, that was no deterrent because at the time I had no scientific reputation to lose.

Despite this opposition, I believed the evidence was piling up that my actinide concept was correct. Starting the series at actinium meant the series would begin in the same column as the lanthanide series, the next row down, and in keeping with the pattern of the periodic table. One test of the idea was to see if it would predict particular electron shell configurations, which would in turn dictate certain chemical characteristics such as oxidation states. The predicted configurations correlated well with what I knew of the chemistry of the corresponding elements. I proposed the actinide concept and this evidence in a Met Lab report in the summer of 1944, and within weeks of accepting it, we began to close in on the activity we suspected was element 95 or 96.

Our early attempts at isolating the alpha emitters we believed were new elements were based on the hypothesis that they would be similar to plutonium and therefore could be oxidized to the VI oxidation state. This oxidation state could then be used in a chemical isolation procedure, as it was with plutonium. But the actinide concept meant that this would not work. If these elements were like their lanthanide homologs (instead of plutonium), then it was unlikely that they could be oxidized above the III state. This insight allowed us to identify almost immediately an isotope that seemed to be a new element.

My collaborators in this work were two young Met Lab chemists who did the separations work, Ralph James and L. O. (Tom) Morgan, as well as Al Ghiorso, in charge of the electronic instruments used in the radioactivity investigations. Ralph had come to us fresh from graduating from Berkeley; Tom interrupted his graduate studies at the University of Texas to join the Met Lab. Both joined me at Berkeley after the war to obtain their doctorates.

We analyzed a sample from Berkeley's 60-inch cyclotron, where plutonium 239 had been bombarded with alpha particles. I noted in a report: "There was found in this material a new radioactivity, emitting alpha particles of range about 4.7 cm, which seems to be due to an isotope of element 96 or 95." This turned out to be element 96, formed by the plutonium nucleus absorbing the two protons in the alpha particle (thereby moving two places up on the periodic table).

A crucial step in identifying this new element, in addition to the separations work, was to trace its decay path. Nuclear scientists speak in terms of "genetic" relationships, in which an isotope decays into what is referred to as its daughter. These genetic relationships are an important identification tool. We knew our element was an alpha emitter—that is, it decayed by emitting particles made up of two protons and two neutrons—because we could measure the alpha particles it gave off. After our unknown isotope emitted its alpha particle, we found a known, recognizable isotope—plutonium 238. It was a matter of simple logic that an element that emits an alpha particle and turns into element 94-238 must be the isotope of element 96 with atomic weight 242.

Before the war ended, we had begun to isolate element 95 from the material from the reactors at Oak Ridge and Hanford. This element was being formed by the capture of a neutron by a plutonium atom, followed by the transmutation of the neutron to a proton. The actinide concept predicted that these elements would have a stable III oxidation state and would greatly resemble the lanthanide elements. Both predictions proved true. In fact, these elements resembled the rare earths and each other so closely that we experienced a great deal of difficulty trying to isolate them. Element 95 was first isolated in the fall of 1945 by Burris Cunningham at the Met Lab. Element 96 was not isolated until the fall of 1947, after we'd returned to Berkeley, by Louis Werner and Iz Perlman. We were confident we had correctly identified them before the isolations were complete.

The world first heard about these elements much more quickly—and quietly—than it did about plutonium. We demonstrated immediately that neither of the two new elements was fissionable, so neither would have military importance. Because it lacked military use, the information about the existence of element 96 was quickly declassified. Element 95, however, was considered more sensitive because it had first been synthesized in the reactors, as a result of bombarding plutonium with neutrons, and, since neutrons were the key to the chain reaction, any element made through a neutron reaction was considered security-sensitive. To get around this stumbling block, we found an alternative way to synthesize it through alpha-particle bombardment. We were allowed to write up this information for publication, although we had to acknowledge that we were not describing the actual discovery, the details of which were still classified.

I was getting ready to present a paper revealing these new elements at an American Chemical Society meeting when I was invited to appear on a radio program called *The Quiz Kids*. One of the Quiz Kids asked me if any additional new elements had recently been discovered. I replied that we had just discovered elements 95 and 96, and students could tell their teachers that there were now more than the 92 elements listed in textbooks. Judging from the mail I later received from many schoolchildren, their teachers were rather skeptical of this information.

We announced names for the elements in April 1946. During the search for them, one researcher in our group called them "pandemonium" and "delirium" because of the difficulties they caused. But we deferred to precedent in the way their homologs among the lanthanides had been named. Element 95 occupied the box under europium, so we followed the precedent of using the geographic area where it was discovered and named it americium. The homolog of element 96 was named gadolinium for a Finnish chemist who had done a great deal of work on the rare earths, so we named element 96 curium after Pierre and Marie Curie, whose pioneering work on radioactivity had done so much to advance our field.

The initial significance of americium and curium was that they demonstrated the accuracy of the actinide concept, which pointed the way to the discovery of other elements in the future. And the more information we gathered about the chemistry of these new elements, the clearer the accuracy of the actinide concept became. This concept led to the last realignment of the periodic table, and for that reason was, I believe, my greatest contribution to basic science.

The process demonstrated well the three stages of scientific discovery. In the first stage, people call your idea crazy and say you'd be a fool to propose it. In the second stage, with the evidence mounting, people say it just might be correct. By the time you have enough evidence to offer proof, you are at the third stage, when people say that the idea is so obvious that of course it's true, any idiot could have seen that.

In retrospect, it seems obvious that the inner electron shell seen in the lanthanide series should repeat, and repeat in the same region of the periodic table. But at the time it went against everything that we had learned in school about the periodic table, and it required the reassignment of several elements from positions they had occupied for years.

While radioisotopes have been lifesavers in medicine, americium has come to save lives in a completely different fashion. It is a key component of smoke detectors. Americium is an alpha emitter, constantly giving off ions that travel only four or five centimeters to where they hit a detector. It takes very little to interfere with them: if smoke gets into the detector, it deflects some of the alpha particles, the interruption of the flow of the alpha particles setting off the alarm. The presence of a smoke detector in your house increases your chances of surviving a fire by 70 percent.

For nearly a year after the war's end, I remained at the Met Lab, continuing with our studies of americium and curium and developing an improved process for the isolation of plutonium that captured the uranium as well.

# TWELVE

# BACK TO THE RAD LAB

Throughout the war, I had been on leave from my post as a newly minted assistant professor at Berkeley. I'd come to Chicago as a young, unknown commodity. I had run a large lab there successfully, and I had proposed a theory that led to the discovery of two new elements. The plutonium project was regarded as an unqualified success—and now I found I was in demand. The University of Chicago asked me to stay. They had treated me exceedingly well, and Arthur Compton was not only an amiable supervisor and talented scientist but also a friend. The university planned to convert the wartime facilities on the outskirts of the city to the high-powered Argonne National Laboratory, a research laboratory that could attract talent at the level of Enrico Fermi.

When I told Berkeley's Wendell Latimer of the University of Chicago's interest, he asked me to refrain from accepting any offers until he could talk to me in person.

Chicago responded to my hesitancy by sweetening its deal. Its president, Robert Hutchins, offered me a full professorship at an annual salary of $10,000, nearly four times my assistant professor's salary. I still remember the words that accompanied this offer: "You deserve the good life." More important than money, I would direct a laboratory that included academic staff and graduate students.

On my next trip west, I met with University of California president Robert Gordon Sproul, the man I'd barged in on as an undergraduate student to urge the creation of a graduate school at UCLA. Sproul was willing to make me the first person in the university's history to jump directly from assistant to full professor (although the salary was less than half what Chicago offered). I could bring back with me several Met Lab staff members as professors and graduate students; Ernest Lawrence would create additional nonfaculty positions at the Rad Lab. The Rad Lab, with its cyclotrons and promise of continued growth on the cutting edge of science, pulled me strongly. Ernest was not only an innovator in science but unrivaled as an administrator and fund-raiser.

Finally, I preferred Berkeley's status as a public rather than private university. The University of California had been my only option out of high school. The opportunities it had given me had made all the difference in my life; I liked the idea of devoting energy to building public education to give others similar opportunities.

In all, about twenty of us transferred from the Met Lab to Berkeley, many returning "home," as I was. The cream had really risen to the top during the war. Our team had moved among assignments at Chicago, Oak Ridge, and Hanford developing a diversity of skills, so it was an extraordinary opportunity to put together a complete research team in one fell swoop. Nearly everyone had been segregated from the "regular" workforce for several years and was looking for new opportunities. For example, Stan Thompson joined us to study for his doctorate rather than returning to Standard Oil. Al Ghiorso, too stubbornly nonconformist to work for a degree higher than his bachelor's in electrical engineering, returned as a research associate. More than fifty years later, he's still at it. Iz Perlman was offered an associate professorship, and he picked up where he'd left off as my right-hand man at the Met Lab, a researcher and organizer willing and able to accomplish any task.

Ernest appointed me director of the nuclear chemistry division at the Radiation Laboratory, practically a dream job. The new Atomic Energy Commission gave it reliable financial support in the postwar years, and Ernest built one high-energy machine after another, constantly pushing the frontiers of physics forward.

In his autobiography, Luis Alvarez described the Rad Lab's postwar period well:

> We had gone away as boys, so to speak, and came back as men. We had initiated large technical projects and carried

them to completion as directors of teams of scientists and technicians. We were prepared to reassume our subordinate roles with Ernest as our leader once again, but . . . he signaled that we were to be free agents. We made all our own technical and personnel decisions, and for the first few years after the war we had unlimited financial backing from the [Manhattan District]. Although Ernest showed a keen interest in what we were doing, . . . wise parents let their children solve all the problems they can but stand by to help when a problem proves too difficult. Ernest was always a wise scientific parent; all of us who were fortunate enough to be his scientific children remember with gratitude the help and understanding he offered when we needed it as well as the freedom he gave us to solve our own problems when it seemed that we could eventually succeed.

I believe that during this period ours was the premier nuclear chemistry research group in the world; at least nobody beat our productivity. Over the next twelve years, we discovered six elements and did intensive research into their isotopes. We demonstrated fission could occur in lighter elements than previously believed. Our studies of subjects such as alpha decay were extremely useful in making scientific advances. With the 60-inch cyclotron alone, we discovered about 25 isotopes of transplutonium elements and more than 100 isotopes of other elements. The 184-inch cyclotron produced a similar number.

Among our first major discoveries were elements 97 and 98. For 97, Stan Thompson, Al Ghiorso, and I collaborated. Stan did the chemical work, and Al handled the radiation detection end. I thought the actinide concept would predict the element's properties so precisely that making the chemical identification would be relatively easy. That may have been true—but it took three years of overcoming obstacles to get into position to do the chemical separations.

It was slow in part because, just as at Chicago, we were in many ways constructing a new laboratory. We not only had to build up a stock of equipment, we also had to come up with innovations to solve new problems such as the intense radioactivity we encountered in many experiments. These innovations included glove boxes (in which you put your hands into lead-lined gloves to manipulate reagents in a protective box), "junior caves" (in which we made separations behind a moderate amount of shielding and handled the radioactive material with tongs), and "caves" for highly radioactive materials (in which we worked over the top of thick lead shielding with tongs, using overhead mirrors to see what we were doing).

We thought we could produce elements 97 and 98 by bombarding elements 95 (americium) and 96 (curium) with helium ions, thereby adding two protons to the nucleus of each. But first we had to produce americium and curium in large enough amounts to be used as targets for bombardment. Eventually we produced the americium and curium through prolonged neutron bombardment of plutonium. But before we could use them as targets, we had to develop techniques to separate them from the plutonium mixture. This separation was difficult because of americium and curium's intense radioactivity, even in submilligram amounts, which necessitated the use of such awkward apparatus as the caves.

Once the americium and curium targets were separated and bombarded with helium ions, the next set of separations required the development of wholly new techniques. The separation of plutonium had been based on exploiting plutonium's many oxidation states, an approach that also worked for americium and curium. But we did not expect it to work for elements 97 and 98 because they were not likely to share this chemical characteristic. Plutonium could be oxidized all the way to a plus-seven level; on the basis of the behavior of their homologs in the lanthanide group, we anticipated that the new elements could not be oxidized past the plus-three level.

The technique that proved to be the key to their discovery was called ion-exchange adsorption-elution. In this method, you find a resin that your target material will attach itself to (in the argot, you adsorb your target material on an ion-exchange resin). Then you place this material in an eyedropper-like tube called a column. You add an eluent (solvent) to the column that selectively picks the target off the resin and dissolves it. The heaviest materials fall out of the column first, emerging a drop at a time. Or, more formally stated, your target materials drip out of the column in the inverse order of their atomic weight onto a series of plates at the base of the column.

We could calibrate our instruments by running an experiment using the rare-earth homologs to these elements; they would be so similar chemically that the new actinide elements should elute in the same order and place as their rare-earth homologs. On the basis of these column calibration experiments, we expected element 98 to elute onto collection plate number thirteen in the twenty-fifth and twenty-sixth drops of eluent—and that's where we found it.

Having the suspected element's location closely narrowed down made it much easier to identify it through its radioactive decay pattern. While Stan was becoming so expert in these chemical techniques, Al was matching him with innovations in radiation detection. He developed terrifically sensitive instruments for detecting the kinds of radioactive decay we expected of these elements (X-ray-emitting electron capture and alpha emission). More and more Al was demonstrating how to measure the distance and energy of alpha particle emissions as a signature for each isotope. For example, an alpha particle emitted with an energy of 6 million electron volts at a certain half-life would be unique among the two thousand known isotopes.

Stan and Al performed the first actual identification experiment for element 97 on December 19, 1949. The bombarded americium target came off the cyclotron that morning, and Stan began the chemical separation. By early evening, he had eluted the fraction we expected to contain element 97 off the separation column, and the fraction was showing the alpha and X-ray activity we expected for element 97.

As I watched Stan elute the drop containing element 97, my heart began pounding furiously. Not knowing whether the palpitations signaled simple excitement or a dangerous condition, I called one of the lab's physicians. He came to my office, where his examination revealed what he thought was a gross heart irregularity. He summoned an ambulance to take me to the hospital.

Al telephoned me there the next day to say he'd confirmed a definite pattern indicating we had found element 97. The hospital kept me under observation for several days without finding any heart problems—now that was an exciting discovery!

Our elements seemed to be coming in pairs—we discovered element 98 just two months later. This discovery was relatively painless, as the chemical preparations we used for element 97 applied almost as well to element 98, and our predictions of 98's radioactive and chemical properties were so accurate that they led us to it without a single misstep. Our techniques were getting so sensitive that we identified element 98 based on the presence of a total of only some 5,000 of its atoms. (Kenneth Street, one of my graduate students who had just been hired on the faculty, joined our team as a co-discoverer.)

Element 97's homolog among the rare earths is terbium, named for the town of Ytterby in Sweden, where many of the rare earths had been found and identified. Naming our new element analogously after Berkeley practically leaped out at us. I telephoned the mayor of Berkeley to share what I thought were glad tidings that the city would thus be immortalized on the periodic table as berkelium, news that he greeted with a complete lack of interest. Stan and Al suggested that berkelium's chemical symbol should be the letters Bm, because it had been such a stinker in resisting chemical identification for so long, but cooler heads prevailed to choose Bk.

We could glean no guidance for the name of element 98 from its homolog in the rare earths, dysprosium, from a Greek word meaning "hard to get at." We went through a long list of possibilities before settling on californium, to honor the state and university where the work had been done.

*The New Yorker*'s "Talk of the Town" poked fun at our new names:

> New atoms are turning up with spectacular, if not downright alarming, frequency nowadays, and the University of California at Berkeley, whose scientists have discovered elements 97 and 98, has christened them berkelium and californium respectively. While unarguably suited to their place of birth, these names strike us as indicating a surprising lack of public-relations foresight on the part of the university, located, as it is, in a state where publicity has flourished to a degree matched perhaps only by evangelism. California's busy scientists will undoubtedly come up

with another atom or two one of these days, and the university might well have anticipated that. Now it has lost forever the chance of immortalizing itself in the atomic tables with some such sequence as universitium (97), ofium (98), californium (99), berkelium (100).

We wrote back:

"Talk of the Town" has missed the point in their comments on naming of the elements 97 and 98. We may have shown lack of confidence but no lack of foresight in naming the elements "berkelium" and "californium." By using these names first, we have forestalled the appalling possibility that after naming 97 and 98 "universitium" and "ofium," some New Yorker might follow with the discovery of 99 and 100 and apply the names "newium" and "yorkium."

The *New Yorker* staff's reply was brief: "We are already at work in our office laboratories on 'newium' and 'yorkium.' So far we just have the names."

# THIRTEEN

# THE H·BOMB AND OPPENHEIMER

In the summer of 1946, Congress passed the Atomic Energy Act, which moved America's nuclear program from military back to civilian control. A five-member Atomic Energy Commission took over the vast enterprise of the Army's Manhattan Engineer District.

The transfer came about largely due to lobbying by Manhattan Project scientists. The Manhattan Project forever changed the relationship between science and government. Never before had a scientific concept been taken from theory to practical application in such a short time, and with such a massive infusion of money and talent. The government became so heavily involved because it was a question of national defense, but this large-scale and sensitive technology called out for continued government leadership and support. The AEC's activities cut across a broad spectrum, from defense to medicine to industry to power, effectively nationalizing these efforts in what has been called "an island of socialism."

President Truman appointed only one scientist with experience in the nuclear field to the AEC. That decision meant that much of the technical expertise would lie outside the commission itself, in the hands of a General Advisory Committee.

In December 1946, I received a phone call from AEC Commissioner Robert Bacher inviting me to be a member of the GAC, and I accepted immediately. It was a powerhouse committee, and I felt honored to be in the company of the other eight members: Robert Oppenheimer, Enrico Fermi, James B. Conant, Isidor I. Rabi (a nuclear physicist at Columbia),

Lee DuBridge (president of the California Institute of Technology), Cyril S. Smith (director of the Institute for the Study of Metals), and two industrialists—Hood Worthington of Du Pont and Hartley Rowe of United Fruit. As a group, we had been involved in every phase of the Manhattan Project and understood every aspect and impact of nuclear science.

The AEC commissioners had decision-making authority, but they lacked the grounding. The GAC's prestige and influence were so great that the commissioners didn't tell the committee what to do; we told the commissioners what to do. Our putative role was to respond to their requests for advice, but we went well beyond this. If we thought a subject needed action, we brought it to the commissioners' attention, often with strong recommendations.

For example, at one meeting we recommended a major reorganization of the AEC. It was nothing we'd been asked to look into, and Chairman David Lilienthal made no attempt to hide his unhappiness when we presented our advice. Nonetheless, he must have recognized that our ideas were on the mark, because within a few months a reorganization took place that was remarkably similar to the one we'd recommended.

Robert Oppenheimer's performance at Los Alamos made him the natural, almost automatic, leader of the GAC. Because of a weather delay, he arrived late to our first meeting and found that he had already been elected chairman. Oppie's leadership of the committee was masterful. At the end of each meeting the commissioners would join us for a briefing, and Oppie would present an eloquent summary of the proceedings. His evenhanded summations of our discussions, giving each person's perspective, were much better than the written record. And he provided real leadership in guiding a committee with strong egos, high-level intellects, and pet projects toward the nation's real priorities. We expected nucleonics to change the world and took very seriously our opportunity to shape its growth. The panel was designed to meet quarterly, but we found so much to do we came together monthly, which was quite a time commitment.

At the end of the war, the United States had demobilized remarkably fast, and this included the nuclear enterprise. Just as the soldiers were eager to come home, the Manhattan Project's top leaders moved back to their previous interests or on to new ones. However, unlike the airplane or tank manufacturers, which could close down or return to making cars and trucks, the atomic-bomb production facilities had to continue if we were to have a stockpile—an objective that gained in importance as our relations with the Soviet Union quickly deteriorated. Yet the postwar dislocations and cutbacks left that effort in serious disarray, and one of our first tasks was to tell the AEC how to get it back on track.

In addition to the military work, we tried to get the commission to recognize the importance of fundamental nuclear research and its applications. As scientists, we knew the significance of the radioactive isotopes being produced in the AEC facilities, and fought to have them distributed among universities to maximize their applications in research. In these early years, the AEC instigated its marvelous program of support of basic research in U.S. universities and colleges and helped to establish national laboratories for the large-scale research that needed to be done.

We also encouraged the development of the emerging civilian nuclear power program, although our forecasts regarding its future were seriously overpessimistic. (In one report, we said "decades will elapse" before nuclear power could be a significant power source.) It was a case of seeing the daunting problems without anticipating the breakthroughs that would make nuclear power possible. We also wrongly presumed that nuclear fuel would be in short supply, when in truth, we learned, uranium had seemed rare only because no one had ever had a reason to look for it.


A major issue after the war was that of secrecy. To overgeneralize, most scientists argued for openness against the armed forces' (and many politicians') emphasis on secrecy. In general, the GAC fought to diminish secrecy and pressed for more openness in the operation of the AEC.

The Manhattan Project had generated a tremendous amount of scientific knowledge, most of which had nothing to do with the atomic bomb and could be scientifically useful. Yet much remained classified. We worked hard to have as much as possible declassified, and also to limit the amount of secrecy in laboratories and about imminent discoveries. (Many of these discoveries would now be government-supported and thus, potentially, government-controlled.) The Pentagon wanted to keep as much information as possible secret, in the belief that this would make it more difficult for the Soviets to build the bomb. But as scientists are fond of saying, there are no secrets in science: the only secret about the atomic bomb was whether or not it would work, and that question had been answered. Or, as Albert Einstein put it: "What nature tells one group of men, she will tell in time to any group interested and patient enough in asking questions."

When my colleagues and I discovered plutonium, we kept it secret voluntarily. We knew this was a single, useful piece of information. But when the plutonium bomb exploded over Nagasaki, the world learned of the element's existence, and Soviet scientists knew as much as they needed to know to build an atomic bomb.

In the Franck Report, we'd forecast that the U.S. nuclear monopoly could last only a few years. The Soviet Union exploded its first atomic bomb in August 1949, some four years after Hiroshima. Some people were surprised at how quickly they had managed to do it—but those of us familiar with the Manhattan Project were not particularly surprised. We knew the Soviet Union had capable scientists.

I first heard about the Soviet bomb at the GAC meeting in September 1949, and I immediately remarked that it illustrated the futility of secrecy. Our system thrives on open sharing of discoveries; greater openness would benefit us. It was counterproductive to put ourselves in a straitjacket in hopes of gaining or keeping a lead of a year or two on the Soviets. For example, the AEC had an excellent fellowship program to support students for a year of study, but its effectiveness was hindered by a requirement that each student be cleared by the FBI, whether or not they would be coming anywhere near classified material.

It's true that there was spying at Los Alamos—but as the above timetable shows, it didn't make all that much difference in speeding the Soviets' way to the bomb. And is the ability of spies to penetrate our most secret laboratory an argument for or against the value of secrecy? Could any enterprise as large as the Manhattan Project keep all its secrets?

The Soviet bomb forced President Truman to turn to the question of whether America should try to keep a lead by building a much more powerful weapon, the hydrogen bomb. We didn't know for certain whether the hydrogen (or thermonuclear) bomb was feasible, but if it was, we expected it to be as much as a thousand times more powerful than an atomic bomb. The GAC was asked to consider whether the United States should begin a crash program to build what was commonly called the Super. The decision was not simple. There were valid objections. There was no guarantee of success, which meant we could squander significant resources and impede the continued development of atomic weapons. The military usefulness of the Super was questionable. And was a crash program needed?

The GAC meeting to consider this question was planned for that October. I missed it because I was in Sweden, where I'd been invited by the Royal Academy of Sciences to give a series of lectures on the transuranium elements. The clear implication was that they were looking me over for the Nobel Prize, so I wasn't about to miss the trip.

I expressed my opinion in a letter to Oppie. I said that the idea of another horribly destructive weapon was disheartening, but that we had no choice but to develop the Super because the Soviet Union certainly would. I thought long and hard about this letter, and I intentionally couched a key sentence in the double negative: "Although I deplore the prospects of our country putting a tremendous effort into this, I must confess that I have been unable to come to the conclusion that we should not. . . . I would have to hear some good arguments before I could take on sufficient courage to recommend not going toward such a program." The only thing worse than our building the bomb would be the Soviets having it when we didn't.

In my absence, the remaining committee members voted unanimously against a crash program. In addition, six members stated, "We believe a super bomb should never be produced." In a kind of minority report, Fermi and Rabi noted that the bomb's force would be such that "by its very nature it cannot be confined to a military objective but becomes a weapon which in practical effect is almost one of genocide." They urged that the United States "invite the nations of the world to join us in a solemn pledge not to proceed in the development or construction of weapons of this category."

Both of these reports maintained that the H-bomb would add little real military advantage; the United States' stockpile of atomic bombs would provide plenty of firepower for retaliation in the event of an attack. (And scientists were not the only ones who questioned the Super's military value. In *Dark Sun*, Richard Rhodes reports on a meeting between the Joint Chiefs of Staff and the AEC in which a participant described General Omar Bradley's reaction: "Instead of being infatuated with the possibility of a bomb 1,000 times as powerful as our first A-bombs, he thought such a weapon would be useless against most military targets and that its value would be mostly 'psychological.' ")

In a split vote, the AEC commissioners also voted against a crash program. But Truman had other advice, including that of the congressional Joint Committee on Atomic Energy, which recommended a crash program. In January he announced his decision to initiate a vigorous program to develop the hydrogen bomb. In retrospect, it was a good decision because the Soviet Union turned out to be working very fast, and in some ways achieved a workable H-bomb before the United States did.

Apparently, Oppenheimer did not present my letter for discussion at the GAC meeting. This failure, his later contention that the GAC recommendation was unanimous, and his overall role in opposing the Super were all factors cited when his security clearance was suspended a few years later. Whole books have been written about this affair, so I won't try to rehash the details, but since my letter was specifically mentioned in the bill of particulars against him, let me give my perspective.

The Oppenheimer case was part of a pattern of hysteria that began to grow after the war and culminated in McCarthyism. This illness infected the University of California in 1949, when the regents decided that the university must have a loyalty oath. All faculty members were required to sign a pledge that we weren't communists and would not try to overthrow the government. This was a frivolous, irrelevant distraction for the regents to be meddling in, and it sparked a storm of protest. It also cost the university some important talent. From the Rad Lab, we lost Pief Panofsky to Stanford, where he set up a tremendously successful rival nuclear laboratory. A young professor named David Saxon left (he was hired back years later as university president). There were many more examples, but just these two show the high price the university, which is supposed to be a bastion of academic freedom, paid for engaging in such foolishness. (Courts later declared the oath unconstitutional, and the state had to pay damages to those fired for refusing to sign it.)

While I thought that the oath was an extremely unwise policy, the extent of my protest against it was to sign it on the last possible day. I saw nothing to be gained by refusing; getting fired wouldn't make it go away. There was also nothing to be gained by alienating Ernest Lawrence, who had been turning increasingly to the right after the war. I believed in saving my political capital for more productive fights, such as working quietly to get rid of some of the unneeded secrecy rules. We were trying to get more of our work declassified and to remove some of the more annoying obstacles. (For example, all our work with plutonium had to be performed in a secure building, separate from our other work.)

We all had to have our security clearances renewed periodically, and a constant source of irritation was the attitude of the security people toward one of our most important staff members, Al Ghiorso. Al's success in science has stemmed from the fact that he has always been an original and creative thinker (he found television so banal that he brought up his children without it, and now his children have done the same with theirs). His unwillingness to adopt a "go along to get along" attitude and his undiplomatic insistence on pointing out the ludicrous nature of some of the security regulations only made the security people more intransigent. Al is perhaps the most liberal person I know, the only one who describes Franklin Roosevelt as a conservative. ("Of course he was a conservative," Al says. "He saved capitalism, didn't he?")

The security people complained that before the war his wife Wilma had been a communist. Even if that had been true, during the Depression years, when capitalism had thrown millions out of work on what appeared to be a permanent basis, it was not unusual for people to have socialist or communist leanings. Many friends at UCLA and Berkeley had urged me to join them at their meetings and rallies.

In those years, Wilma had even dragged my future wife, Helen, into a "subversive" activity. In those segregated days, touring bands would perform on different nights for "whites" and "coloreds." Wilma and Helen had the audacity to go on the "colored" night because the music was better than the watered-down version the bands played for the white crowds.

By the early 1950s I'd worked and socialized with Al on a daily basis for a decade. I never detected a hint of anything that would make anyone suspect any disloyalty, yet sometimes I had to fight like hell to keep the AEC security people from revoking his clearance.

That was the kind of climate we were living in when Oppenheimer's loyalty was called into question in late 1953. While Oppenheimer had had some problematic dealings in his past, the whole issue would never have come to a head had he not made a bitter enemy of Lewis Strauss, who become AEC chairman in May 1953.

Oppenheimer made Strauss look foolish too many times. I saw him alienate Strauss at a GAC meeting. An AEC lawyer told me about a congressional hearing where Oppie took apart Strauss's position on an issue and, in doing so, implicitly skewered the man himself. Oppie turned to the lawyer and asked, "How did I do?" The lawyer replied, "Too well, too damn well."

I was familiar with Oppie's power to make you feel small and foolish. As this affair began to brew, I tried to warn him that they were out to get him, a comment that he met with a withering "I can take care of my own affairs, Glenn."

Unfortunately, he couldn't. When his security status was challenged, he could have avoided the whole fiasco by letting his clearance expire. He could have waited out his opponents until the political winds changed, and his security clearance could have been reinstated after the whole thing blew over. But in his pride, he demanded a hearing.

Ironically, Oppie's great leadership of the GAC, his persuasiveness and influence, were suddenly given dark motives as part of some subversive campaign against the hydrogen bomb. (His detractors had to ignore all the times that this persuasiveness moved the GAC in a positive direction that no one could quarrel with.)

Before the hearing, lawyers from both sides interviewed me. I told Oppie's lawyers that I was certain he was not a security risk, but if the government asked me I would say that it had been a grave mistake not to show my letter on the Super to the GAC. I told the government that I had known Oppenheimer for years and had absolutely no doubt about his loyalty and devotion. To my relief, neither side thought my testimony would help. When he took the stand in his own defense, my letter was among the weapons used to entrap him in self-contradictory testimony.

The lone scientist on the three-member board that heard his case voted in his favor, the nonscientists voted against him, and the AEC commissioners upheld the hostile verdict. In their decision my letter was cited as one of six instances supposed to illustrate his "want of character."

To say that the man who led the Los Alamos lab lacked character was outrageous. It was shameful on the part of the government to confront and humiliate a man who had done such tremendous service for the country. At the time, Oppenheimer's only position in the government was as a consultant. I. I. Rabi said during the hearing, "If you don't want to consult the guy, you don't consult him"—but there was no need to humiliate him by yanking his security clearance and dragging his name through the dirt. He deserved better treatment for the work he'd done for a country he'd served with dedication and conspicuous ability.

I could never comprehend the attack on Robert Oppenheimer in terms of national security, only in terms of personal vendettas. It was a chilling lesson for me about the consequences of making enemies, about powerful egos reacting to slights and retaliating. It showed the importance of personality, of the way personal interactions can influence what should be policy and professional matters. After witnessing a Strauss-Oppenheimer interaction, David Lilienthal noted "how much the course of events is affected by wholly personal quirks, by what seem at the time little personal things." The lesson was to become important for me, as my life was drawn more and more into the political arena.

The Oppenheimer episode should be a lesson to the country about how obsession with secrecy and security—and their political use and abuse—can harm your security rather than help it. Oppie's brilliant leadership had not ended with the war. He led the General Advisory Committee equally brilliantly, and his contributions strengthened our country and improved the nuclear weapons program that some of his enemies feared he opposed. Cutting him off from making further contributions deprived us of the energy and talent of a formidable intellect without providing a shred of additional security.

When I became AEC chairman, I would find a way for the country to make some amends toward Robert Oppenheimer.

# FOURTEEN

# BIG PRIZES: CHILDREN, ELEMENTS, AND A NOBEL

Helen and I started a family right after the war. Helen was about seven months pregnant when we took the train back to Berkeley in May 1946. We'd been home for ten days when we took an automobile trip up to the Napa Valley to scout out golf courses—I was now a golf addict, given its efficacy in my cure in Chicago. It was a trip I regret, for Helen awoke that night with cramps that signaled premature labor. When I called the obstetrician who was taking care of Helen, he coldly refused to meet our emergency.

I was in a quandary until Helen remembered the name of a colleague's obstetrician. About two in the morning, I frantically called Dr. Josephine Borson and pleaded for her help. To our vast relief, Dr. Borson sent an ambulance immediately. At about four, a nurse emerged from the delivery room to show me a tiny three-pound-seven-ounce daughter, on the way to be put into an incubator. There was continued activity in the delivery room, however, and about fifteen minutes later they brought out a four-pound-seven-ounce boy.

We sent out announcements that said, "Mr. and Mrs. Glenn T. Seaborg announce the production of Paulette Jeanne and Peter Glenn. Two Fragments, But Not Fission." When I first saw plutonium I'd compared my feelings to those of a new father, but they were nothing next to the thrill of real fatherhood. The dangerously small and premature babies remained in the hospital for several weeks. With the doctors' assurances that they were doing well, I left on a business trip in June, only to be called back with the horrifying news that Paulette had died.

Paulette's death was so devastating that when Peter finally came home a month after his birth I was almost obsessively protective, worrying when Helen took him on the most innocent of outings. He continued to gain weight and improve, though he never became a robust child.

Our daughter Lynne was born in 1947, and Helen was expecting again in April 1949. On a Friday night, she began having labor cramps. I called Dr. Borson, positioned the car at the bottom of the porch steps, and went to help Helen down from our upstairs bedroom. She was in obvious distress, and when she stepped out onto the porch, she announced she wasn't going any farther. The baby was going to be born right then and there. It was more a matter of catching than delivering him, as he emerged head first and face down, which I later learned was the normal way. I announced it was a boy, and Helen got up and walked inside to the couch.

When I called Dr. Borson again with the news that the baby had been born, she said she'd get right down to the hospital, and I told her that wouldn't be necessary, we were still at home. I went into the kitchen to put some water on to boil because in books and movies, that's what they always tell the father to do. When Dr. Borson arrived in just a few minutes, I greeted her with a grin and the comment "Boy, am I wise to your racket." The ambulance that Dr. Borson had ordered then whisked away Helen and the baby, with the umbilical cord still attached. The baby, whom we named David Michael, seemed none the worse for his unusual arrival in the world.

That year we purchased a lot in Lafayette, a suburb on the sunny eastern side of the hills that ring San Francisco Bay. More than a half dozen other families from the lab moved into the same neighborhood. We even teamed up with two neighbors, including Iz Perlman's family, to build and maintain a swimming pool together.

In September 1951, Arne Tiselius of Sweden's Uppsala University gave a set of lectures at Berkeley. Despite the fact that we'd moved into our new house only a month before and had not even a couch in the living room, Helen and I hosted a dinner party in his honor, and as he was leaving he told Helen he looked forward to seeing her in Sweden. Helen responded that we hoped to visit Sweden someday but had no plans at this point. "Well," Tiselius said, "it may be sooner than you think."

With that bit of tantalization, I was wound up when November's season of Nobel Prize announcements came around. As I drove to work one morning, the news came over the radio that the Swedish Royal Academy of Sciences was in the process of voting, and the rumor was that I would win in chemistry. I managed to keep the car on the road until I got to work.

As was our custom on pleasant days, a group of us were eating lunch at a picnic table outside the lab when a secretary called me inside to take a phone call. A Swedish reporter told me that the 1951 Nobel Prize in chemistry would be awarded jointly to Ed McMillan and me.

When I broke the news at the lunch table, there was complete silence. My first congratulations came in the form of a quip by Iz Perlman: "You seem awfully happy for a man who just lost half a Nobel Prize." (I hesitate to include his joke lest anyone think it might imply that Ed's work didn't deserve equal credit. It certainly did. In addition to his work on neptunium and plutonium, his inventions and refinements relating to particle accelerators made much of the Rad Lab's future work possible.) Congratulatory phone calls, telegrams, and cards poured in. Lord Cherwell, the eminent British scientist, wrote, "I suppose if you can't find new elements you just have to make them." My childhood friend Clayton Sheldon asked for a loan. Our hard-to-impress five-year-old son Peter asked if anyone had ever won two Nobel Prizes. I said no, then corrected myself when I remembered Marie Curie, which sparked his disdainful reply, "A *girl?*"

The prize committee did not recognize Ed and me for the actual discovery of transuranium elements; instead, our citation referred to our "discoveries in the chemistry of the trans-uranium elements." The committee adopted this careful wording because Enrico Fermi had already been awarded the 1938 prize for the discovery of the transuranium elements. Fermi's "transuranium elements" turned out to be fission, instead, but the committee couldn't bring itself to award two prizes for the same discovery.

It was particularly gratifying for us Berkeley boosters that with the addition of Ed and me, the Berkeley faculty had the most Nobel laureates of any university. Helen and I traveled to Stockholm for the ceremonies with Edwin and Elsie McMillan and Ernest and Molly

Lawrence. Our group had especially close bonds because Elsie and Molly were sisters and Helen had been Ernest's secretary. Ernest finally delivered the Nobel lecture that World War II had prevented him from giving. Ed bought all the formal trappings for the ceremonies, and his white vest became a Berkeley tradition. Emilio Segrè borrowed it when he won the prize in 1959, as did Donald Glaser in 1960. By 1961, when Melvin Calvin made the trip, the vest was so well known that the Swedes asked him about it.

One striking characteristic of the Nobel ceremony is the tremendous formality—even the photographers in the audience are clad in white tie and tails. It's traditional to answer the king with a toast at the formal dinner, and when it was my turn I spoke in my best Swedish, which I'd been practicing for the occasion. It had never occurred to me that my parents both spoke in a distinctive regional accent, but the Swedes noticed it instantly. It was as if a Swede had "y'alled" in English with a Southern accent. The next morning's newspaper proclaimed: "Seaborg Answers King in Ringing Dalarna Accent."

Naturally enough, incidents like that one engendered a special relationship between me and the Swedish people, who sensed my affection and took pride in my achievements, almost as if I were native-born. When we visited cousins in my ancestral region, the town flew Old Glory alongside the blue-and-yellow Swedish flag. Children popped in where we were eating, politely bowed or curtsied, and asked for an autograph. Delegations of small-town officials and interested onlookers greeted us, seeming touched by the fact that I was exploring my roots. And I met many relatives for the first time. I was talking on the phone with one cousin who kept insisting that I put Helen on the line, despite my protests that she didn't speak Swedish. When I finally gave in, she put the receiver to her ear and said, "Ja . . . ja . . . ja . . ." for several minutes and handed the phone back to me. My cousin admonished me, "What do you mean, she doesn't speak Swedish?"

I got to know The Svedberg, a Swedish Nobel laureate. As we talked, we discovered that his grandfather had been a manager at the same ironworks plant where my great-grandfather had been foreman (and where my grandfather worked before emigrating). The's grandfather was named Theodore—my father's name and my middle name—and we wondered if our names had common origins.

I found I hadn't mastered all the customs, however. On December 13, St. Lucia Day, Lucia singers walked into our suite at the Grand Hotel to begin our day with coffee and rolls. Not expecting any such greeting, Helen and I were sleeping when they strolled in; the photographers' flashbulbs were a little unnerving.

That evening I had the honor of crowning the Stockholm Lucia queen and her ten princesses at the City Hall. In addition to pinning an emblem on the Lucia queen I was required to kiss her; this time the photographers' presence wasn't so bad, as they insisted I repeat the act several times because they claimed I wasn't doing it correctly. An official escorted Helen to a balcony to view the pageantry and commented, "Dr. Seaborg is enjoying himself so much," then realized what he'd said and quickly added, "Oh, but he is only doing his duty."

A half-share of a 1951 Nobel Prize amounted to $16,000. This windfall added a couple of rooms to our house for our growing family and paid off our mortgage. That I would pay off a loan offered at the low interest rates then prevailing instead of investing in stocks is a good example of how scientific and financial acumen often seem mutually exclusive, but seeing mortgagees evicted from their houses during the Depression had given me a powerful aversion to debt.

I proudly displayed the Nobel medal on my desk for several months, until some joker, I think it was Burris Cunningham, insinuated that if he needed some gold foil, he knew where to find a good source to roll some out. Not sure how far any practical jokes might go, I took the prize home immediately.

A Nobel Prize can be a mixed blessing. Because suddenly you're an authority, reporters seek your opinion and comments even on subjects you know little about. You're showered with speech and lecture invitations. Some recipients have gotten so caught up in the renown and demands on their time that their scientific productivity has plummeted. I was fortunate to escape any major disruptions, perhaps because I was still young enough to add to my schedule, perhaps because I loved my research too much to be distracted. I wish nonscientists could get a taste of what it's like to go to the lab in the morning with high expectations, never knowing what discoveries might await that day.

These discoveries could come from the most unexpected sources. Our quest for berkelium and californium had required years of carefully developing procedures and equipment. The next elements literally dropped out of the sky. The clue that led us to them came in the form of a telegram from the AEC classification office.

The first full-scale test of a thermonuclear, or hydrogen, bomb was held in the Pacific in November 1952. On December 4 we received the telegram, informing us that a new isotope of plutonium had been discovered in the test debris and requesting that we keep secret any evidence we might have of its existence. Evidently, the head of the classification office sent the telegram because he was aware we had been looking for just such an isotope, plutonium 244. We'd been trying for years to make it by bombarding plutonium 239 for long periods in a reactor. If this report was true, it meant that the uranium 238 in the bomb had captured a half dozen neutrons in the explosion, forming the plutonium isotope instantly!

We had been looking for plutonium 244 because we expected it to undergo beta decay—that is, it would emit electrons as its excess neutrons transmuted into protons. Neutrons transmuting into protons meant the atoms would be moving up the periodic table, forming new elements. If plutonium 244 could be found in the test debris, perhaps there were new elements to be found there as well.

We quickly contacted friends who were closer to the weapons effort and obtained a piece of filter paper from a plane that had flown through the blast area to collect samples. In just over a week after we'd received the filter paper, Stan Thompson and Al Ghiorso had adapted the ion-exchange experiments we used to find elements 97 and 98 to identify an isotope of element 99 by looking for its characteristics as predicted by the periodic table. Within another month, we'd identified element 100. That identification was noteworthy because we did it with a sample that contained only about 100 atoms. (Further confirmation of 99 and 100 came when tons of coral were mined from the explosion area and examined.)

The Argonne National Laboratory in Chicago and the Los Alamos laboratory performed similar experiments on the debris and reported similar findings. The three laboratories began arguing about which group was entitled to be called the discoverers before agreeing that the most reasonable solution was to share the credit. We named element 99 einsteinium, after Albert Einstein, and element 100 fermium, after Enrico Fermi. While Einstein is well known, Fermi is not, at least among

The microchemists Louis Werner and Burris Cunningham in Room 405 of Jones Laboratory at the University of Chicago on August 20, 1942, the day they isolated a tiny precipitate of a plutonium compound, the first time a synthetic element was "beheld by the eye of man."

The balances used in the first Manhattan Project experiments to isolate plutonium each consisted of a quartz fiber with a tiny sample holder to weigh "invisible material."

An aerial view of the barracks in Hanford, Washington, in 1944; some 40,000 workers lived there during the construction of the reactors and plutonium separation plants.

The mess hall at Hanford, where workers were fed in shifts. When Seaborg ate lunch there, people were talking about a murder committed the night before.

The Hanford extraction plant. In three years, the tools for isolating plutonium went from tiny balances to the industrial scale of the separation process here, a billion-times scale-up.

Single-shell tanks under construction at Hanford to hold the radioactive waste produced in reactors. This shows the scale of the operation and gives an idea of the haste with which the tanks were built. They were never improved.

Seaborg on the *Quiz Kids* show, where he revealed, in response to a question from one of the children, the previously secret news of the discovery of two new elements, November 11, 1945.

Al Ghiorso in front of, and Art Jaffey behind, a pulse (radiation) analyzer at the Met Lab.

Stanley Thompson, using a mirror to watch his own work from behind the protection of lead bricks, at the Met Lab, February 1946.

Isadore (Iz) Perlman, 1942.

Albert Ghiorso, 1950.

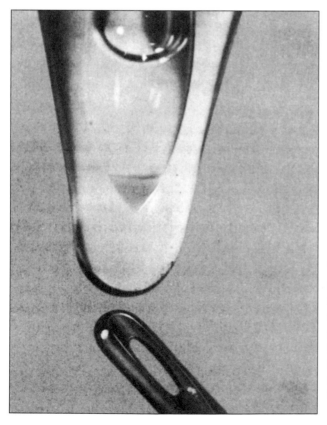

The first photograph of an americium compound, next to the eye of a sewing needle to give an idea of scale. Americium (element 95) was first isolated in the fall of 1945 at the Met Lab, and is now commonly found in smoke detectors.

As the size of its machines grew, so did the Radiation Laboratory: the newly constructed 184-inch cyclotron building high above San Francisco Bay.

Seaborg receiving the Nobel Prize from King Gustav VI with Princess Sibylla looking on, December 1951.

Stanley Thompson and Seaborg in 1948 with a centrifuge during their work that led to the discovery of elements 97 and 98.

The heavy ion linear accelerator (HILAC), which came on-line in 1957 and was used in the discovery of elements such as 102 (nobelium).

Inside the HILAC.

Seaborg watching behind two football players at California's opening game of the 1958 season—his first as chancellor. The Golden Bears lost this one to the College of the Pacific, but unexpectedly went on to play in the Rose Bowl.

With seven Nobel laureates on its faculty, Berkeley led the world. Seaborg; Owen Chamberlain (physics, 1959); chemistry prize recipients Edwin McMillan (1951), William Giauque (1949), John Northrop (1946), and Wendell Stanley (1946); and Emilio Segrè (physics, 1959), all together for the first time, met for a group portrait, March 31, 1960.

the general public. But in my ranking of the greatest scientists I have met, he and G. N. Lewis are the best.

The complexity of modern physics forces even the most brilliant to choose between specializing in theory or in experiment. Fermi is generally recognized as the only twentieth-century physicist equally at home with both. After the war, I would save my most puzzling problems to present to him when I saw him at conferences or government committee meetings. He would be happy to help, giving patient explanations that were always so clear that one could easily understand them. If we were working on a calculation and needed to plug in an obscure formula, the rest of us would go scurrying to look it up in a book, but Fermi would derive the formula himself from basic principles and have it faster than we could find it. At the first atom-bomb test, which he witnessed in New Mexico, he measured the distance the blast had moved some strips of paper he dropped and from this made quick (and accurate) calculations on the yield of the bomb. Once, when we were out by San Francisco Bay, Helen watched him sighting at the Bay Bridge along his arm. He knew the size of his thumb and the length of his arm, and could make instant measurements of the bridge's length, height, and other aspects that intrigued him.

He was fully aware of these abilities but displayed none of the arrogance that so often accompanies brilliance. During the war, we scientists in Chicago formed a buying club to share books, and Enrico would periodically appear at our door to deliver one, always smiling, always pleasant. The football coach Tom Landry, who explained his own famous stone-faced expression by saying, "You can't smile and think at the same time," obviously never met Enrico Fermi, who was always smiling and thinking circles around the rest of us.

When we settled on the name fermium for element 100, Fermi was ill with cancer. It was an accident of timing that he died before the name was officially accepted. It never occurred to us that there was anything untoward about naming an element after a living person, an issue that would come up some forty years later. The name fermium for 100 turned out to be a happy coincidence because it proved to be the last element synthesized using neutron-capture reactions, a subject that Fermi studied extensively.

Our next element came thanks to a sudden inspiration Al had in the midst of an airplane flight—he grabbed the only writing material at hand and did some calculations, literally on the back of an envelope. Al's figures showed that if we could get a billion atoms of einsteinium (element 99) and bombard them with helium ions, in each bombardment an average of one atom would absorb an ion's two charges and become element 101. We spent several months developing the new separations— the einsteinium would have to be used quickly because its half-life is about 20 days—and the new bombardment techniques that would be needed.

It took two or three years of bombarding plutonium in a reactor to synthesize einsteinium. I arranged to get the einsteinium samples from the largest nuclear reactor of the time, the AEC's Materials Testing Reactor in Idaho. In addition to Al and Stan Thompson, our team included a staff researcher, Bernard Harvey, and a postdoctoral fellow, Gregory Choppin. After several unsuccessful attempts that helped refine the techniques, the definitive experiments occurred during the night of February 18, 1955. A typical experiment went like this: The separated einsteinium was placed in the accelerator on an invisibly thin layer of gold foil. A helium ion beam was sent through the foil from the other side, so any atoms of element 101 that formed would be knocked (recoil) onto a second thin gold catcher foil. As soon as the bombardment was finished, Bernie and Al ran in to the accelerator's target room and put the catcher foil in a test tube. Bernie ran the foil to a makeshift lab where Greg heated it in a solution to dissolve the gold. Bernie then carried the test tube outside to where Al was sitting in his Volkswagen with the engine running. The experiments were done at night in part to avoid traffic—Al had a mile-long drive to the Radiation Laboratory, where Stan was waiting to run the solution through an ion-exchange column. This step isolated the element 101 and provided chemical identification. The drops from the column were caught one by one on platinum plates and dried under a heat lamp. The plates were taken to a room where Al had special counters set up, one counter to each plate. Any element 101 present on a plate would reveal itself by giving off energy as it decayed.

Each energy pulse would signify the exciting evidence of a new element, but a long time would elapse between pulses. Rather than hover over the equipment, Al wired the counters so that an energy pulse would set off the building's fire alarm. The bell rang, the research team cheered, and Al turned off the alarm.

The team reran the experiment a dozen times, finding a total of some 17 atoms of element 101. It was the first time that an element had ever been identified one atom at a time.

After working all night, the tired researchers went home for a nap, leaving their apparatus in place. When an atom decayed unexpectedly the next morning, the fire alarm sounded again. A fire in a building stocked with radioactive material could be catastrophic, so some worried day-shift workers began to evacuate while others searched wildly for the fire until someone noticed Al's wiring arrangement. A note from Ernest Lawrence congratulating us on the discovery included a stern admonition that we were not to tamper with the fire alarms even for work as important as the discovery of a new element.

We thought it fitting that there be an element named for the Russian chemist Dmitri Mendeleev, who had developed the periodic table. In nearly all our experiments discovering transuranium elements, we'd depended on his method of predicting chemical properties based on the element's position in the table. But in the middle of the Cold War, naming an element for a Russian was a somewhat bold gesture that did not sit well with some American critics. It was noticed in the Soviet Union, of course. I happened to meet with Vice President Richard Nixon when he was preparing for his 1959 trip to the Soviet Union (the one that featured his famous "kitchen debate" with Khrushchev) and told him about mendelevium. He evidently found an opportunity to use the information, because I soon received a package mailed from the American embassy in Moscow. It contained this letter from a Soviet citizen:

> In this friendly act of the American scientist each Soviet citizen discerns a great respect toward our people and its culture, as well as one of the steps toward the liquidation of the absurd, according to Nikita Sergeevich Khrushchev, tense state of "cold war" between two great nations. May I present you, in commemoration of your remarkable discovery and your noble act, the book by Dmitri Ivanovich Mendeleev, "Fundamentals of Chemistry," with his autograph.

The inscription read: "To my deeply appreciated colleague, Dr. N. I. Bistrov, in commemoration of saving my son. D. Mendeleev, 1889." The book is one of my most treasured possessions.

The tremendous growth and scientific progress continued at the Radiation Laboratory throughout the 1950s. Ernest Lawrence became more involved with weapons research. He was instrumental in establishing a new laboratory at the site of a wartime air base in nearby Livermore, which was meant to compete with Los Alamos. At first, our nuclear chemistry division was responsible for the chemical work at this new laboratory. We supplied many graduating Ph.D. chemists, and eventually Kenneth Street moved from our staff to be head of nuclear chemistry there.

But most of the work of my group was not weapons-related; my colleagues and I were really interested in basic science. We had to work hard to get our building declassified, a move that was resisted by the government secrecy experts because we did perform a small amount of sensitive work.

But the defense tie-in meant that our work was well supported by the Atomic Energy Commission, and we had access to a series of increasingly powerful accelerators. Built before the war, the 60-inch cyclotron could accelerate deuterons to an energy of 20 million electron volts. The 184-inch cyclotron, which came on-line in 1947, could accelerate deuterons to 180 million electron volts; the bevatron, on-line in 1953, could impart 6 billion electron volts to particles.

But the largest particle these machines could accelerate was about the size of a helium nucleus. If we were to continue to find heavier elements, we needed a new approach. As the synthesis of mendelevium illustrated, moving up the periodic chart one or two elements at a time was increasingly impractical—it required synthesizing a short-lived and hard-to-make new element, then using it for a target. A better approach would be to bombard more abundant elements, such as uranium or plutonium, with larger ions in order to move up several steps at once. The question was how to accelerate these larger ions.

In addition to his cyclotron, Ernest Lawrence had also built the first linear accelerator, which was basically a cyclotron that had been un-wound into a straight line. Al Ghiorso and I convinced Ernest that for accelerating heavier ions, the linear accelerator was the way to go. The linear accelerator could strip more electrons from the accelerated particle (allowing use of a heavier ion), and a straight beam of ions was much easier to aim at a target than one spiraling out of a cyclotron. In 1957, the heavy ion linear accelerator (HILAC) was put in operation, capable of accelerating ions as large as neon, element 10.

The HILAC made possible the discovery of element 102, a discovery that was clouded by controversy. An international team working at the Nobel Institute in Stockholm claimed the discovery in 1957. However, neither a Soviet group nor our group could duplicate their experiments, and the Nobel Institute claim was eventually found to be erroneous. In 1958, we managed to synthesize the real element 102 in the HILAC by bombarding curium (element 96) with ions of carbon (element 6). We identified element 102 through another atom-at-a-time collection tech-nique. The half-life of the new element seemed to be about three sec-onds; with these short-lived elements we depended increasingly on the collection and identification of their daughters (the isotopes they decayed to) rather than on chemical identification. The age when one could actu-ally do any chemistry with the new elements seemed to be drawing to a close. Though we were the first to identify it clearly, research groups in the Soviet Union later corrected some of our interpretations, so the credit for the discovery should be shared by these groups. The original, incor-rect discovery team had suggested the name nobelium, after Alfred Nobel, for element 102. By the time our claim as discoverers was recog-nized, this name was so well established in the literature that there seemed no point in changing it.

# FIFTEEN

# A CHANCELLOR'S

# THREE CHALLENGES

Throughout the 1950s, I often slipped out of the lab to indulge my passion for golf. My scores tended toward the atomic numbers of the elements I worked on, but so were my partners'. Ben Hogan's book *Better Golf Without Practicing* worked as the title promised, however, shaving several strokes off my game. But I kept my baseball-style swing that Al called "a thing to behold." He maintains that despite my horrible form, I stayed competitive by psyching out my opponents with trivial comments, something that it is perhaps best to neither confirm nor deny. But we mild-mannered scientists could be as competitive as anyone on the athletic field.

One person I could consistently beat was the physicist Luis Alvarez, the most creative and versatile scientist I have ever known. During World War II, he worked on radar, then on the intricate implosive system for the atomic bomb. His work with the bubble chamber and his pioneering use of high-speed computers to process information led to a tripling of the known subatomic particles in just a few years (work for which he won the 1968 Nobel Prize in physics). At an age when many people retire, he then teamed up with his geologist son and another colleague to propose that the sudden extinction of the dinosaurs was caused by the impact of a huge meteor, a theory that has gained increasing currency.

It seemed to me that Luis could invent anything, and perhaps it was his frustration at losing to someone with form as bad as mine that led him to invent a golf practicing machine. Luis' machine had photo cells and strobe lights that produced a set of images he used for analyzing his swing, to ensure that he held to correct form. The improvement in Luis' game under the influence of the machine was noticeable, and he even sent a copy of it to the First Golfer, President Eisenhower, although I never heard if there was any reaction.

My graduate students later confided that they considered my avid support for Berkeley's football team so predictable that they relied on it for a harmless subterfuge: if I planned to be in the lab on an autumn Saturday morning, they knew to show up and to be seen there at least until I headed for the stadium; then they'd have several hours free, perhaps to attend the game themselves, as long as they slipped back in before their professor returned to be duly impressed with their Saturday dedication.

It was my obvious love of sports that led me out of the lab and on to a new career course. When Clark Kerr was appointed to the newly created position of chancellor of the Berkeley campus of the University of California in 1952, he asked me to serve as faculty athletic representative, a post I held for six years. My duties included academic supervision of the student athletes, ruling on their eligibility and ensuring they complied with entrance requirements; attending meetings of the Pacific Coast Conference and the National Collegiate Athletic Association; and, of course (this was the tough part), attending as many intercollegiate sporting events as my schedule would allow. I would also do what I could to help coaches recruit by having an open door to meet with potential student athletes. The message that a faculty leader would take the time to meet with you, that Berkeley took its athletics as seriously as its scholarship, didn't hurt in attracting the kind of students we wanted.

I greatly enjoyed the new social circle into which my duties brought me. I often traveled with the teams to games, and this led to some lasting friendships with coaches and players. Many of the players later told me how amazed they were that a faculty member would spend this time with them. For example, one such player was an end named Jim Hanifan, who went on to be head coach of the St. Louis Cardinals, among other positions in the NFL. Some thirty years after he graduated, when he was offensive line coach of the Washington Redskins, he took Helen and me on a fascinating tour of their facilities.

In 1956, my fellow Pacific Coast Conference representatives appointed me press spokesman, which should have meant little more than conducting the press conferences after our meetings. That routine duty became a challenging one when scandals erupted at several of the schools, and it became known that UCLA, USC, and Washington were paying athletes under the table. Relations among the schools in the conference were already rocky, with conflicts over admission standards; schedule preferences (smaller schools wanted more in-conference games while the "majors" wanted dates free to play high-profile teams like Notre Dame); and the conference's unwieldy constitution, which many schools found excessively rigid. The next year, the conference broke up.

In the following months, I devoted a great deal of time to negotiating with other schools about putting together a new conference. In 1958 we formed the Athletic Association of Western Universities, consisting of USC, UCLA, Berkeley, and the University of Washington, soon joined by Stanford. The AAWU's philosophy was to have less rigid governing rules and rely more on the integrity of the members, an approach that proved successful. (The AAWU evolved into today's Pac-10.)

Clark appreciated the leadership and resistance to pressure I'd shown in this rather sensitive work. So when he became the University of California's president, he asked me to replace him as chancellor at Berkeley, saying he wanted somebody he could trust to handle the campus there so well he wouldn't have to worry about it.

Clark ignored my protests that I wasn't interested because I already had a job I loved, and he persisted over a period of several months. Finally, the time came for him to take on his responsibilities as president, and he still hadn't named a replacement. He called me in for one more meeting and asked what it would take for me to accept the job as chancellor. I gave him a list of what I assumed would be unacceptable conditions, the main deal breakers being that I would have to continue to have graduate students and carry on with research, that since the chancellor's house on campus was no place to bring up kids we would stay in our house in Lafayette, and that I'd remain as associate director of the Radiation Laboratory. When I finished, Clark asked, "Is that all?" Then: "No problem." I was dumbfounded.

I was left with no honorable way out. But when I discovered how tremendously rewarding the job was, I realized that Clark had done me a great favor. I'd been at the lab for twelve postwar years and was ready for a new challenge. The expanded horizon of a faculty athletic representative was nothing compared with the new social realm in which Helen and I found ourselves. As chancellor, I met the leading lights in every field, as well as visiting lecturers and dignitaries ranging from the English writer C. P. Snow to Queen Frederika of the Netherlands, plus successful alumni and contributors to the university.

It was the most difficult job I ever had, harder even than my next job as chairman of the Atomic Energy Commission. At the AEC, I was responsible only to the President of the United States and Congress; I had authority to make a decision and carry it out. As chancellor of a public university campus, I had an endless number of bosses in the form of interest groups to keep happy, any of whom could make my life miserable: the faculty, the university president, the regents, the governor, the legislature, the alumni, the students, and the students' parents. A chancellor has to rely on persuasive ability and consensus building to get people to go along to carry out a program.

The way decisions are made and carried out in running a large university is rather peculiar. There are voluminous written regulations, procedures, bylaws, manuals, and directives designed to ensure that everything is run aboveboard, in the manner of a civil service. Yet a tremendous amount of power is implicit, vested in the traditions of collegial shared authority. Some decisions must be made through highly formal and visible processes, with widespread consultation and recorded votes. Other decisions are remarkably casual—a few words exchanged in a corridor or over the phone. The chancellor's trick is to recognize which decisions require formal steps; which advice must be taken (and which can be ignored); when to act quickly and when to delay. The challenge is to find the path between appearing dictatorial and becoming paralyzed among the layers of advice and cumbersome machinery of overlapping approvals.

Decisions that lack support can easily be lost in the maze of being implemented: there were eighty-four committees and subcommittees responsible in varying degrees to the chancellor, not to mention committees and boards of the student government, Academic Senate, and alumni association. Just appointing the members of administrative committees was a big job, requiring hundreds of letters a year written to faculty and students. There was a Committee on the Opening Exhibit for the Art and Anthropology Building, an Advisory Committee on Computer Facilities, a Special Committee on Fraternity Problems, a Committee to Screen Applications for Summer Employment of High School Students, an Advisory Committee on Discrimination . . .

But cumbersome as all this may sound, the committees enabled us to spread the large administrative burden: on a campus with 22,000 students, 1,600 faculty, 6,000 staff, and an annual operating budget of $50 million, our central administration consisted of three vice-chancellors (all of them part-time, adding this work to their faculty duties), three part-time faculty assistants, a budget assistant, and about twenty secretaries, typists, and file clerks.

During the 1950s, the university was developing new campuses around the state, which required changing its administrative system. Clark and I managed to work out most issues of centralization vs. autonomy in remarkably informal fashion, in meetings and chats. That informality contrasts sharply with today, when the chancellors at each UC campus preside over complex, large administrative organizations with hundreds of executive and management positions. Yet most of the problems of running a campus haven't changed since those days. Clark Kerr summed up the three main ones as "athletics for the alumni, parking for the faculty, and sex for the students."

I was blessed when it came to the alumni's priority; my term was the golden age of the Golden Bears. Berkeley's rugby team went undefeated in 1959 and 1960; its trophies included the World Cup series. Cal teams won the International Regatta Association championship in 1960, the California Intercollegiate Baseball Association championship in 1960, and the AAWU water polo championships in 1959 and 1960. The highest-profile wins were the NCAA basketball championship in 1959 and the Pacific Coast Conference football championship in 1958—our last trip to the Rose Bowl. Did I have anything to do with this unprecedented spurt of athletic success? My standard response is that it never happened before and it's never happened since. I rest my case.

I do take pride that this golden age came immediately after my years as faculty athletic representative. I became so closely identified with

Berkeley sports that the famed San Francisco *Chronicle* columnist Herb Caen pointed out that Seaborg is an anagram for "Go Bears." And I'm also proud that the triumphs came without deviating from the tradition described by Robert Gordon Sproul: "At Berkeley we want to have students who are engaging in athletics, not athletes who are playing at being students."

The championship basketball team was notable for its lack of stars. Not a single player made All-American or even all-conference. They won with a tenacious defense, as coach Pete Newell chewed on a towel and gave strategy a new meaning. Every opponent was held to one of their lowest point totals of the season, and then complained of having an "off" night—it was amazing how many of these off nights just happened to be against the Bears. In the Final Four, our team faced a University of Cincinnati team led by Oscar Robertson in a game played on the university's Charter Day. The ceremonies included my inauguration as chancellor, followed by a banquet to honor the Alumnus of the Year. As I ate dinner, I tried to pay attention to the conversations around me, while discreetly listening to a transistor radio. The game was in its final minutes when I had to put the radio away because Clark Kerr rose to speak. Fortunately, the head of the alumni association came out and whispered the good news that we'd won. I wanted to break the news to the audience, but Clark overheard me getting it, pulled rank, and made the announcement himself. (I could watch the next game on television, when our boys beat Jerry West's West Virginia by one point.) Despite losing six of its seniors, the team returned to the finals the next year, where they lost to an Ohio State team that featured Jerry Lucas, John Havlicek, and Bobby Knight.

The football team was led to the Rose Bowl by the indomitable Joe Kapp, whose distinctive rough-and-tumble playing style made the Minnesota Vikings a force to be reckoned with for years; the only thing that kept us from winning the Rose Bowl was that our opponent outscored us. The next year was disappointing, and football coach Pete Elliott accepted a job at the University of Illinois. Hiring a new coach would normally have been the athletic director's responsibility, but the university was in the midst of changing the administration of its sports program, and the task fell on my shoulders. I was surprised at the level of football!

obsession at an academically oriented school like Berkeley. I received the largest outpouring of advice I have ever seen on any subject: letters, telegrams, phone calls, personal visits, newspaper columns, and letters to the editor. People stopped me on the street, whispered advice during meetings on unrelated subjects, and spoke in hushed tones in late-night phone calls at home. Some messages were threatening; one offered a handsome bribe. It was as if there was more at stake than just hiring a person to coach a few dozen players. This person seemed to play a mystical role in people's lives; his leadership somehow extended vicariously to a wide circle of deeply involved alumni and others.

If you could get the alumni this energized about hiring professors, you could find the talent to win a Nobel Prize every year. One alum offered to donate a million dollars to the football department if I hired his candidate; no one ever told me that they'd endow a chair if I hired a certain professor. If ever proof was needed of our emphasis on sports over academics, this process provided it—even at a university that no one expected to be a football powerhouse.

One front-running candidate had coached at Navy for nine years and been an assistant coach for the San Francisco 49ers. The first search committee not only recommended him but reported that they had no other strong alternatives. Despite, or perhaps because of, his background, I didn't think this man was right for Berkeley. Fortunately, a powerful regent, Ed Pauley, who was an owner of the Los Angeles Rams, adamantly opposed him, and his opinion carried enough weight to give me cover to buck the recommendation.

We soon began to hear about the thirty-four-year-old coach of the University of New Mexico. His 7–3 records for the past two seasons were impressive, but his personal credentials were even more so: Phi Beta Kappa, student body president, and eight letters at Coe College, followed by a master's in history from Harvard. Marv Levy arrived in Berkeley for an interview on February 2, and on February 5 we announced that we had hired him. I spent most of a day on the phone explaining our decision process and dealing with people's emotions. Reactions ranged from words of encouragement to disappointment and even anger. I can't imagine a more likable coach and a better fit for the campus, but unfortunately there was no happily-ever-after ending. In Marv's four years at Cal, his best record was 4–5–1. He later recalled that after that season, he met with the athletic director and told him the program's future was bright. The athletic director agreed, saying, "That's why I'm in a strong position to bring in a new coach."

Perhaps this proved for the best for Marv, however. Given the situation at Berkeley, I doubt anyone could have had much football success—and no one did for years afterward. With help from Pappy Waldorf, a former Cal coach who was then with the 49ers, Marv landed the head coaching job at the College of William and Mary. He rose through the ranks, ending his career with the Buffalo Bills, which he led to a record four consecutive Super Bowls. I still take pride in the fact that we "discovered" him. And as a further aside, Marv had a young assistant coach at Cal named Bill Walsh, who would help create the 49ers dynasty.

Clark's second issue for a university head, parking for the faculty, was always an issue on a campus surrounded by a city on three sides and steep hills on the fourth. Any expansion was difficult, and parking had been tight for years. Of all things, a controversy was sparked by a federal loan of more than a million dollars that would allow us to *add* parking facilities on a massive scale, nearly 1,700 spaces.

The loan came with the requirement that we charge fees for the parking places, and the regents set the fee for faculty members at fifty dollars per year. This set off a small revolt among some professors. Rancorous meetings of the Academic Senate passed loftily worded resolutions objecting that the fees would help pay for facilities for others.

As for Clark's third issue—sex among students—one big brouhaha on that topic involved the student humor magazine. *The Pelican* pushed the boundaries of taste so consistently that we administrators looked forward with trepidation to each month's issue. The magazine's low point came when it published an article entitled "A Modest Proposition," calling for a campus brothel. This would, it claimed, make male students more efficient in their studies by offering an easy way to deal with one of their obsessions, and in addition it would "provide the Departments of Psychology, Economics, Sociology, and School of Business Administration with a perfect laboratory for controlled experiments." Lest we think his proposal benefited only males, the author noted that a woman student would have "a chance to obtain an easy job one or two nights a week which will provide her with extra money and, indeed, be as beneficial to her as it is to the male."

These days, the sexist tone of this proposal is so notable that it makes it hard to remember how shocking the very idea of sex among students was in those days. There was a tempest of criticism, with the phrase "beyond the pale" coming up again and again, and strident calls for the administration to "do something." My options were pretty limited because it was a student-controlled publication, and the only way to have much effect was to take measures much more drastic than appropriate. But it was important to appear to do something.

After a regularly scheduled lunch with the student publications staffs, I had a private conversation with *The Pelican*'s editor. We had a rather cordial exchange, in which I asked him what he would do if he were in my shoes and warned him that trouble was brewing for his magazine, including pressure to suspend publication. After that, when a concerned parent, regent, or other party protested to me about this matter, I could tell them that I had called the offending editor into my office, "and did I give him a talking-to!"

I felt it was important to keep abreast of student concerns, so I held twice-monthly office hours during which any student was welcome to stop in and talk. The number of them who did was quite manageable. A high proportion of my visitors had no problem, but were curious as to whether they could truly walk in and chat with the chancellor. The problems ranged from a student who thought it was unfair that she had to pay to park twice (once in the daytime and then again when she came back at night to study) to a physics major who complained that a new residence hall rule that required sophomore women to be in an hour earlier interfered with studying in the library at night. One graduate student had trouble making readings on a galvanometer because his glasses hit the instrument's eyepiece. He complained that the School of Optometry turned down his application for contact lenses because they were "too busy" and he was "not a football player or track athlete." Our investigation of his complaint led to some improvements in meeting students' needs (and he received his contacts).

For me, the students always came first. One of my assistants at the time remembers accompanying me as I gave some regents a tour of our laboratory. I ran into a graduate student who was having problems, and stopped to confer with him, leaving my assistant to take charge of the tour of the facility he barely knew. He faked it as well as he could until I caught up with them.

One great benefit of serving as chancellor was that it afforded an opportunity to influence society and social policy in ways not directly related to education. For instance, the university could give a boost to the budding civil rights movement by quietly enacting antidiscrimination policies. And indeed, we gave the college's fraternities and sororities an ultimatum: they would have to eliminate discriminatory language from their charters if they wanted to maintain their status as "recognized student groups." The housing office removed from its list of approved housing a boardinghouse that practiced racial discrimination. We refused to play football games at universities where our black athletes might be treated any differently from our white players.

In 1957, the Chicago *Tribune* asked fifty educators and administrative officers to rate the top ten American universities. They rated twenty-four of Berkeley's twenty-eight departments as "outstanding" and ranked Berkeley third overall (behind Harvard and Yale). And in 1964, when the American Council on Education conducted the first major postwar survey of higher education, they called Berkeley "the best-balanced distinguished" research university in the nation. That was remarkable: Berkeley was a mass-education campus that could match and surpass the most elite private institutions in its quality.

We were part of a grand experiment, and we were proving that it was possible to provide high-quality mass education, a much bigger challenge than that faced by the smaller, elite Ivy League schools. In the late 1950s, our enrollment was about 20,000 and growing at about 6.5 percent a year. I was proud that California had taken the lead in supporting high-quality higher education, and it's worth a look at how this came about. One key, of course, was money.

There's a phrase that's gained currency—"throwing money at a problem"—that seems to imply that there's something wrongheaded about spending money to address problems, that you might solve them without spending money. But you can't have quality education without money, and in these fortunate times, funding was relatively easy.

In October 1958, the Soviet Union launched the Sputnik satellite—and for the first time since World War II the United States lagged in an area of scientific endeavor. The Sputnik-inspired National Defense Education Act increased federal funds for education programs and student loans. Meanwhile California's population was growing by leaps and bounds, and the first of the baby-boom generation was approaching college age. California responded to its prosperous times and growth with bond issues; in November 1958 voters approved $200 million, largely for new buildings at the University of California and the state colleges.

At Berkeley, buildings were going up at a never-before and never-again rate. Probably no major long-established university has ever built so much as Berkeley did starting in the late 1950s. The five-year building program in 1958 listed sixty-two projects with a price tag of more than $129 million—back in the days when a million dollars was real money. The new classroom, research, library, administrative, and cultural facilities affected every field of study and extracurricular activity. The first large residence halls were completed, beginning the move toward making Berkeley a much more residential campus. All this went remarkably smoothly.

Of course, it is faculty, not buildings, that make a university great, and the prestige of our faculty continued to grow. In 1959, Emilio Segrè and Owen Chamberlain were jointly awarded the Nobel Prize in physics for their discovery of the antiproton. The next year, Donald Glaser won the physics prize and the chemistry prize went to Willard Libby, a Berkeley graduate and former faculty member, now at UCLA, for his work in carbon-14 dating. In 1961, the chemistry prize went to my friend Melvin Calvin for his work in elucidating the mechanisms of photosynthesis. (The fact that Libby's and Calvin's awards both involved radiochemistry reflected the growing importance of this field.) That made four Berkeley winners in three years, an unprecedented Nobel harvest. When Edwin McMillan and I won in 1951, Berkeley had moved ahead of all other institutions, with six winners on the faculty. Now we were almost in a class of our own.

One of the rights and responsibilities of winning a Nobel Prize is the opportunity to nominate others for the prize. I took this responsibility seriously, and every year submitted letters. Segrè, Chamberlain, Glaser, and Calvin were all among my nominees. Another, Luis Alvarez, had been inexplicably overlooked when Glaser won the award for collaborative work. That omission was finally rectified when Luis won the physics prize in 1968.

That kind of faculty quality didn't happen by coincidence. People like G. N. Lewis had begun building their departments from the time they arrived. Part of a chancellor's job is recruitment; I took particular pleasure in having Donald Glaser at Berkeley, because I had worked hard to convince him to join our faculty shortly before he received the Nobel Prize, just as Wendell Latimer had worked to bring me back from Chicago. It made a difference to potential faculty to have a chancellor express interest in their joining a faculty, and I sought out these people. The price of excellence was eternal vigilance.

A month or so after I assumed the chancellor's post, Clark Kerr sent me an article from *Esquire* titled "The Brightest Young Men in Science" (yes, in the 1950s they were all still men). The article described eleven promising scientists, none over the age of thirty-six. Kerr attached a note to the article asking why there were no University of California faculty members on the list. Our inquiry revealed that ten to fifteen years previously, such a list would have included several people from UC. While we had many eminent scientists in the forty-to-fifty-year bracket, it was a serious matter that we weren't getting more youthful contenders.

Several months of study produced no easy resolution, although the discussion itself served Clark's purposes, giving him a chance to educate the regents on problems they would face and on the continuous struggle for excellence. For one thing, it made clear that our insistence on the loyalty oath had kept us from landing a couple of bright young scientists. Another problem was money. UC had historically paid well, but other universities had become more competitive. Some of the brightest young professors were being wooed with high salaries, which raised a potential problem: do you offer the young "stars" more money than your established faculty members, many of whom were equally productive?

In general, the best scientists are motivated by many factors besides money, such as facilities and the quality of colleagues. Those two considerations are definitely what had drawn me to Berkeley. The cyclotron had made Berkeley my mecca. But other institutions were now upgrading their facilities. And as for the quality of colleagues, strength attracts strength. When you try to improve a department, one of your greatest obstacles is often resistance from current faculty members. It's the "big fish in a little pond" syndrome, the human tendency to want to be the best or most prestigious in a department, even if one has to shrink the pond. People like that will find all kinds of reasons to stop you from bringing in a bigger fish. Your only countermeasures are to enlist the real faculty leaders to fight for better recruitment, for doing the right thing, for putting the university first.

True faculty stars don't want to be surrounded with mediocrities; they are secure enough to welcome the challenge of bright colleagues, who can bring out the best in each other. A bigger pond gives them the opportunity to grow themselves. Our physics and chemistry departments were so strong that Donald Glaser's potential colleagues saw him not as a competitor but as someone they were eager to team up with.

Almost as soon as I assumed the chancellor's post, we lost one of the leaders who'd built Berkeley into a physics powerhouse when Ernest Lawrence died of colitis. He was just fifty-seven years old, and we all felt a terrible loss. He had always been a bundle of energy and optimism, always a lift to be around. For a quarter century, his teaching and example had profoundly affected my way of thinking and approach to research. It was terribly moving that my first major task as chancellor was to choose a successor to head the Radiation Laboratory that Ernest Lawrence had built and that had made my whole career possible.

The choice turned out to be fairly easy. Luis Alvarez phoned me early on to take himself out of the running and voice support for Ed McMillan. Ed had certainly demonstrated his ability over the years. He was a charter member of the Rad Lab who'd taken on larger responsibilities as time went on and consistently contributed to its success, particularly with his innovations in high-energy machines. He served with distinction as director until his retirement in 1973. (The Rad Lab's name was soon changed to the Lawrence Berkeley National Laboratory, the lab in Livermore to the Lawrence Livermore National Laboratory.)

Lawrence's inventive vision had changed history, and many of us thought he deserved a lasting memorial. I strongly believed that the only fitting memorial would be a science museum and education facility. The museum could house Lawrence's original cyclotron and the other apparatus that had so profoundly affected the course of science. But the memorial shouldn't be something static aimed only at preserving the past. It should be something that could grow and contribute to society, that could keep science education and the public understanding of science advancing into the future, that could display a wealth of scientific equipment and demonstrations, worthy of an international reputation.

As naturally happens when you push for an idea, especially one as grandiose as this, I found myself assigned the task of moving it toward fruition. I soon found strong backing for my idea among some powerful regents, and one of them, Ed Pauley, suggested a funding source. The AEC paid the university substantial fees for managing the nuclear laboratories, and the state government claimed a sizable portion of them: part of this money could be directed to this project. After all, the state got the money because of the laboratories, and the laboratories were there because of Lawrence.

The Lawrence Hall of Science turned into a very long-term project. Eventually it opened in 1968, in a large building with a commanding view of the Bay Area and a futuristic "molecule" design that became a distinctive feature of the Berkeley hills. The Lawrence Hall has grown into one of the country's major science museums and education facilities, with a rich offering of classes, activities, films, tours, hands-on learning experience, service to schools, teacher training, and curriculum development.

In January 1959 I was invited to become a member of the newly created President's Science Advisory Committee. The committee required monthly trips to Washington for two-day meetings, but this was an unparalleled opportunity for me—not only to serve the country but to gain contacts that would be invaluable to my work as university chancellor. The committee's chairman, George Kistiakowsky, who was also President Eisenhower's science adviser, asked me to head a panel examining the relations between basic research and graduate education. I enlisted the help of a dozen leaders in science education, including the vice president of research at Bell Laboratories, the director of the Oak Ridge National Laboratory, the provost of Stanford, and professors at various universities. The report of the Panel on Basic Research and Graduate Education became known as the Seaborg Report, although it was very much a collaborative effort. McGeorge Bundy, dean of the faculty of arts and sciences at Harvard, did the actual writing of the report, a masterful job of synthesizing disparate ideas. In this process, we formed a friendship that may have brought me to the attention of the Kennedy administration.

A main argument in the report was that the federal government must continue its central role, which it had taken on after World War II, in support of basic research, but that the nature of the role needed to change. The government generally paid for specific research projects through targeted contracts. This separated research from education, and it ignored the training of new scientists, encouraging universities to free some of their faculty to do research alone and to pass on the burden of teaching to others. The committee's argument was that graduate education and basic research belonged together at every possible level, because research and teaching are inseparable parts of training scientists:

> The federal government should act in . . . areas of scientific promise because no other agency of our society is responsible for the national security and the general welfare or has the financial strength to provide the necessary support . . . . Whether the quantity and quality of basic research and graduate education in the United States will be adequate or inadequate depends primarily upon the government of the United States.

Universities also needed to change. Most American universities were founded for education, and most still maintained the same artificial division between research and teaching that bedeviled the government's relations with the universities. Universities needed not only to correct this imbalance but to ensure that their own standards of freedom and excellence were maintained as their connections with government grew. Universities needed to stop fearing that federal grants would mean federal control, but government agencies needed to be more flexible in providing long-term, unrestricted grants.

The report also noted that the number of major universities doing excellent work in basic research and graduate education needed to double from twenty to forty in the next fifteen years. The burden for this effort could not be borne by the federal government alone; more and more private resources would also be needed.

The report became a widely adopted basic blueprint for graduate education for the years to come. And the number of influential universities did grow, as the baby-boom generation arrived.

By the end of the 1950s, students were showing the first signs of awakening from the silent generation. Clark Kerr had begun a slow liberalization of university policies to allow more student freedom of expression. He was a politically astute maneuverer, guiding a board of regents composed of successful, generally conservative business people and politicians toward more liberal policies. One way he did this was through the codification of some rules, which came to be known as the Kerr Directives. Many of them were simply formal statements of long-standing policies. Some were actually liberalizations, but adopted with an eye to the regents, since the directives' regulatory structure would serve as a reassuring framework, restricting just how far this new freedom could go.

In this way, after a trial run, Clark convinced the regents for the first time to allow political candidates and their supporters to appear on campus (though this seems like a rather obvious part of educating citizens). He explained that he believed in making students safe for ideas, rather than making ideas safe for students. (Eventually, he even convinced the regents to drop their ban on communist speakers!) However, the university restricted the students' own political activity (in their life as *students*, as opposed to as individuals). A long-standing policy prohibited the student government (ASUC) from taking stands on off-campus issues, for example. ASUC membership was compulsory, and because a student had no choice but to be a member, we believed it was improper for those who participated in student government to purport to represent the viewpoint of every student.

More than one history of the student movement traces its first stirrings to a Berkeley student group called Slate. Slate was a socially pro-gressive group that favored greater activism for students in student and political affairs. It was determined to push the rules to the limits, then push some more.

Slate managed to elect only one student body president, David Armor, and despite our official disagreements, he and I had a good relationship. We would have lunch or dinner together regularly to talk things over, even if only to review our divergent positions. But we did have at least one noteworthy clash, in the case of the "free love" professor.

An assistant professor of biology at the University of Illinois had written a letter to his campus's student newspaper with some advice to students that included this sentence: "A mutually satisfactory sexual experience would eliminate the need for many hours of frustrating petting and lead to much happier and longer-lasting marriages." This was a scandalously radical position to advocate several years before the advent of the birth control pill and the sexual revolution. The president of the University of Illinois recommended to its regents that the professor be fired because the letter was in unacceptably bad taste. The obscure biologist briefly became an object of national debate.

The ASUC executive committee, led by Slate, passed a resolution condemning the University of Illinois for firing the professor, on the grounds that dismissing a faculty member for expressing his views was a violation of academic freedom. They had a point about academic freedom, but most of us thought their action willfully violated the university policy against outside political action. And of course their point about academic freedom was overshadowed by the appearance of defending the professor's views on free love.

I came under pressure from all sides. An assistant chancellor began pressing for the university to take disciplinary action against the students. An ACLU lawyer called to say he would have "serious questions" if any disciplinary action were taken. A group of professors issued a statement backing the students. Many alumni simply resented the fact that the students had "embarrassed" the university. Clark Kerr even raised the possibility of making membership in the student organization voluntary, which would have devastated it.

I knew I had to do something, and wracked my brain for a way out. I finally decided that I needed to give every appearance of taking decisive action (although any real action would merely exacerbate the situation). I sent a letter to the student body president:

> Since the Executive Committee of the Associated Students of the University of California, Berkeley, in its action of May 3, 1960, exceeded the limits of its authority, I hereby declare this action null and void and am so informing the president of the University of Illinois by carbon copy of this letter.
>
> I regret that the Executive Committee chose this deliberate action and am extremely disappointed in those responsible for it . . .

The students were furious, in the way that you get when you are powerless to respond. The San Francisco *Chronicle* reported: "Seaborg Vetoes UC Student Stand." Administrators and regents were placated because I could say that I had undone the students' action. In walking a fine line among university interest groups, the appearance of doing something was often more important than real action. And most important of all was to refrain from overreacting.

One unwelcome trait that Slate introduced to campus was a disrespectful, needling, and mocking rhetoric that often infuriated administrators more than their actions or positions did. One outcome of the 1960s that I regret is that in many ways this tone has won out and mutual respect and civility have been lost. This letter essentially settled the controversy, which in any case was quickly overshadowed by another event that is often considered the first salvo fired in the battles of the 1960s.

The House Un-American Activities Committee (HUAC) was a holdover from the McCarthy era that made a show of holding hearings around the country that followed a repeated format. The congressmen would take testimony from a traveling panel of witnesses who varied little from hearing to hearing; they were self-proclaimed reformed communists who would describe the tremendous reach and threat of the "communist menace." Then the committee would subpoena local alleged "subversives." These persecuted souls would generally refuse to testify on the grounds that they were protected by the Fifth Amendment from having to incriminate themselves and occasionally disrupt the proceedings. Conservative groups would support the hearings, while civil liberties defenders and other liberals would be vocal in their opposition.

One Berkeley student was among those subpoenaed. His subversive acts included joining a Congress of Racial Equality picket line protesting stores with segregated lunch counters and walking the eighteen miles from San Francisco to San Quentin prison to protest the execution of Caryl Chessman, a popular cause at the time.

As HUAC began its show at San Francisco City Hall, audience members selected by the committee were allowed to enter while the subpoenaed witnesses' family members and fellow students were barred. Such provocative actions and attacks on individuals' rights were typical of HUAC. The people left outside battered the doors until they were dispersed by police. The next day the crowd outside was larger, and the police used fire hoses; in the ensuing melee, sixty-eight protesters were arrested, most of them students, thirty-one from Berkeley. The following day, the crowd was even larger, as was the police presence. Fearing another outbreak of violence, the committee adjourned and departed through a rear exit, never to return to San Francisco.

An official report by the FBI's director, J. Edgar Hoover, described an elaborate pattern of "communist" strategies and planning that led to the riot: "The communist conspiracy operating on American soil is part and parcel of the world conspiracy and the thousands of communists in the United States are for all intents and purposes foreign agents on American soil who are dedicated to our destruction." Whatever happened to those thousands of communist agents, nobody seems to know.

Other observers perceived the event as a group of people who were frustrated in their attempt to demonstrate peacefully and who responded to HUAC's provocations. A judge dismissed the charges against most of those arrested, although he said there were "ample grounds" for convicting them.

We heard the usual demands to "do something" about these students, to "control" them because their actions had "embarrassed" and "cast discredit upon" the university. There were warnings that such student activity would cause an adverse reaction in the state legislature. In addition, a right-wing film called *Operation Abolition* alleging that the communist conspiracy had led to the City Hall riots stirred up emotions among conservatives of the John Birch persuasion. I took care to respond to communications from alumni in particular.

In this case, our policies on student activities helped; we succeeded in treating the matter as an off-campus issue. As Clark Kerr said, "We cannot take complete charge of the student's life. Students have rights as citizens beyond the university." This approach benefited most of the students involved, but it backfired in the case of a few who could be pressured from other quarters. For example, the Immigration Service threatened to deport a Scottish graduate student who had not rioted or been arrested but had merely picketed the HUAC meeting. The student received a reprieve only after a Member of Parliament appealed to the Secretary of State.

One of Slate's main objectives was to change ROTC from compulsory to voluntary, and that fall they picked up their protests.

I was no more impressed by compulsory ROTC than I had been in my UCLA days when I had joined the band to avoid it. It seemed it had been scarcely updated; its obsolescence was confirmed by Berkeley graduates who'd joined the armed forces, and reported that the topics covered so superficially in ROTC were taught much more effectively in basic training. For the average student, the ROTC curriculum was a waste of time; the national defense could be better served by replacing the time spent in ROTC with four units of science, or perhaps learning about the physics of ballistic missiles.

But the fall of 1960 was not a time when such a topic could be debated rationally. Richard Nixon and John F. Kennedy were locked in a tight race for the presidency and sharply debating issues of national security. It would be a difficult time to make any changes because ROTC's proponents always tried to paint any move to weaken the program as motivated by some lack of patriotism.

The issue was already on the regents' agenda, but any pressure from the students made it all the harder for the regents to take a dispassionate approach. They couldn't appear to cave in to vocal pressure such as demonstrations, without giving ammunition to the "soft on communism" side. However, any advice to the students that demonstrations would harm their cause was taken as stalling by the administration, the equivalent of patting them on the heads and telling them to behave. Slate was bent on confrontation, and the officers who ran the ROTC program often seemed to do all they could to rile up the students, meting out harsh military punishments for minor infractions and asking inappropriate questions about a student's political affiliation before handing him a failing grade.

After Kennedy won the election, I had a phone conversation with Edwin Pauley, who was generally considered the most powerful behind-the-scenes Democrat in California. Pauley opposed changing the ROTC requirement at that point because such a change could be construed to mean that the incoming administration was soft on defense. All these considerations over whether freshman and sophomore men should have the right to choose whether to take a couple of courses! The regents put off the issue until September 1962, when they voted to make it voluntary. That was a key issue at the dawn of the 1960s. But we would see in coming years that the controversy over ROTC on campuses would only intensify, as it became an irresistible focus of demonstrations against the Vietnam War.

As might be expected, by the mid-1960s students considered Clark Kerr too conservative and many regents considered him too liberal. It's doubtful there would have been any way to stem the tidal wave of student activism of the 1960s that began with the civil rights movement and mushroomed with the antiwar movement. In any case, Clark's careful course was swept away in the flood tides.

Among the casualties of the student movement's mass confrontation were the academic traditions of good behavior and reasonable respect for authority. With the new informality that emerged on campuses, with students and faculty addressing each other by first names and abandoning most rules and traditions of dress, civility became a victim, and this caused lasting harm. Disrespect for authority and ridicule of others' opinions assumed prominence in the arsenal of rebellious students. The public backlash could be strong enough to tip the electoral scales toward a new conservatism.

In California, that meant the election of a new governor named Ronald Reagan. Reagan dismissed Clark Kerr for his perceived failure to rein in the students during the Free Speech Movement and other incidents of campus unrest. His customary wit intact, Clark noted that he left the job the same way he came into it, "fired with enthusiasm." Of course, Reagan's hard-line style was, if anything, less successful when it came to keeping order.

After the campuses became more peaceful, the once shared traditions of tolerance and respect were never quite regained, and their absence had a chilling effect on the free exchange of ideas.

I've wondered at times how I might have coped as head of a restive 1960s campus, but as fate would have it, I would not spend that decade at Berkeley.

# SIXTEEN

# KENNEDY'S CALL: A MOVE

# TO WASHINGTON

Monday mornings were among my most enjoyable times as chancellor, because I spent them at the Radiation Laboratory. On January 9, 1961, a German crew was filming for a television special, so my visit stretched into the afternoon. Just after one o'clock, I was summoned to the phone—to my amazement, President-elect John F. Kennedy was on the line, calling to ask if I would join his administration as chairman of the Atomic Energy Commission.

"Take some time to think about it," he said. "I'll call you back tomorrow." He said he needed a qualified candidate quickly to head off a favorite son of a powerful member of the Joint Committee on Atomic Energy.

I could barely contain my excitement; I doubt I gave the German crew my most cogent interview.

That evening, Helen and I discussed at length the prospect of moving to Washington. It would be not only a huge change in direction for my career but a completely new environment for the family, which had grown to six children. The kids demanded a vote. The outcome was seven to one against moving, but I had doubts about the validity of fourteen-month-old Dianne's vote. Rather than challenging the results, I exercised the veto inherent in the powers of the head of a democratic institution.

I was convinced that the advantages far outweighed the disadvantages. I would be in charge of a national program of great importance, for which my background had prepared me as well as all but a handful of people in the country. I would be in a position to advance causes I believed in deeply: nuclear science, especially research; nuclear electric power; a nuclear weapons test ban; and international cooperation. And, despite the children's resistance, a couple of years in the nation's capital—I would complete the two and a half years remaining on outgoing chairman John McCone's term—would be an interesting experience for them.

The excitement that Kennedy was bringing to the country was palpable and contagious. Some of my friends had been named to top posts in the new administration. On a trip to Washington the month before, I'd had breakfast with Sargent Shriver, Kennedy's chief recruiter, and given him information and advice on potential appointees. I had noted in my journal: "Shriver told me something about how JFK's cabinet is developing. One gets the impression of a dynamic, new, young energy in this administration."

My appointment was almost derailed by a congressman who told Kennedy that I was an ardent Nixon supporter. He'd probably seen an issue of *U.S. News & World Report* from the previous August which listed me among "Nixon's Idea Men." I had no inkling of the source of the story, but I had noted in my diary when the magazine came out: "As a lifelong Democrat, it is uncomfortable to be described as a 'Nixon man.' Helen, who is always a shade more liberal than I, will probably be outraged." (She was.) I quickly got the word back that I'd considered myself a Democrat since Franklin Roosevelt's first campaign, although my public persona was apolitical. That approach worked better for a scientist and university administrator, and kept me from alienating any politicians it might be helpful to talk with—at times I had had policy discussions with Nixon during his eight years as Vice President.

I came east months before my family, taking up residence at the University Club on Sixteenth Street. I purchased a house in the Chevy Chase section of Washington after simply asking the real estate agent to find a house large enough to fit six children and within walking distance of grammar, junior high, and high schools. This location worked well for me also, as it was between the AEC's downtown office and its main building in Germantown, Maryland. Helen and the kids joined me after school let out.

The period of our separation brought home to me the extent to which I depended on Helen. In the division of labor in our marriage, she skillfully handled all the family matters, leaving me free to focus on my career. As the wife of a chancellor, she had taken on a semi-official role within the university community, hosting and appearing at functions with grace and aplomb. Now, as the wife of the AEC chairman, she would have a similar, even more challenging job, which she fulfilled with uncommon distinction. I owe an immeasurable amount of my success to her—and am fond of pointing out that I consider her my greatest discovery.

Kennedy's eloquent inaugural address was especially thrilling when heard from the official seating on the steps of the Capitol. (The poet Robert Frost's appearance was particularly exciting: for some reason a fire flared briefly on the rostrum at that point.) I met John Kennedy for the first time on the reviewing stand for the inaugural parade, when I introduced myself to Attorney General–designate Robert F. Kennedy, who greeted me cordially and introduced me to his President brother.

Our real acquaintance began when President Kennedy visited AEC headquarters within a month of taking office. Our staff had rehearsed an hour-long briefing. It was strictly timed and moved quickly to cover each department. The program stretched to more than two hours, however, because Kennedy interrupted repeatedly with incisive questions. This was no going-through-the-motions politician's briefing, but a lively response to an intellectual challenge. His questions displayed a probing intellect and quick grasp of some rather technical subjects.

This was my first exposure to his natural drive for firsthand knowledge and curiosity that to me were reminiscent of the scientist's approach. On a trip to the Nevada Test Site, we flew in a helicopter over a crater created by a nuclear explosion. Kennedy was fascinated by the size of the hole, 1,400 feet in diameter and 400 feet deep. The pilot had difficulty convincing him that it would be too dangerous to land on the crater's edge, where the dust was so deep it would interfere with taking off. Kennedy settled for a low-level flight around the lip of the crater. And at visits to nuclear facilities, he was eager to try his hand at some of the remote-controlled operations.

That drive for information combined with a natural informality constituted a striking personal style. He thought nothing of calling a lower-level official for direct information on an issue; the incredulous reactions of those who picked up the phone to find the President on the other end apparently delighted him. Once when he called me at home, the son who answered got distracted by one of the many things more important to him than a parent's phone call. When he finally got around to telling me, I found the President waiting patiently.

Kennedy's probing questions at the AEC briefing reflected a first-rate intellect, a mind of a caliber equal to that of the best scientists I have known. One striking example occurred when I invited him to Berkeley to give the Charter Day speech. On the plane ride out, I briefed him on the background of the university, the various people who would be in attendance, and the many connections which members of his administration had with Berkeley. (Secretary of State Dean Rusk had studied law there; Secretary of Defense Robert McNamara had studied business; there were more people from Berkeley than Harvard in his administration.) As I ran through the list of names and described their connections, Kennedy listened with one ear as he leafed through his speech. To my astonishment, he made a lengthy introduction to his speech with flawless references to the many people I had briefly mentioned on our flight. Then he delivered the speech with such fleeting glances at the text that I would have thought he was speaking extemporaneously if I hadn't seen the text. It was one of the most impressive feats of memory I have ever witnessed.

His Charter Day speech was as eloquent as every speech I ever heard him make. His eloquence was matched with an unfailing wit. He received a tremendous reaction at the White House dinner he held for Nobel Prize winners when he made his famous ad-libbed comment: "I think that this is the most extraordinary [collection of] talent that has ever been gathered together at the White House"—we all puffed up our chests proudly—"with the possible exception of when Thomas Jefferson dined alone."

One aspect of his administration that has not received adequate attention was his commitment to arms control. Perhaps his greatest, most durable foreign policy contribution was the Limited Test Ban Treaty, a treaty that would never have come to fruition were it not for his personal passion for the subject. Kennedy began working on it from the moment he took office.

There were three nuclear powers at that point, the United States, the United Kingdom, and the Soviet Union. The three had observed a voluntary moratorium on nuclear-weapons tests since they'd begun serious negotiations on a test ban treaty in late 1958. Diplomats from the three had been brought to the table after the public outcry over radioactive fallout from the extensive earlier tests; radioactive debris knew no national boundaries. But the negotiations had bogged down over disagreements about a system for verifying compliance, a problem that would continue to dog the treaty. The United States wanted an extensive system because it feared that the Soviets would cheat; the Soviets resisted such controls because they suspected we would use them for espionage.

Of course, it was much easier for the Soviets to say that verification was not necessary. In our open society, with its free press, we could not keep tests secret, but in the Soviet Union the press was controlled, as was travel: there were vast territories to which foreigners would have no access. Just the same, their sensitivity on the verification issue also stemmed from the fact that we had many more missiles than they did, which made information on the opponent's missile sites much more advantageous to our side than to theirs.

The negotiators had almost reached a compromise in the spring of 1960 on a treaty to bar all tests considered to be verifiable. (The treaty would have allowed underground tests that produced signals of less than 4.75 on the Richter scale.) But when an American U-2 spy plane piloted by Francis Gary Powers was shot down over Soviet territory in May 1960, tensions between the countries ended any hopes of an agreement during the Eisenhower administration.

Kennedy immediately instructed his top advisers to hammer out a U.S. position, a process in which I participated. The President was convinced that the United States could make concessions in some areas to meet Soviet objections without impairing U.S. security, and a good part of the discussion centered on the practical aspects of getting an agreement.

I found myself in a challenging position. I personally strongly favored arms control in general and a test ban in particular. However, I could not discount the opposite views held by many AEC people, who thought that national security would be better served by keeping the freedom to test and thus to improve our weapons. Although there were risks involved in a test ban agreement with the Soviet Union, the risks of not reaching an agreement might be even greater. The opposing views of the administration leadership and much of the AEC community waged war in my head and conscience for the entire period of the test ban negotiations. I tried to play the honest broker, calling attention to the valid points raised by each side. I also worked with an eye toward keeping the treaty acceptable to the Joint Committee on Atomic Energy, which tended to be more hawkish than many in the administration and would have the power to block the approval of any treaty.

In April 1961, the United States and the United Kingdom introduced a treaty proposal. It was similar to the 1958 proposal in that it banned all but small underground tests. It also proposed a worldwide detection system operated by an international staff with headquarters in Vienna and including 180 manned detection stations. Up to twenty annual inspections would be allowed on the soil of each party.

The Soviets rejected this treaty, calling the number of inspections "artificially high." Each side had negotiators in Geneva working on the text, but the Soviets were unresponsive to any concessions we suggested. The reason for their unresponsiveness became clear at the end of August when they broke the test moratorium with a massive series of dozens of atmospheric tests with accompanying fallout. Their action—supposedly negotiating a treaty while preparing this test series—was a shattering experience. In later years, I often heard it cited as a reason that the Soviet Union "couldn't be trusted."

Nuclear-weapons technology was in its infancy in those days and racing ahead. Testing was an integral part of improving it, and during the moratorium we'd developed many weapons that some were eager to test. Both the United States and the Soviet Union were pursuing such goals as reducing the weight of warheads, improving the weight-to-yield ratio, and testing new designs and systems, such as smaller weapons for battlefield use or submarine launches.

The Soviet tests raised the specter that they could overcome our lead in nuclear weapons. About two weeks after the Soviet tests began, we responded by resuming underground testing. Pressure grew on Kennedy to match the Soviets' atmospheric testing, which was more environmentally hazardous than underground testing but more technologically productive.

The Sunday-morning television show *Meet the Press* had been trying to get me to appear for months. I'd already put off appearances twice to avoid sensitive times, but finally agreed to appear at the end of October. As luck would have it, the week before my appearance the Soviets announced they would test a fifty-megaton bomb. A bomb that large had questionable military value, except for intimidation, but it was the kind of easily understood "progress" certain to focus the press panel on the question of whether the Soviets were gaining on us. It would increase the pressure on Kennedy, who was still considering his options, to respond with our own atmospheric tests. When I consulted him on how I should cope with this situation, Kennedy gave me the helpful instruction that I should be very forthcoming, but not reveal anything of substance. Perhaps he could master that style for his famous press conferences; for me, with my few months of on-the-job training, it made for a very uncomfortable half hour.

When our analysis indicated that the Soviet tests had been technically productive, Kennedy felt he had no choice but to authorize our own atmospheric tests. We conducted a series of atmospheric tests in the Pacific between April and November 1962 with a total yield of approximately twenty megatons, about a tenth of the total of the Soviet tests. Progress toward a treaty was suspended during these long months, and in the meantime, in October, relations deteriorated to the brink of war.

The crisis broke on October 15, when U-2 photographs disclosed evidence of a medium-range missile site in Cuba. By October 17, launchers and missiles could be seen, and it was clear the missiles could be fired within two weeks. On October 22, the President broke the news to the country, and announced that the United States would impose a naval blockade on Cuba. This was a bold step with unforeseeable consequences; if we tried to stop a Soviet ship, the U.S.S.R. might well view it as an act of war. The following day, I informed my fellow commissioners that AEC operations had been placed under Phase I Alert, with instructions to check that communications were in order, twenty-four-hour duty for communications personnel, and additional security measures.

At the AEC, we faced a personal choice that focused our minds considerably. After the President's speech, AEC employees who had been enjoined by secrecy were allowed to discuss with their spouses plans for the safety of their families. The AEC's main office building had been constructed in Germantown, one of Washington's outer suburbs, as part of President Eisenhower's plan to disperse critical government functions to blunt the effects of an atomic attack. The building included a reinforced underground structure with sophisticated communications systems. This Emergency Relocation Center (ERC) contained compartmentalized sleeping facilities to house 120 people with a cache of food and water to last several weeks. In an emergency, a group called the Initial Cadre, consisting of the commissioners and "essential staff," were to take shelter there and carry on whatever functions were still possible. From time to time there'd been mock exercises using the ERC, exercises that most officials treated as nuisances interrupting their busy schedules, but that suddenly took on an important reality.

The commission had adopted a policy that excluded the families of the Initial Cadre from the ERC, ostensibly because the presence of our families might distract us from our duties. As the crisis came to a head, however, it became increasingly clear that abandoning our families to go to the presumed safety of the shelter was a difficult option, duty or no duty. One of my assistants in particular pointed this out to me; he'd discovered that his wife had set up a makeshift fallout shelter in their home—could he abandon them to this shelter when greater safety awaited him? But he had checked with the AEC's general manager, who said that the commission's decision on the ERC would be impossible to reverse under the circumstances. My assistant had, however, discovered an alternate plan when he had inspected the ERC. One of the senior personnel there had said, "There are no instructions to refuse admittance to the family of any member of the Initial Cadre. If you or your family were to show up at this door, you would not be turned away." Of course, this was not general knowledge. What would happen if some people showed up with their families and others had thought it was not an option? Helen and I had serious discussions on our proper course should the situation materialize but, fortunately, never had to make a decision.

After one of the longest weeks in history, on October 28, the Soviet Union agreed to remove its missiles from Cuba under United Nations

inspection. Kennedy's complete control and coolness throughout this crisis was remarkable to behold. Anyone who lived so close to the brink of
a nuclear war could not help being changed by the experience; it proved
to be a turning point in the relations between Kennedy and Khrushchev
and a major factor in making the test ban treaty attainable, for the treaty
followed a path that paralleled that of the personal relations between the
two leaders.

In their meeting in 1961 in Vienna, Khrushchev had been bullying
and bellicose. It was a sobering experience for Kennedy, and people speculated that Khrushchev took his counterpart's measure there and had
been encouraged to try such adventures as placing missiles in Cuba.

Now the near-calamity of the missile crisis forged a bond between
them. They each understood the other better. As Kennedy said in an interview with *Saturday Review* editor Norman Cousins, "One of the
ironic things about this entire situation is that Mr. Khrushchev and I occupy approximately the same political positions inside our government.
He would like to prevent a nuclear war but is under severe pressure
from his hard-line crowd, which interprets every move in that direction as appeasement. I've got similar problems. Meanwhile, the lack of
progress in reaching agreements between our two countries gives
strength to the hard-line boys in both, with the result that the hard-liners
. . . feed on one another, each using the actions of the other to justify his
own position."

With that in mind, they avoided making the other look bad. They
consulted each other more frequently, and instituted the hot line. During
the crisis, fateful decisions were being made several times a day, but it
had taken about four hours to code, decode, and translate the average
transmission. The system had been so cumbersome that open broad-
casts had been used for some important announcements, including
Khrushchev's final offer to withdraw the missiles. By the next summer, a
direct, private teletype link had been established.

Another consequence of the crisis was a great rise in Kennedy's prestige among Americans, who were impressed with the way he stood up to
the Soviets. His improved credibility gave him political capital to use in
advocating the test ban treaty. Meanwhile formal negotiations dragged
on in Geneva, and Khrushchev was his belligerent rhetorical self in the
spring of 1963.

That May, in this ambiguous atmosphere, I led a delegation to the Soviet Union that focused on the peaceful uses of atomic energy. I was
deeply convinced of the value of scientific and technical exchanges in fos-
tering understanding between the two countries, so I'd begun working
in this direction from the time I arrived in Washington. Kennedy lent us
Air Force One for the trip, and we flew eight and a half hours nonstop
from Dulles Airport to Moscow. (Simply allowing a direct flight from
the United States was an unusual concession from the U.S.S.R.) Kennedy once said that anyone who wonders why a person would want to be
President hasn't traveled on Air Force One, and after the comfort of that
flight (including taking a nap on the President's bed), I understood what
he meant.

We had proposed visiting facilities no foreigners had seen. Our hosts
accepted our itinerary without hesitation, and even included additional
sites they thought would interest us. We were the first foreign group to
visit the Soviet reactor testing station at Ulyanovsk and the first Western
visitors since World War II to visit the Radium Institute in Leningrad.
Everywhere we went we were treated with the warmest hospitality.

Soviet nuclear science was obviously ambitious and competent, with
one glaring omission. In the United States, nuclear reactors for generating electric power are surrounded by airtight, reinforced containment
structures to prevent the spread of radiation or contaminants in the event
of an accident. The Soviet reactors lacked such containment because, my
hosts explained, they believed that once a reactor had been safely designed, accidents could not happen. I expressed disbelief at this attitude,
but my hosts' confidence was unshakable. Their miscalculation became
tragically clear in the Chernobyl accident. There were other missing
safety features, but it was mainly the lack of containment that made
Chernobyl so devastating. The Chernobyl tragedy was not caused by any
inherent danger of nuclear power, but was the preventable result of bad
design.

Regardless of nation, scientists share a common language. Exchanges
help scientists of different countries find commonalities that break down
barriers. Trips like ours were important in cutting through the Soviet
Union's extreme insularity so that our counterparts would realize that
we were actual people on the other side of the arms race. (One sign of
this Soviet isolation was that the chairman of the Soviet State Committee

on Atomic Energy told me I was the first American he had ever met.) These bonds make it more difficult for militarists and others to use ultranationalism or other dangerous tools to move a country in a reckless direction.

Soviet insularity became even clearer when my hosts proudly said that they had made an appointment for me with the chairman of the Presidium, a position we might roughly translate as President. I had never heard of the man, but was assured he was a high official destined to play an even more important role in Soviet government. And so I became the second American whom Leonid Brezhnev ever met, the first being the head of the American Communist Party, Gus Hall. (I was later told that this was the only personal discussion he held with a noncommunist American until he met with Secretary of Agriculture Earl Butz in 1972.)

Brezhnev and I discussed our delegation's visit for about an hour, when Brezhnev said he wanted to leave the subject of science. I quote from my journal:

> He said that I would doubtless meet with President Kennedy upon my return and that he wanted me to tell the President that Khrushchev means what he says . . . about peaceful coexistence and peaceful cooperation. "This is not propaganda," he said, "it is the sincere desire of our government, our people, and of our party, which leads the country. I can't say any more than that. I hope that this area will be as successful as your scientific contacts. Please tell President Kennedy this, even though I don't know him. And give my best wishes to him and his family." I replied that I would give this message to the President, who is a fine man. I said that Brezhnev would feel this way if they ever had the opportunity to meet someday. Brezhnev ended this conversation by declaring that if they met he thought the President would like him because of his candor and openheartedness.

Brezhnev's manner was warm and friendly, and he seemed more "Western" than many of the Soviets I met. Intrigued at being a go-between with a message that diplomats could endlessly dissect and reinterpret, I reported this exchange to Kennedy, along with my impression that Brezhnev would likely be easier to deal with than many of the other Soviets we had met. Brezhnev would replace Khrushchev as First Secretary of the Communist Party less than a year and a half later.

The Soviets had conducted a second series of tests, but Kennedy's store of political capital was such that, rather than answering with tests again (which would have been more symbolic than substantive anyway), he seized the "peace" initiative. Following a suggestion of British Prime Minister Harold Macmillan, he proposed that the United States and Britain send high-level emissaries to Moscow to discuss a treaty in private, bypassing the stalled negotiations in Geneva. Two days after receiving notice of Khrushchev's willingness to receive such negotiators, Kennedy gave his extraordinary commencement address at American University.

This speech was a marked departure from the standard American fare that demonized the Soviet Union: "No government or social system is so evil that its people must be considered as lacking in virtue. As Americans, we find communism profoundly repugnant as a negation of personal freedom and dignity. But we can still hail the Russian people for their many achievements." Kennedy called attention to Soviet sacrifices and sufferings in World War II, in which "at least 20 million lost their lives. A third of the nation's territory . . . was turned into a wasteland." Such recognition was almost unheard of in those days, but the speech was an attempt to begin reordering relations by turning away from confrontation and replacing it with a recognition of "a mutually deep interest in a just and genuine peace and in halting the arms race."

Kennedy ended by making two major announcements:

> First: Chairman Khrushchev, Prime Minister Macmillan, and I have agreed that high-level discussions will shortly begin in Moscow looking toward early agreement on a comprehensive test ban treaty. Our hopes must be tempered with the caution of history—but with our hopes go the hopes of all mankind.

Second, to make clear our good faith and solemn con-
victions on this matter, I now declare that the United States
does not propose to conduct nuclear tests in the atmosphere
so long as other states do not do so.

The speech drew remarkably little attention at home, but it seemed
to have a profound effect on his target audience, the leadership of the Soviet Union. The Soviet press printed the entire speech, including the sections that criticized Soviet policies and analyses of history. That set the
stage for the negotiations.

Kennedy demonstrated his usual political acumen by selecting Under
Secretary of State Averell Harriman to head the U.S.-U.K. delegation.
Harriman had been American ambassador to Moscow in the crucial
years 1943–46, and was highly respected by the Soviets for his consistent,
forthright approach. He was instructed that the main objective was the
achievement of a comprehensive test ban, and failing that, a ban on testing in the atmosphere, in space, and underwater. But before our delegation even arrived in Moscow, Khrushchev ruled out any on-site inspections, which put the comprehensive test ban out of reach.

Just the same, Harriman said that Khrushchev set a positive tone:
"Khrushchev was very jovial in our first meeting. He said, 'Why don't
we have a test ban? Why don't we sign it now and let the experts work
out the details?' So I took a blank pad which was in front of me and I
said, 'Here, Mr. Khrushchev, you sign first and I'll sign underneath.'
That was the jovial way in which we were talking."

In twelve days in Moscow, Harriman (under daily supervision from
Kennedy) negotiated an agreement. It was always arduous to negotiate
anything with the Soviets. Each side would state and restate its positions
a hundred times with neither side budging. In order to get toward a
compromise somewhere in the middle or simply to move the negotiations along, you would soften your terms in hopes of seeing some flexi-
bility in response. Instead, the Soviets would accept that as the new
American position without budging a hair from their starting point, and
expect the negotiations to continue from there.

In addition to giving up the comprehensive test ban, the other main
concession Harriman had to make was to drop a provision that allowed
for tests for the Plowshare program for peaceful applications. In ex-

change for giving up this provision he obtained one that allowed for withdrawal from the treaty.

Harriman also followed a sensitive instruction from Kennedy to feel out Khrushchev about the possibility of a joint preemptive strike against China's nuclear capabilities. Khrushchev, however, belittled the likelihood of China's becoming a formidable nuclear threat. He said it would be years before China would have nuclear weapons, and even then not in amounts approaching U.S. and Soviet stockpiles. China in fact exploded a bomb within sixteen months; one can only speculate on how history might have changed had Khrushchev had a more perspicacious assessment of China's nuclear future.

Dean Rusk invited me to fly back to Moscow as part of the delegation for the pageantry of the signing ceremony. I came away impressed with seeing the Soviet leadership in action; they were prepared with well-written, appropriate speeches at the drop of a hat. Nikita Khrushchev, despite his rotund appearance in photos, seemed to be in the best of physical condition, full of bounce and good humor. He had an amazing sense of timing and was a master of repartee. He greeted me as "my old friend," which, since we had never met, I took as a reference to the trip we had made a few months earlier and the warm relations it had engendered—perhaps a window on how the news filtered up through the Soviet hierarchy.

From the moment agreement was reached (just six weeks after his American University speech), Kennedy began his campaign to ensure that the Senate would ratify the treaty. The senators invited to join the delegation to Moscow were chosen with an eye toward their influence, but it was a sign of the uphill battle ahead that not a single Democrat from the Armed Services Committee agreed to go. Kennedy put on a full-court press for ratification, seeking not only the required two-thirds Senate majority but a margin that would demonstrate a strong endorsement. He took his case to the public, encouraging creation of a Citizens' Committee for a Nuclear Test Ban and giving advice on its campaign, such as which senators to target in constituent mailing campaigns. He took every opportunity at his press conferences to tout the treaty in realistic terms. Polls showed that he succeeded in turning public opinion from lukewarm to overwhelming support.

The signing in Moscow was followed within a week with Senate hearings on ratification of the treaty. Dean Rusk, Robert McNamara, and I were the first three witnesses before the Foreign Relations Committee. We were each questioned for an entire day. A main point of Mc-Namara's testimony was that without a treaty continued atmospheric testing would help the Soviet Union erase our technical lead in nuclear weaponry.

The most important aspect of my testimony related to my belief that the treaty would not exclude the continuation of the AEC's Plowshare program, studying the peaceful uses of nuclear explosions, which I described as including "civil engineering projects such as digging canals, harbors, passes through mountains for transportation purposes . . . aids to mining, aids to the recovery of low-grade oil, [and] the development of underground water resources." Several senators had let it be known that their support of the treaty had lessened because its ban on atmospheric testing seemed to exclude the possibility of Plowshare explosions. I like to think that my optimistic testimony helped move some of them from a doubtful to a favorable position. (Unfortunately, I was too optimistic; as will be seen, the test ban treaty imposed large obstacles on the Plowshare program.)

Another key to gaining support for the treaty among skeptics was the administration's adoption of four "safeguards" that the Joint Chiefs of Staff promulgated as the price of their support: continuation of an aggressive underground testing program, maintenance of modern nuclear laboratory facilities, maintenance of the capability to have atmospheric tests should they become necessary, and improvement in our ability to monitor compliance with the treaty.

The Senate approved the treaty by a vote of 80–19. It was Kennedy's proudest accomplishment, and the first arms control treaty with the Soviet Union in the eighteen years since World War II. But at the same time, it was limited in its ends, and the failure to achieve the comprehensive test ban that had appeared within our grasp was a world tragedy of the first magnitude.

Supporters held four principal hopes for the limited test ban treaty: it would reduce the health hazards of radioactive fallout, it would slow the arms race between the superpowers, it would be followed by further arms control agreements in the direction of nuclear disarmament, and it would slow the proliferation of nuclear weapons to other countries. Of these, only the reduction in fallout clearly came about. Most people consider that to be success enough, for as the head of the AEC's division of biology and medicine put it, if weapons testing had continued at its rate in 1958, "civilized man would have been in trouble."

But even the decline in fallout had its price, because, ironically, with fallout off the public's radar screen, the other objectives became more difficult to reach. Elimination of the concern about fallout "made the continuation of uninhibited weapons development politically respectable," in the words of two leading analysts. Testing went underground, figuratively as well as literally. Underground testing was invisible to the populace—out of sight and out of mind as a threat to their lives.

The number of announced U.S. nuclear detonations for the period 1945–80 was 638. Of these, 345 (54 percent) took place after the effective date of the treaty. Of the 298 Soviet tests announced by the United States through 1980, 168 (56 percent) took place underground after 1963. These tests added significantly to the variety and sophistication of nuclear weapons.

Yet the test ban treaty did indeed pave the way for future arms control agreements—the Outer Space Treaty, the Seabed Treaty (prohibiting nuclear weapons in outer space and on the ocean floor, respectively), a Biological Weapons Convention, and the SALT strategic arms limitation accords. But these treaties were peripheral to the main problem of the arms race and for the most part prohibited actions no nation wanted to take anyway. The arms race continued unabated with the introduction of larger, more sophisticated, and more terrible weapons.

"When you stop to think of what the advantages were to us of stopping all testing in the early 1960s when we were still ahead of the Soviets it's really appalling to realize what a missed opportunity we had," Averell Harriman pointed out, in an interview he gave me when I was doing research for a book on the test ban treaty. A comprehensive test ban could have saved untold amounts of money and prevented the introduction of more dangerous and destabilizing weapons. We missed the opportunity because we were afraid of the risk—or perhaps because we were obsessed with one risk and ignored another. We gave great weight to the worry that the Soviet Union would cheat and develop weapons behind our backs, and ignored the equal or greater risk in continuing the arms race.

The hard-line position—that the path to greater security can only be found by building more and larger weapons—made it politically impractical to gain approval for a treaty that did not allow for such weapons. But this position does not take into account the fact that more and larger weapons do not necessarily increase national security when the opponent is free to match your buildup. Nor that larger, more sophisticated nuclear weapons can be a destabilizing rather than a stabilizing factor.

How big a risk would it have been to accommodate the Soviet position on inspections in order to gain a comprehensive test ban? We believed that for a comprehensive test ban to be enforceable, on-site inspections would be necessary, that if we detected suspicious seismic activity the Soviets said was an earthquake, an inspection could determine the cause. Khrushchev always maintained that no such inspections were necessary, but at one point he was willing to agree to three per year. He later said that he offered three merely as a political concession to Kennedy, knowing that Kennedy would need some inspections to get the treaty through the Senate. His offer was based on a conversation with a Western official who implied that three would be acceptable to the United States. He'd gone out on a limb with his own people in agreeing to any on-site inspections at all, so when we treated his offer as a bargaining position instead of grabbing for an agreement, Khrushchev said he felt betrayed. It caused him acute embarrassment at home when we hadn't accepted his offer, so henceforth he was unwilling to agree to any inspections. Considering that we had been willing to go as low as six inspections and that we could never establish any scientific basis for a particular number of inspections, the difference between three inspections and six seems minuscule in retrospect, especially considering the cost of no agreement.

Even with no inspections, a comprehensive test ban would likely have been to the advantage of the United States. Our concern about the likelihood and consequences of Soviet cheating was exaggerated (I was among those who failed to realize this at the time). Khrushchev was probably right that no on-site inspections were necessary. To have been

caught cheating would have caused tremendous political embarrassment, and the Soviets would not have known with any certainty what
tests we could detect. Our detection technology advanced so quickly that
it's doubtful they could have performed enough clandestine tests to have
made truly significant military advances, certainly not enough to have
erased our advantage.

But through underground testing, they did. Perhaps in the early
1960s we'd already passed the point where nuclear war becomes un-
winnable. As Khrushchev said:

> President Kennedy once stated . . . that the United States
> had the nuclear missile capacity to wipe out the Soviet
> Union two times over, while the Soviet Union had enough
> atomic missiles to wipe out the United States only once. . . .
> We're satisfied to be able to wipe out the United States the
> first time around. Once is quite enough. What good does it
> do to annihilate a country two times over?

As we developed larger and more destructive weapons, we may have
had more megatonnage or throw weight than the Soviet Union, but
any perceptible advantage disappeared. As Winston Churchill put it:
"What's the point in making the rubble bounce?" Or Henry Kissinger:
"What in heaven's name is nuclear superiority?"

The American fear of taking a risk led to much greater risks farther
down the road. The risk of Soviet cheating was a smaller one than the
risks inherent in a world of MIRVs and other offensive weapons. The
new, more sophisticated weapons, rather than giving more security, were
instead destabilizing, and aroused more fear of a first strike from the
other side. Lastly, perhaps worst, by continuing our weapons testing and
improvements, the United States lost any moral authority to discourage
the proliferation of nuclear weapons on the part of other countries.

Kennedy considered the limited test ban a step toward a comprehensive
test ban, which he continued to hope might be achieved. The test ban
treaty was so important to Kennedy that he once remarked that he

would gladly forfeit his reelection for its sake. He told Harriman that if he were reelected, the principal thrust of his second term would be to seek improved relations with the Soviet Union. And Khrushchev said that the treaty had helped build a "fund of confidence" that would encourage further moves toward reducing international tension. If Kennedy and Khrushchev had survived in office, such a treaty would have been possible. But, of course, neither leader was given the time needed for any further steps. To me, that is a little noted but important aspect to the tragedy of Kennedy's assassination.

A delegation of Soviet nuclear scientists paid us a return visit in November 1963. The tour included a stop at our lab at Berkeley, which of course meant a look at our heavy ion linear accelerator. Ironically, I was standing on the very spot where I'd been when called to the phone when President-elect Kennedy offered me the AEC chairmanship; this time, I was called aside and given the tragic message that President Kennedy had been shot.

The news threw us all into a turbulence of emotion and confusion. Our Soviet guests seemed as overwhelmed as we—they offered to cancel the rest of their tour if we wanted them to. The situation was especially touchy because of speculation that the Soviet Union had been involved in the assassination. Local authorities even recommended that we remove them surreptitiously from their San Francisco hotels—we felt like spies smuggling them out through the kitchen of the Fairmont. I canceled the Soviet group's scheduled stops over that weekend, and arranged for them to visit Yosemite National Park instead while I flew to Washington. The following Monday the Soviets resumed their schedule, which took them to the National Reactor Testing Station in Idaho. There they asked for a television set so they could watch the President's funeral (later telling me they were touched to see me among those at the service at Arlington Cemetery). Back in Washington before their departure, they laid a wreath on President Kennedy's grave.

This reaction on the part of the Soviets was quite endearing; they cooperated without hesitation with spur-of-the-moment changes and gave clear signs that Kennedy had meant something special to them. For me, the personal shock was so great that I questioned whether I wanted to stay on in Washington.

# SEVENTEEN

# LBJ: A PRESIDENT

# AND A FRIEND

President Kennedy had appointed me to fill out a two-and-a-half-year term at the AEC that had expired in June 1963. He had then sent me a telegram expressing delight that I had consented to being reappointed. I couldn't remember having discussed it with him, but I felt I couldn't turn down the President of the United States.

Now, when Lyndon Johnson assumed the presidency, he asked Kennedy's appointees to stay on for the sake of the country. I knew Johnson slightly because I was a member of the space council that he chaired, and in his first actions as President, he gained my immediate respect. I'd made an appointment to brief him on the sensitive matter of the plan to cut back in the production of nuclear weapons material. Throughout the 1940s and 1950s, the United States had produced fissionable bomb-core material as fast as we could, but by now we had a considerable stockpile and were producing more than we needed.

Reducing production could, however, adversely affect the economy. The material was produced in huge industrial facilities that employed many workers. At their peak, the gaseous-diffusion plants for enriching uranium to bomb grade consumed nearly 10 percent of the nation's total electric power. The economic consequences of cutting back had appalled President Kennedy. He so feared the effects of large layoffs rippling through the economy that he had decided to put off any cutbacks until after the 1964 elections, wanting to avoid damaging not only his own chances but those of Democrats in the affected states. Kennedy had an agreement with Henry (Scoop) Jackson, the Democratic senator from

Washington who was facing reelection, to hold off. The remoteness of Hanford, a production site that had been chosen precisely because of its location, amplified the local importance of the jobs there.

When I told President Johnson of the need for the reductions, and of Kennedy's decision to put them off because of economic concerns, he was remarkably unmoved by the political effects. He looked me in the eye and asked, "Is it the right thing to do?" When I said it was, he said that we should move ahead without concern for the political fallout. I came to learn that, despite his reputation as a master politician, that question, "Is it the right thing to do?" was typical of him. (We gradually stopped the operation of all but four of the fourteen plutonium production reactors, in a manner that avoided layoffs.) When I observed that Congress would resist the cutbacks for a variety of reasons, Johnson replied matter-of-factly, "Don't worry about Congress; I'll take care of them." And take care of them he did, in a manner largely invisible to the public.

In the public eye, Johnson suffered because he was as poor a speaker as Kennedy was brilliant. What the public did not see was that no one was more effective than Johnson when he was one-on-one or in a small group. I could almost feel energy emanating from his body. Helen described the experience of talking with President Johnson as a feeling of being surrounded. His approach reflected his oft-repeated line, "Let us reason together." His effectiveness stemmed from an uncanny ability to reason the other person around to his way of thinking, to persuade with persistent arguments. He would put his arm around a member of Congress at a reception and start talking him into something. And when he moved on to his next victim, you could almost see the congressman shaking his head in bewilderment, wondering how the President had convinced him to agree to whatever he had just agreed to. This is the image that comes to mind when I hear the phrase "the Johnson treatment."

But he was himself amenable to being reasoned with. One evening, on the way home, I stopped at the University Club for some exercise. As was customary there, I was swimming in the nude when an attendant told me that the President was on the phone. President Johnson was decisive, the sort to reach a verdict and move on to the next issue. I forget the exact matter that was discussed that evening—an ill-advised choice for an appointment or something else I needed to talk him out of—but I felt foolish, standing there naked and dripping wet and trying to argue with the President. But I knew I'd get one shot and had to be quick with my arguments; so, embarrassed as I was, I managed to dissuade him.

Another time when I was resisting an idea of his, he glowered at me and asked, "Glenn, what are you trying to do here? Are you resisting carrying out the wishes of the President of the United States?"

By then I knew his tactics well enough to shrug the intimidation off with a smile and reply, "Yeah, I guess I am."

The time to settle the budget came at the end of the year, when Johnson generally went to his ranch in Texas for the holidays. Every year I would make a trip there to make appeals to him on items in the AEC budget that had been denied by the Bureau of the Budget.

The ranch was an informal place; generally, the President himself or his wife, Lady Bird, would drive out to the ranch's landing strip to pick us up. We'd have a traditional southern meal of black-eyed peas and such at their dining table— a real family meal, with their children and grandchildren and Lady Bird, whom LBJ clearly adored.

I know the stories about Johnson driving around the ranch at breakneck pace are true, because sometimes I went on those trips. We'd climb into his white Chrysler station wagon for these too exhilarating tours of the ranch, with the dog in the back seat and LBJ in the driver's seat with his six-month-old grandson on his lap. He was proud of the collection of exotic animals he had on the ranch, including English deer, Japanese deer, an Indian antelope called the nilgai and other antelope, as well as the native white-tailed Texas deer. Once when the President climbed out of the car and with difficulty shooed some quail back into an enclosure from which they had escaped, my comment that this was probably as high-priced help as had ever chased quail seemed to tickle him.

In the appeals sessions, the Budget Director would explain why a particular item had been deleted, and I would present my case for why it was needed. Almost invariably, LBJ ruled in my favor. This did not stem from any eagerness to spend money. Because of his Great Society programs, Johnson has sometimes been painted as a big spender, but this contrasts with another public image of him as a strangely frugal miser who wandered the White House at night, turning out lights. He was very conscious of not wanting to waste taxpayers' money; he was willing to take the heat for cutbacks in weapons-material production because of his fiscal responsibility.

At one meeting, he admonished a roomful of subcabinet-level officials to treat the government dollar as carefully as their own. He was cutting "the light bill in the White House from $6,000 to $3,000 per month," he said to illustrate the impact a little cost-consciousness could have, and asked us to check our telephones, for example, to be sure we didn't have more than we actually needed. He put it in a powerful context, asking us to bear in mind that we were acting for the President of the United States and would be judged as his personal representatives. At an important meeting on a topic unrelated to finances, he interrupted the conversation to glare at me and demand to know why I was still riding in a Cadillac, when we had been given a directive to exchange our chauffeur-driven Cadillacs for smaller, cheaper, less ostentatious Chevys. I quickly assured him I had made the switch as soon as directed.

Dean Rusk described Lyndon Johnson as "a man of great personal kindness. He was always ready with words of encouragement and appreciation." I agree with that completely. He often made it clear to me that he thought I was doing a good job, and I treasured the message each time. I believe he trusted me because he came to realize that I had no political ambitions and no hidden agendas, but simply was trying to do my best and what I thought was best for the country.

I'm not sure how much my success in gaining his approval of my budget appeals depended on the power of my arguments and how much on our personal bond and his trust. I remember one day in particular when my secretary told me I was wanted for a meeting at the White House. After we'd finished the substantive discussion, the President just kept shooting the breeze. An assistant brought in root beer and cookies, and after a while, Johnson gave an impromptu press conference with the reporters whose job it was to hang around and wait for news. I left the White House that day with the impression that he mostly called the meeting because he just wanted the companionship that we all take for granted but that must be difficult for a President to find.

Because of this personal friendship, and because his presidency accomplished so much in the way of progressive legislation, it was particularly saddening to see its potential dissolved in Vietnam. I found his ensnarement in that difficult war understandable after I had attended some cabinet meetings and heard his military advisers' unfailingly optimistic predictions, Johnson being continually drawn in by their telling him that victories were just around the corner, that a few more troops would make the difference. I was as influenced as he by these constant favorable predictions.

By late 1967, Robert McNamara, an architect of the original escalation of America's war in Indochina, had become so disaffected that Johnson eased him out as Secretary of Defense. His replacement, Clark Clifford, was instrumental in convincing the President to de-escalate the war. My children were opposed to American involvement in the war, and I came around to this view at about the time when Johnson announced his decision not to seek reelection (a decision that completely astonished me); the military officers were still giving the cabinet optimistic briefings.

Johnson achieved great success with the civil rights and voting rights acts, but perhaps more revealing of his character and commitment to these issues was his behind-the-scenes work to promote equal opportunity. At one of his first meetings with regulatory and independent agency heads, he emphasized the value of women in government and his desire to see more women occupying high places in government. He requested a report from each of us in a month about what we had done to bring women into our agencies.

At the AEC, my fellow commissioners and I were told to help the President find a woman and an African American that could be appointed to the commission. Eventually, the commission came to include Mary (Polly) Bunting (president of Radcliffe College) and Samuel Nabrit (president of Texas Southern University), both of whom served with distinction. Times were truly different then: a prominent executive in the nuclear power industry phoned me to inquire into Polly Bunting's qualifications; he was concerned because he had heard that the commission's meetings could get rather heated, and wondered about a woman's presence at them. Was this the proper environment for a lady, and could gentlemen conduct business in their customary manner with one present?

The Johnson administration passed a great milestone by negotiating the Nuclear Nonproliferation Treaty (NPT). This achievement was particularly gratifying to me because Johnson did not bring to the presidency the passion for arms control that Kennedy had. He appreciated the Limited Test Ban Treaty's environmental benefits, but doubted its value as an arms control measure. Nor was he impressed with my arguments about the importance of a comprehensive test ban treaty. Moreover, he was skeptical of the value and place in government of the Arms Control and Disarmament Agency.

Kennedy had created the ACDA, whose job was to work ceaselessly for opportunities for disarmament. The rationale was that disarmament was a legitimate interest that, like defense, labor, commerce, or agriculture, deserved representation within government councils. With the armed forces always asking for more weapons, it made sense to have a government agency that advocated restraint. The ACDA had adopted as its number one objective the prevention of the proliferation of nuclear weapons to any further countries. For the first few years, progress was stymied because the State Department was working at cross-purposes: it hoped to create a Multilateral Force (MLF), a NATO naval force manned by personnel from several nations and equipped with nuclear weapons. And it hoped that by giving our NATO allies greater involvement in planning their own defense, the MLF would preserve Allied cohesion against the Soviet threat and encourage the movement toward a united Europe.

There was also an idea that participation in the MLF would help to dissuade other nations from wanting to be independent nuclear powers—particularly West Germany, which always seemed to occupy center stage when it came to discussion of nuclear nonproliferation. It often seemed to me that the Soviet leaders were interested in an NPT mainly to obtain West Germany's renunciation of nuclear weapons, repeatedly declaring that they would ratify the NPT only when West Germany did.

West Germany, of course, felt threatened by the Russian bear looming over Western Europe. It had the technical ability to make nuclear weapons and was wary of counting on permanent U.S. protection, and thus was hesitant to forswear the possibility forever. The United States wanted to cooperate with the West Germans to retain the cohesion of NATO, but also wanted to make sure they would sign an NPT were it negotiated.

Meanwhile, whereas West Germany was cautiously interested in the MLF, Great Britain was opposed to it. The Soviet Union was appalled at the thought of any force that put a German finger on the nuclear trigger. And the MLF conflicted with one of the main objectives of a nonproliferation treaty, which was to prevent nuclear powers from sharing weapons and technology with nonnuclear countries. Eventually, President Johnson did his own evaluation of the MLF, which like the ACDA he had inherited from the Kennedy administration, and decided against it. This was one of the steps taken to clear the way for the NPT.

Nuclear proliferation received little attention in the first months of the Johnson administration, but discussions on this subject changed worldwide in October 1964, when the Chinese Communist government exploded its first atomic bomb. France had joined the nuclear club in 1960, so the nuclear powers now numbered five. The Chinese test had long been expected, but the reality of it shook up the whole international equation. China's rival India considered its need for a bomb, which made India's enemy Pakistan think of following suit. Even Australia began to stir. Suddenly, the threat of a domino effect in nuclear weaponry focused the minds of government leaders.

Within the American government, the Chinese bomb even sparked questions as to whether a nonproliferation treaty should be pursued at all: since China had the bomb, the argument went, perhaps it was better for countries such as India or Japan to be able to defend themselves. If our enemies were going to pursue nuclear weapons anyway, why should we keep them from our enemies' foes? I argued strenuously against this position, pointing out that once we started making exceptions, we'd lose control, and no one knew where it would end. This point of view quickly prevailed.

Some of us in the administration hoped to make the NPT a priority, but negotiations continued to lag largely because of the lack of presidential involvement, with Johnson preoccupied by the escalation of the Vietnam War in 1965.

At times, personal factors got in the way of policy. In 1965, for example, when Johnson agreed to speak at ceremonies commemorating the twentieth anniversary of the United Nations, he was expected to address the issue of nuclear nonproliferation in an important way. I was excited about the prospect, and had helped to supply some passages drafted by AEC people. On the plane flight out to San Francisco, the President gave me a copy of his speech, and I was disappointed to find that almost all the AEC material had been omitted. A Johnson aide took me aside and confided that it had been dropped at the last minute because of Robert Kennedy's long-awaited maiden speech as a senator, given the day before. Evidently someone had leaked an internal report to the senator, because Kennedy's speech included some of the very same passages that were in Johnson's draft. As far as I'd ever seen, Johnson's relations with John Kennedy had been cordial, cooperative, and based on mutual respect, but Lyndon Johnson and Bobby Kennedy simply seemed to dislike each other from the first. The episode with the speech certainly illustrated how Bobby Kennedy could get under the President's skin, and Johnson's irritation was no doubt amplified by his great dislike of leaks.

The absence of commentary on nonproliferation weakened the President's speech considerably, so when he asked me how I liked it, I could muster enthusiasm only for a section where he referred to the prospects for a better future through science. "Is that the only part you liked?" he asked, annoyed. The audience also seemed rather disappointed with the speech, which was shorter and less substantive than expected, which annoyed him further.

(During the ceremonies, I sat next to Adlai Stevenson, then U.S. ambassador to the United Nations, and Stevenson unburdened his soul to me with a long recitation of the trouble he was having with the President, who, he complained, was not very knowledgeable of or sympathetic about international affairs. A photographer got a shot from below of Stevenson, in his academic robes, with his legs crossed, a hole in the bottom of his shoe clearly visible. The photograph received national play—cropped to include my right ear.)

In 1966 there were further pressures to get President Johnson to focus on nuclear nonproliferation. The Senate held some hearings on it, and then passed a unanimous resolution urging "additional efforts . . . for the solution of nuclear proliferation problems." Some of us in the administration worked through Johnson's aide Bill Moyers to make the case for the urgency of getting a treaty. Something worked, because Johnson began to make comments at press conferences about the importance of having a nonproliferation treaty. These simple statements energized the U.S. negotiators carrying on the talks in Geneva.

By the end of the year, the United States (negotiating on behalf of our allies) and the Soviet Union reached agreement on the first two articles of a treaty. The first article forbade states having nuclear weapons from transferring them "to any recipient whatsoever." Article II forbade states not having nuclear weapons from accepting their transfer or manufacturing them.

The provisions obviously ruled out the multilateral force and could have been a stumbling block to a united Europe. At this point we put into play a tactic that was quite useful in glossing over apparent differences. We prepared a series of treaty interpretations which, we told the Soviets, would accompany the treaty when it was submitted to the Senate for ratification. The Soviet Union did not have to agree formally to them, but if it did not object too greatly, it could simply maintain silence. The most important interpretation claimed that the treaty would not prevent a federated European state, if one should ever develop, from inheriting the nuclear weapons of Britain or France, an eventuality perhaps sufficiently remote to allow the U.S.S.R. to take a chance on it.

The treaty provisions that remained the biggest challenge to work out concerned the question of allowing for the spread of nuclear *power* without the spread of nuclear *weapons*. The nuclear power industry was developing rapidly because it was increasingly attractive for both industrialized and developing countries. However, reactors used to generate electrical power could be used to produce a low-grade bomb material as well. How could the international community have faith that nations generating electricity with nuclear power weren't diverting nuclear materials to weapons manufacture? The answer was to monitor the nuclear materials through a system of international "safeguards" checking on a country's nuclear program: examination of records documenting the movement of nuclear materials; surveillance at key locations by means of cameras and other instruments; the use of seals and other techniques to guard against unauthorized movement of material; and outside inspectors taking independent measurements and observations. The International Atomic Energy Agency, now almost a decade old, was fully capable of performing these tasks.

Several nations that were developing nuclear capabilities with an eye toward exporting their technology objected to inspections. Allowing foreigners to roam through their nuclear facilities would leave them open to industrial espionage, they charged. And it was not a level playing field, since the existing nuclear powers would not be subject to inspections (for the obvious reason that there was no point in inspecting nations that already possessed nuclear weapons). Many of us in the administration proposed that the United States could overcome this objection by opening its own peaceful nuclear facilities to inspection. We eventually convinced President Johnson that this was the right course. I worked my contacts in the industry to get their acquiescence. At my suggestion, President Johnson made his dramatic announcement that the United States would agree to on-site inspection of its peaceful nuclear facilities on December 2, 1967, the twenty-fifth anniversary of the first chain reaction. The British immediately followed our example. By January 1968 our allies and the Soviet Union had agreed on the draft text of Article III of the treaty, the safeguards article.

The superpowers had agreed on the three-article treaty, but the nonnuclear countries, which were after all the main objects of the treaty, greatly resented what they called the discriminatory nature of this draft. They pointed out that they were being asked to renounce their right to add nuclear weapons to their arsenals, while the United States and the Soviet Union were giving up nothing. The United States and the Soviet Union found themselves in an unaccustomed alliance against the demands of the nonnuclear states, which resulted in the addition of three more articles to the treaty.

Article IV states the right of all countries to pursue the peaceful uses of atomic energy and the obligation of more advanced countries to give technical assistance to them. Article V requires nuclear states to make available to nonnuclear states explosives for peaceful uses such as excavation and mining. Both Brazil and India had objected to the earlier draft treaty because it precluded their developing such explosives. When I visited Brazil in 1967 and discussed this objection with its leaders, I pointed out that the AEC was willing to offer a peaceful explosives service at a fraction of what it would cost them to get it for themselves. These discussions convinced me that the Brazilians' avowed interest in peaceful explosives was a cover to keep alive a nuclear weapons option, a belief supported by their continued refusal to sign the treaty even after Article V was added. In Article VI, the nuclear powers pledged "to pursue negotiations in good faith on effective measures regarding cessation of the arms race and disarmament."

The Treaty on the Nonproliferation of Nuclear Weapons was opened for signature on July 1, 1968, in Washington, London, and Moscow, and immediately signed by the Big Three and more than fifty other countries. When the Senate ratified it the following March, it went into force, having been ratified by the requisite number of countries—the Big Three plus forty. The treaty has been an impressive international accomplishment.

For years following the passage of the treaty, only one additional country was known to have exploded a nuclear device—India in 1974. Then, some thirty years after its passage, India and Pakistan both tested nuclear devices. (Add to these countries Israel, generally acknowledged to have the bomb, and South Africa, which dismantled its nuclear capability.) Considering the possibilities we were facing in the 1960s—John Kennedy once said, "I see the possibility in the 1970s of the President . . . having to face a world in which fifteen or twenty or twenty-five nations may have these weapons"—that's an amazing record.

"I am not really thinking of [developing] nuclear arms," Mohammad Reza Pahlavi, the Shah of Iran, once said, "but if twenty or thirty ridiculous little countries are going to have nuclear weapons, then I may have to revise my policies." When he said that in 1975, the Shah was a staunch U.S. ally. What if, instead of pursuing strict nonproliferation, we had adopted an attitude of letting allies go nuclear? It's frightening to think of what might have happened had nuclear weapons fallen into the hands of Ayatollah Khomeini. The treaty provided the security that made it unnecessary for the Shah to think about developing nuclear weapons.

The NPT requires review conferences to be held every five years. At the conferences in 1975, 1980, 1985, and 1990 many countries complained vociferously that the superpowers were not negotiating in good faith to end the arms race. There was concern that this dissatisfaction might threaten the renewal of the treaty at the 1995 conference, but it was extended by acclamation, and the nations with nuclear weapons committed themselves to concluding a comprehensive test ban treaty, which they have done (the United States has not ratified it). The treaty's 178 parties account for 98 percent of the world's installed nuclear power capacity, 95 percent of the nuclear power capacity under construction, and all the world's exporters of enriched uranium.

The NPT story illustrates how arms control agreements can best be negotiated, in particular the effectiveness of negotiating in secret. Most arms control proposals announced publicly by either side were insincere, with features that the proposer knew in advance were unacceptable. The side making the proposal had the cynical propaganda motivation of gaining credit in world opinion while making the other side look intransigent.

For example, at one point President Johnson proposed a "verified freeze on the number of strategic nuclear offensive and defensive missiles." A freeze would have not only locked in an American advantage but required inspection of secret facilities. The Soviet Union counterproposed that the major powers destroy all their bombers; this was unacceptable to the United States, with its large lead in bombers. The United States responded with a proposal that both sides destroy an equal number of bombers, which would have increased the proportional U.S. advantage.

Secrecy also enables each side to make concessions without loss of face and, just as important, to understand the other side's sensitivities better. The argument over the multilateral force illustrates this point. In public, we could not condone the Soviet Union's abhorrence of a West German finger on a nuclear trigger without showing disrespect to our ally; in private, we could accept this point of national sensitivity. Our relations with our allies required that we hold out for the possibility of future European unity; the Soviets understood this but could not acknowledge it publicly. The delicate device worked out, in which we issued an interpretation of the treaty about which they remained silent, could only have been arranged in private between negotiators who understood and trusted each other.

Sometimes this trust became so strong that the negotiators were almost conspirators. At one point a compromise was reached on the safeguard-inspection issue, but neither side could submit it to its government because both delegations were under instructions not to budge from previous positions. They eventually decided that each side would submit the proposed compromise to its government as a suggestion from the *other* side. The American government decided to accept it, but, since it was inconsistent with the allied position, the United States resubmitted it to the North Atlantic Council as a *Soviet* suggestion. This fiction was necessary because Dean Rusk had promised the West German Foreign Minister that the U.S. proposal would not be changed without prior consultation.

Another lesson to learn was how critically important presidential leadership is in attaining these agreements. The test ban treaty owes its existence to John Kennedy's passionate commitment. The NPT didn't move until Lyndon Johnson made it his priority. Because he came around to seeing its importance, it became one of his greatest international legacies. Johnson's dedication to opposing communist expansion was obvious, but he also recognized that "while differing principles and differing values may always divide us, they should not, and must not, deter us from rational acts of common endeavor."

# EIGHTEEN

# TROUBLES WITH NIXON—AND
# A LOOK INSIDE THE AEC

I thought that Richard Nixon's victory over Hubert Humphrey signaled the end of my time with the AEC. Though my term as commissioner technically did not expire until 1970, the choice of who would be chairman was up to the President, and not until after Nixon's inauguration in January 1969 did I learn that the new President intended to ask me to stay on as AEC chairman. There were only two or three other carryovers in high-level positions, all of them in the more technical agencies, such as NASA.

By then, I'd been acquainted with Richard Nixon for more than twenty years, and I'd never admired his politics. We had first met in Chattanooga, Tennessee, at a banquet honoring us both along with eight others as the U.S. Junior Chamber of Commerce's "Ten Outstanding Young Men of 1947." Nixon was then a thirty-four-year-old congressman from California, gaining fame (and notoriety) for his role in the Alger Hiss case. I noted in my diary, "Nixon suggested to me that we should remain in touch with each other and 'stick together.'"

In 1950, he was in the midst of his red-baiting smear campaign for senator against the Democrat Helen Gahagan Douglas when he visited the Radiation Laboratory. After I gave him a tour through the chemistry research labs, his aide announced that now Nixon and I were scheduled to go to the Claremont Hotel for a photo session. Such photographs would be seen as my endorsement of Nixon's candidacy, so I undiplomatically blurted out some contrived excuse about why I couldn't go. Nixon quickly and graciously accepted the excuse. My clumsiness continued at another meeting a few months later, when we ran into each other at the Rose Bowl and I introduced him to my companion as Jim Nixon. (James Nickson was a physician at the Met Lab during the war.)

When Nixon was Vice President I took what opportunities presented themselves to talk to him about subjects like education and loyalty oaths. I described the success of federal aid to science at the university level and the need for federal assistance in the construction of new buildings. Nixon was surprisingly supportive of my position on the loyalty oath; despite his virulent anticommunism, he recognized the problems involved. At one memorable meeting in December 1959, the talk turned to the coming presidential campaign. He predicted that either he or Nelson Rockefeller would win the Republican nomination. He thought the Democratic nomination would go to either Senator Stuart Symington of Missouri or Adlai Stevenson, and I noted in my journal that Nixon "had a low opinion of the former but regards the latter as an intelligent and formidable adversary." Interestingly, he did not consider Kennedy a likely nominee.

In 1969 I soon got a sense of how different from the Kennedy and Johnson years this administration and my work in it would be. At my first meeting with the new President, Nixon gave me specific instructions on what to say to the press about our conversation. This was my first taste of his almost obsessive desire to orchestrate his administration's press relations—a hallmark of his presidency.

A few weeks later, a meeting was held to consider whether to continue support for the Seabed Treaty, which banned the emplacement of weapons of mass destruction on the ocean floor. When Nixon asked what I thought, I replied that I favored the treaty and began to explain why I thought it would be a mistake to reverse the American position on it. The President cut me off, saying that I should confine my remarks to my technical judgment, that I was not there to give my political opinion. I responded that it was difficult to separate the two in this case, but that the treaty would not impede our development of nuclear weapons.

Both the content and the delivery of Nixon's remark stunned me, and left me with much to ponder. Apparently my eight years in Washington and experience working with Congress and negotiating numerous international agreements meant nothing to him. My possession of scientific expertise disqualified me from having any political judgment.

During the Eisenhower, Kennedy, and Johnson administrations, the

AEC chairman had been an active participant in formulating arms control policy. The AEC chairman, after all, headed the agency that helped to develop and test many of the weapons that were the subject of arms control talks. Such a person might have some useful knowledge. So from an administrative, policy-making standpoint, Nixon's attitude made little sense. And from a personal standpoint, I hated being left out of this policy area because having an influence on it was the most rewarding aspect of being AEC chairman; it hurt to have that taken away.

As time went on, I noticed more and more an antiscience or antiscientist bias in the administration. In his public statements, Nixon avowed interest in and support for science, but this interest seemed restricted to the grandiose spectaculars, such as our landing a man on the moon or developing supersonic transport airplanes, which generated attention and prestige. When it came to the accumulation of scientific knowledge in the many thousands of research projects in government facilities, universities, and private laboratories across the country—the day-to-day nittygritty that makes the spectaculars possible—he displayed little interest. On the few occasions when I discussed science with Nixon, I sensed a discomfort, and he resisted acknowledging any difficulty in understanding the subject under discussion. In a similar situation President Kennedy asked questions that challenged the scientist to explain more clearly, and exuded confidence that he could grasp an issue if only it were explained properly. I thought Nixon's reaction stemmed from a basic lack of self-confidence.

Henry Kissinger reinforced this tendency. Kissinger simply radiated intelligence, but apparently scientific subjects blocked that radiation like a lead shield. Spurgeon Keeny of the Arms Control and Disarmament Agency noted that Kissinger seemed uncomfortable in the presence of scientists for reasons similar to those I ascribed to Nixon.

According to Nixon's science adviser, Lee DuBridge, Kissinger had convinced Nixon that scientists were of no use on matters such as arms control. So it's an open question as to whether Nixon and Kissinger shunned scientists more out of personal discomfort or out of the belief that scientists were inappropriate for high positions. President Nixon also tended to identify scientists with universities, and colleges campuses were the sources of unrest and demonstrations against the war in Vietnam. Eventually, the position of science adviser itself, as well as the President's Science Advisory Committee and the Office of Science and Technology, were abolished. (When Gerald Ford became President, the science adviser was restored and an Office of Scientific and Technical Policy created.)

Of course, Kissinger had another motive in excluding people like DuBridge and me from discussions—namely, to eliminate competitors. He feuded with and frequently humiliated Secretary of State William Rogers in his drive to be second only to the President in international affairs. This kind of internal backstabbing was discomforting to me. My only other experience of how an incoming administration behaved was with Kennedy's, and his group had seemed more focused on the tasks at hand. No doubt, that was due in part to Kennedy's style—not to take himself or his image too seriously—an attitude that filtered down to the rest of us in a way that allowed us to pay more attention to getting the job done and less to who got credit or blame.

The three Presidents I worked for differed greatly in leadership style. John Kennedy was so stimulated by the give-and-take in large discussion groups that someone characterized his approach as "government by seminar." Yet he consciously kept the White House staff small and used it not to insulate himself but to keep himself open to many views. As Theodore Sorensen once explained to me: "He was quite careful to keep the White House staff very small and relatively low-profile and he made sure the staff members confined their role to being advisers and assistants. This restricted substantially their ability to say on the phone that the President insists that you do this or that. That has been a major source of discord in other administrations." (Nixon's lieutenants H. R. Haldeman and John Ehrlichman come to mind.) Sorensen noted that by granting access to his top people, Kennedy kept anyone from feeling "shut out or shunted aside."

In contrast to Kennedy's open "seminars," Johnson preferred to deal with a limited number of trusted advisers. For important foreign-policy and national-security matters, he relied not on the National Security Council but on his Tuesday lunch group, which included the Secretaries of State and Defense, the National Security Adviser, the chairman of the Joint Chiefs of Staff, the CIA director, and the White House press secretary, a small group in which the participants could speak frankly. But it reinforced Johnson's dangerous preference for dealing with persons whose points of view were compatible with his own and of whose loyalty he was certain. By limiting his meetings to people who agreed with him, Johnson undoubtedly shielded himself from difficult decisions and unpleasant news. As advisers became disaffected with his policies and left, the Johnson administration began to take on the characteristics of a court—a dominant figure surrounded by loyal subjects.

Nixon took the tendency to wall off the White House and limit the circle of advisers to the extreme. In *The White House Years*, Kissinger explains that Nixon "was determined to run foreign policy from the White House," which meant excluding the State Department ("its personnel had no loyalty to him") and the CIA ("it was staffed by Ivy League liberals who behind the facade of analytical objectivity were usually pushing their own preferences"). He spelled out the rather convoluted reasoning behind narrowing the circle of decision makers: "One reason for keeping the decisions to small groups is that when bureaucracies are so unwieldy and when their internal morale becomes a serious problem, an unpopular decision may be fought by brutal means, such as leaks to the press or congressional committees. Thus, the only way secrecy can be kept is to exclude from the making of the decision those who are theoretically charged with carrying it out."

Of course, another approach is to try to keep a bureaucracy's morale from becoming "a serious problem" in the first place, but Kissinger seemed to put the importance of secrecy above the importance of arriving at a sound decision by considering the problem from many perspectives. He also ignored the lesson I learned as a university chancellor: that a consensual decision, in which the people who will be charged with carrying it out have some ownership, has a better chance of being implemented.

I have always felt that the ultimate course of the Nixon administration might have been different had Nixon chosen to hear the opinions of a wider circle of advisers. My experience was probably typical—and I share it here not because I think I had particularly good advice to give, but because it illustrates my difficulties in running one of the government's largest agencies.

Seaborg at one of President Kennedy's cabinet meetings. He is at the far end of the table; Attorney General Robert Kennedy is in the foreground.

President Kennedy and Seaborg visiting the nuclear test site in Nevada, 1962. Intensely curious, Kennedy asked a helicopter pilot to fly dangerously close to a bomb crater.

Seaborg and President
Johnson in the White
House Oval Office, 1964.
Sometimes LBJ just wanted
to chat with a friend.

President Johnson
presenting the Fermi Award
to Oppenheimer at the
White House, December
1963, a ceremony that
represented a partial
vindication for Oppenheimer.

UN ambassador Adlai Stevenson
and Seaborg at the ceremony
celebrating the twentieth
anniversary of the United
Nations, 1965. The hole in
Stevenson's shoe received national
press coverage.

The U.S. Junior Chamber of Commerce's "Ten Outstanding Young Men of 1947" (here with Miss America for that year) included California congressman Richard Nixon and Seaborg. Nixon suggested they "stick together."

Seaborg with President Nixon, 1970. Relations between the two were not always this cordial.

Exchanging gifts with Soviet representatives at the Seaborgs' home in Washington, April 1971. Standing, from left: Soviet atomic energy head Andronik Petrosyants; Seaborg; translator R. Lavroff; and Helen, Dianne, and Eric Seaborg.

Seaborg at the blackboard, explaining a basic chemistry formula to a student, January 1972.

Zhou Enlai greeting Seaborg in China, May 1973.

The discoverers of element 106, later named seaborgium, in 1974. From left: Matti Nurmia, Jose R. Alonso, Albert Ghiorso, E. Kenneth Hulet, Carol T. Alonso, Ronald W. Lougheed, Seaborg, J. Michael Nitschke.

President Reagan presenting Seaborg with a plaque—a blowup of the cover of "A Nation at Risk," the report of the National Commission on Excellence in Education, May 1984.

Glenn Seaborg in 1986.

Seaborg in the Oval Office briefing President George H. W. Bush on the "cold fusion" phenomenon, 1989.

President Clinton with the 1993 Westinghouse Science Talent Search finalists at the White House and, at the back, Seaborg, March 1993.

Seaborg with Vice President Al Gore, March 1993.

Seaborg pointing to a new addition to the periodic table of the elements—seaborgium.

I had direct access to both Kennedy and Johnson when a problem warranted it, a privilege I tried to use sparingly. On day-to-day communication, Kennedy's National Security Adviser, McGeorge Bundy, was a trustworthy pipeline to the President's desk and mind. I always felt confident that the President did indeed learn what needed to be called to his attention and, conversely, that Bundy transmitted the President's thoughts back to me.

In contrast, the Nixon administration erected an ever-increasing number of walls between the AEC and the White House, until my day-to-day access was only via a man named Will Kriegsman, who reported to John Whitaker, who reported to Peter Flanigan, who reported to John Ehrlichman, who reported to Nixon. It was frustrating to have to run a large organization when your contact at the White House was a poorly informed staff assistant. One of Nixon's abiding complaints was that he found it hard to control the bureaucracy. But he compounded the difficulty by isolating himself from those who worked for him. I can attest that his style made my job harder to perform.

He also made odd attempts to change the modes of operation used by previous administrations as much as possible, even to the detail that the National Security Action Memoranda issued by Presidents Kennedy and Johnson were replaced by National Security Study Memoranda and National Security Decision Memoranda; the Bureau of the Budget became the Office of Management and Budget. There was a desire to tinker with systems that worked simply for the sake of change itself.

My distance from the White House—and the distance between my relationship with Lyndon Johnson and that with Richard Nixon—was never clearer than when budget time arrived. In my only budget appeals session with Nixon in person, Nixon leafed through briefing papers while I talked, and limited his remarks to calling for the next item. That night I noted in my journal: "I have the impression that President Nixon had his mind made up before I came and will rule against me on practically all of my appeal items." That perception proved to be correct. In future years, I was asked to present my appeals through the Budget Director, who had already ruled against me, which predictably led to no victories for the AEC.

Of course, I was probably not seen as a "team player." At one point, word came down that the White House wanted me to give speeches promoting Nixon's proposed antiballistic missile system. Like many others in the scientific community, I opposed building this system because I believed it would be ineffective, excessively expensive, and dangerously provocative. I believed it was my duty as AEC chairman to oversee the testing of any weapons adopted as part of our national program—and in that capacity I willingly took the heat for some very controversial and unpopular tests associated with planning for an ABM system. But I did not consider it my duty to make speeches in favor of a policy then being debated in Congress. I never stated this position; I simply ignored the requests to make speeches.

Whether my recalcitrance was noted in an administration with a low tolerance for dissent, I do not know. To his credit, Nixon not only changed his mind about the ABM but negotiated a treaty that prohibited the deployment of nationwide ABM systems and limited their development.

My opposition to the ABM was just one more instance of my not fitting with the Nixon crowd. He and his closest advisers had a favorite word for describing the actions and attitude they aspired to: "tough." I certainly lacked the sort of toughness they seemed to favor, as I learned in a clash with John Mitchell's Justice Department.

In February 1969, FBI director J. Edgar Hoover sent a letter to the AEC director of security. In my journal I described it as alleging that "an officer of a certain industrial nuclear facility may have diverted appreciable amounts of enriched uranium 235 to Israel over the last several years." Hoover urged that the AEC revoke this person's security clearance and cancel the facility's classified AEC contracts. The charge was considered so sensitive that the letter named neither the person nor the company involved; the AEC knew without being told, however.

Zalman Shapiro had worked for Westinghouse developing reactors for submarines, and gone on to found a company called Nuclear Materials and Equipment Company (NUMEC). NUMEC processed nuclear fuel, for example, for use in power reactors. The charge, or, more precisely, the problem, was not new to us. As far back as 1965, we had discovered a discrepancy in the amounts of the uranium passing through the plant. Shapiro had claimed that the uranium in question had been lost in processing, and AEC safeguards teams had inspected the plant and accepted that explanation. NUMEC had subordinated the proper processes to the pursuit of profit and adopted shortcuts that led to excessive and irretrievable losses of material. Shapiro was guilty of sloppy materials handling and misleading bookkeeping, but not of diverting any material. Still, the episode was embarrassing because it revealed lax enforcement and a glaring deficiency in AEC safeguards. But by the time of Hoover's letter we had corrected our problems with improved methods, better equipment, and a beefed-up staff.

Through intensive surveillance, including that favorite Nixon administration practice, wiretapping, the FBI discovered that Shapiro had met with such people as the Israeli embassy's scientific attaché. Their chain of reasoning seemed to be that (a) enriched uranium was missing, (b) Shapiro was a committed supporter of Israel, (c) therefore Shapiro had shipped the uranium to Israel. But the giant leap from (a) to (c) was one that no one at the AEC would make without evidence. If you thought Shapiro could slip into the plant at night and fill a suitcase with uranium, you could give some credence to the smuggling charges. But that was preposterous. He would have needed the cooperation of quite a few of his employees (if not the whole workforce) to divert enriched uranium to Israel, and such a conspiracy would certainly leave some tracks.

When we declined to take action, Hoover wrote again to say that we were making a mistake and that the FBI's

> thorough and extended investigation of Shapiro for more than a year [had] developed information clearly pointing to Shapiro's pronounced pro-Israeli sympathies and close contacts with Israeli officials, including several Israeli intelligence officers. . . . The basis of the security risk posed by the subject lies in his continued access to sensitive information and material . . . and the only effective way to counter this risk would be to preclude Shapiro from such access.

The FBI still gave us no evidence; harboring pro-Israel sympathies and meeting with Israelis were still legal activities, as far as I could ascertain.

The matter rested there for about a year, when Shapiro (who meanwhile had sold NUMEC) received a job offer that required him to apply for a higher security clearance. Since questions had been raised about his loyalty by people at high levels, the normal procedure would have been to hold a hearing where he could hear the charges and respond. However, we couldn't hold a hearing without seeing the FBI files that detailed the charges, and the Justice Department refused to release them. Attorney General Mitchell simply told us to deny the security clearance without a hearing. Never in history had any government agency done that, and we AEC commissioners were not about to be the first.

Still, our hands were tied. We could neither issue nor deny the security clearance without a hearing and could not hold a hearing without the files. We had no power to obtain the files. We could not even reveal to Shapiro the whole story of the reason for the delay.

I met with the Attorney General to present the AEC's case. When it came to Mitchell, the watchword "tough" was perhaps better spelled "unpleasant." I explained why we were certain there had been no diversion of uranium; when he responded at all, he never addressed the substance of my arguments but simply repeated his own position. The Attorney General of the United States, the country's top law enforcement official, was not only telling but forcing us to abandon due process and established procedure. (The strength of the Justice Department's evidence may be gauged by the fact that it never said it would prosecute Shapiro.)

I enlisted the help of Secretary of State William Rogers, Henry Kissinger, and presidential science adviser Edward E. David, all of whom agreed that it would be inappropriate to deny clearance without a hearing; they related this opinion to Mitchell. But Mitchell was unmoved, and it would be fruitless to butt heads with him, since he was one of Nixon's closest associates. Mitchell was satisfied simply to let Shapiro fight it out with the government in the courts. Shapiro hired Edward Bennett Williams, one of the most skillful and prominent attorneys in the country, to represent him. He was clearly ready to fight to clear his name, and unless the Justice Department improved its case, Shapiro was going to win.

In addition, the publicity surrounding a court case would have been a political disaster. It would almost certainly spark an outraged uprising of protest from American scientists, who were still smarting from the mistreatment of Robert Oppenheimer. On the international level, what sense did it make to try to prove that the United States had failed to prevent the theft of enriched uranium from a facility under AEC supervision for use by Israel to make a bomb? What effect would this have on the Middle East, which was in the unstable period between Israel's conquests in the Six-Day War of 1967 and the Yom Kippur War in 1973?

After a great deal of stress and discussion, the AEC commissioners eventually found a way to avoid confrontation altogether. Through our contacts in industry, we convinced Westinghouse to make an attractive job offer to Shapiro that did not require any upgrade in his clearance. Westinghouse was glad to hire someone of Shapiro's accomplishments. We indirectly passed the word to him about the difficulties with his clearance request, and he accepted the job and withdrew his clearance application.

When the abuses of power known collectively as Watergate came to light, I thought of the attitude of Nixon's chief law enforcement officer toward Zalman Shapiro's right to due process. Our day-to-day contact at Justice had been Robert Mardian, head of the internal security division. Mardian's measure of fame came when the Watergate investigation revealed the many controversial wiretaps he had authorized.

Shapiro continued in a successful career, occupying positions of increasing responsibility with Westinghouse until his retirement in 1983. But his career might have been even more successful if not for this undeserved blemish on his record. Later in the 1970s, the story came to light after enterprising journalists filed Freedom of Information requests. Unfortunately, however, some of their articles left the impression that Shapiro had in fact diverted the uranium.

Lest I be considered a biased source, with an interest in claiming that no uranium diversion happened on my watch, let me quote from Seymour Hersh's intensively researched book on Israel's quest for nuclear weapons, *The Samson Option*: "Despite more than ten years of intensive investigation involving active FBI surveillance, however, no significant evidence proving that Shapiro had diverted any uranium from his plant was ever found. Nonetheless, he remained guilty in the minds of many in the government and the press. . . . Zalman Shapiro did not divert uranium from his processing plant to Israel." Hersh relates that the "missing" uranium was found during the cleanup of Shapiro's plant: "More than one hundred kilograms of enriched uranium—the amount allegedly diverted to Israel by Zalman Shapiro—was recovered from the decommissioned plant by 1982, with still more being recovered each year." Interestingly, the CIA seized on this missing-uranium fantasy to decide, for erroneous reasons, that Israel possessed nuclear weapons.

The term to which Lyndon Johnson had appointed me ended in August 1970, but because of strong endorsements by industrial and congressional leaders, Richard Nixon reappointed me as AEC chairman. I agreed to stay one more year because there was so much left to be done. My years with the AEC had been both rewarding and fascinating.

The AEC was unique in the history of American government. From the outset, nuclear energy was clearly a discovery whose applications could not be left to the private sector for a host of reasons, in particular the national security aspect of the weapons, but also the enormous costs. Research accelerators and reactors were expensive. An individual could build a steamboat. Corporations could take the technology of the railroad and spread it across the land. But government was the only entity that could develop nuclear technology. The AEC was established to fulfill its promise.

When I came in as chairman, the AEC was a huge enterprise with very broad-ranging powers, from the national security function of critical weapons testing and development to the encouragement of nuclear electric power to sponsoring research in pure and applied science. Its annual budget of $2.7 billion was fifth largest in the federal government; its physical plants represented an $8 billion investment. There were almost 7,000 employees, and contractors employing some 115,000 people.

The AEC was unusual in that it promoted and regulated all aspects of a technology that cut across many disciplines, unlike the more standard government approach of putting agricultural aspects in the Department of Agriculture, medical aspects in what was then called the Department of Health, Education, and Welfare, and so on.

The AEC was an independent federal agency, its position a little like that of the Federal Reserve. The five commissioners were appointed to set terms and could be removed only under extraordinary circumstances, which insulated them from the politics of successive presidential administrations. The President selected which commissioner chaired the commission, however.

And Congress's Joint Committee on Atomic Energy, which served as a legislative counterbalance, had special oversight powers: the Atomic Energy Act required that the AEC keep the Joint Committee "fully and currently informed" on all its activities. (This meant there was an additional outlet for possible leaks of sensitive information, which every administration found continually bothersome.) The AEC budget had to be authorized in detail by the Joint Committee before it entered the normal appropriations process. (According to a custom the committee established, its chairmanship alternated each congressional session between a House member and a Senate member. During my tenure the post moved between California Congressman Chet Holifield and Rhode Island Senator John Pastore.)

A study prepared at George Washington University said that the Joint Committee was probably the most powerful congressional committee in the history of the United States. It credited the committee with an ability to "overthrow executive authority," since "veteran committee members often have more technical knowledge of the atom than AEC commissioners, who might be serving for relatively short times." Some even questioned its constitutionality. According to a *Newsweek* article, Lewis Strauss, one of my predecessors, had complained that the Democrats on the committee treated him like "a valet" and "a schoolboy."

In this situation with its many traps, I managed to survive for ten years, though, and even thrive.

President Kennedy had started me on the right path, urging me to meet as soon as possible with Joint Committee member Senator Clinton Anderson. Anderson had been one of the reasons Kennedy had asked for a quick answer from me about my willingness to serve—Anderson had a crony from his home state he wanted to install as AEC chairman, and Kennedy needed to counter with a strong candidate of his own.

Anderson was a powerful senator who was not to be trifled with. Strauss had alienated him so badly that the two had become bitter enemies. When President Eisenhower had nominated Strauss to be Secretary of Commerce, a battle ensued that could be seen as poetic justice, considering Strauss's role in Robert Oppenheimer's security case. In a fashion reminiscent of the way Oppenheimer created his own problems in his testimony at his clearance hearing, Strauss tripped himself up and contradicted himself at his Senate confirmation hearing when asked about his own questionable dealings. Anderson led the Senate's rejection of Strauss' nomination, a humiliation suffered by only a handful of cabinet nominees in our history.

Washington was a town where they played hardball, so it was with some trepidation that I met with Senator Anderson. At our first meeting Anderson explained his differences with Strauss. In his arrogance, Strauss had often ignored his responsibility as AEC chairman to consult with and inform Congress about his decisions. Having myself witnessed Strauss's conscious destruction of Robert Oppenheimer, I could understand that one might easily come to dislike him.

Soon, our conversation turned to more personal matters, and I learned that one of Anderson's parents had emigrated from Sweden around the same time my mother had. He was as proud of his Swedish heritage as I was of mine, and this link gave us a personal tie that deepened over the years. I cultivated this sort of relationship with other members of Congress, and was in office long enough to form lasting bonds of mutual trust and respect.

One hallmark of my chairmanship was that I made scrupulous efforts to keep Congress and other interested parties posted on actions taken by the AEC that affected them. People will allow you a surprising amount of latitude in carrying out your duties, even actions they don't agree with, if you pay them the respect and courtesy of consulting them. Still, while I tried my best to get along, I didn't shy away from doing what I thought was right. An early example of this concerned Robert Oppenheimer, whose mistreatment in his security hearing some years before had caused a large rift in the scientific community—some scientists would not even speak to Edward Teller because he had testified against Oppie—and the government's actions had alienated many key figures, souring them about continuing to work with the government.

Every year the AEC presented an Enrico Fermi Award for outstanding achievement in the nuclear field. (I'd received the award in 1959.) I decided that the country could make partial amends by having the award go to Oppenheimer. I broached the possibility with Oppie when I saw him at President Kennedy's dinner for Nobel Prize winners. I also asked him if he'd be interested in having his security clearance restored, and he replied, "Not on your life," but he said he would be happy to accept the award. (In 1962, we presented the award to Edward Teller, which put him in a position in which he would seem extremely petty if he objected to Oppenheimer's receiving it the next year.) Then, one of the first things I did was to invite Lewis Strauss to lunch to break the news to him. He looked as if I'd leaned over the table and punched him, but he appreciated the fact that I told him.

I called Oppie's enemies in Congress and told each one of them personally. The Joint Committee convened for a special hearing to grill me about it. There are times when it is proper to be conciliatory or compromising, and there are times to stand your ground. In this case I simply wouldn't budge, and was willing to explain patiently as many times as they asked why I thought that no one deserved this award more than Robert Oppenheimer, given his tremendous contributions to the country. Some committee members were horrified at the prospect of honoring someone they labeled a "comsymp," and they questioned me over and over about his loyalty, and I explained why I believed it had been an injustice to strip him of his clearance. Eventually, I managed to get a majority vote endorsing the award. (Some committee members never got over this, and the committee later pettily cut the monetary part of the award in half; it was never clear to me how punishing future recipients of the award would punish us or Oppie, but I guess it made them feel better.)

President Kennedy established the practice of presenting the award at the White House. His assassination took place just weeks before the presentation of the award to Oppie, and I thought such a controversial moment was hardly one of the first things Johnson would want to face as President. I explained to him why the award was unpopular in Congress and said that it would be easy for him to distance himself—we could revert to the former practice and present the award at the AEC instead. But he gave his usual response—"Is it the right thing to do?"

and "Don't worry about Congress, I'll take care of them." (Johnson continued to present the award in the White House for all the subsequent years he was in office, but Richard Nixon refused to carry on the tradition.)

I have to admit that when I was called before Congress for one of their inquisitions, in a way it was perversely enjoyable. I relished the game of matching wits with the questioners. Some were worthy adversaries, some less so, and, in addition to the challenge of giving them the best information, there was the added challenge of remembering whom you were dealing with.

As I noted in the opening pages, when Senator Gore of Tennessee asked me about laying off machinists, I could answer with humor without fear that he would take offense or imagine that I was trying to make him look bad. He was interested in the question at hand, rather than personal issues. But that was not true of all members of Congress, and for many of them, the personal need to feel they were being treated correctly and not being embarrassed took precedence over policy considerations. At one hearing, a senator from Louisiana who was giving me a particularly hard time climaxed his questions with what he must have thought was the real clincher: "Dr. Seaborg, what do you know about plutonium?" My staff members almost laughed, but I knew that embarrassing this senator by exposing his ignorance would have been courting retribution at budget time. I managed to assure him gently that I did know something about the subject.

When I went before Congress for these inquisition-style hearings, I would try to be prepared—the Scout motto served me through school and beyond. But I would never let on that I didn't know the answer to a question. "I don't know" brought out the knives. But saying, "That's a good question that demands a careful answer," would buy me time to come up with one, and if I couldn't think of an answer, I'd simply answer a different question. I never gave the impression that I wasn't the master of the subject, and I spoke confidently, with a strong voice. Most of the time this worked, because the questioners paid more attention to how you behaved than to your actual answers.

Once, after I'd given one of these answers, Representative Craig Hosmer, a longtime Joint Committee member who knew me well, responded, "Thank you, I think."

I would answer a question of my choosing, but I would never lie. That was an important core principle for getting along successfully: Always tell the truth. If the moral argument that it's the right thing to do is not convincing on this point, there's a simple self-preservation motivation to telling the truth: I'm not smart enough to lie. If you tell the truth, there's only one version you have to remember. When you fabricate a story, later on you may not remember what you said. You'll have to keep track of what you said and whom you said it to. (And the truth will probably come out sooner or later anyway.) My memory is not good enough.

That principle served me in all aspects of life, and it brings to mind the other axioms I live by—and when I examine them I note that any "secrets of success" that have helped me are remarkably commonplace.

The first is to work hard, be prepared, and try to excel. All my life I've been surrounded by people who are smarter than I am, but I found I could always keep up by working hard.

The second is to avoid procrastinating—if there is something that needs doing, do it now. It won't take you any less time to do it tomorrow than today.

Do the worst thing first. When you have several things to do, do the most unpleasant, hardest one first. If you get it out of the way, you can look forward to the rest with the feeling that everything else you do that day will be easier.

Exercise regularly. I learned this at the Met Lab, but had to learn it over again when I came to Washington and initially let the job get in the way of taking care of myself. I took up hiking then, and I have been hiking ever since.

I used the approach I had with Congress in dealing with the press and many interest groups. Have your facts straight, answer all questions as forthrightly as you can, and never lie. And again on the personal level, I got acquainted with the most influential reporters and editors.

The importance of personal relationships and respect colored my approach to the commissioners, too. According to a *Newsweek* article, under Lewis Strauss, AEC "commissioners refused to speak to each other for months at a time." I had no interest in wasting time feuding. There was a certain fluidity in the power among the commissioners. We were supposed to be equal, with the chairman a little more equal, but the chairman naturally had more influence. Rather than following a top-down business management model, I found the collegial approach of campus-style management productive, and probably a major factor in my longevity at the AEC. A majority vote was enough to get a policy adopted or a question settled, but I found it advantageous to work by consensus. I generally wouldn't be satisfied with a majority vote, but kept making small changes and accommodations until I could get unanimous agreement. And when we disagreed, I found it more constructive to refrain from vociferous argument, and instead to point out the areas of agreement, to keep talking and to get along.

Because its reach was so broad, the AEC had been set up with five commissioners to allay concerns about concentrating too much power in the hands of a single individual. Early on in my tenure (1962), we commissioners agreed that circumstances had changed enough to reduce this fear; it was important to have an efficient decision-making process, and we recommended that the commission structure be replaced by a single administrator.

This was a remarkable step—a government administrative body recommending its own demise. But our proposal died because the Joint Committee was adamantly opposed. Later attempts at change were similarly unsuccessful. I must confess I was not too disappointed, because I found that the commission form of administration, although cumbersome, had many advantages, the foremost being that five minds were better than one.

One criticism of the AEC that grew throughout the 1960s was that it both promoted and regulated the peaceful uses of atomic energy, which was a conflict of interest, especially in the AEC's work with commercial nuclear power plants. One of my first official acts as chairman was to sign a reorganization order that removed the regulatory function from the supervision of the agency's general manager and placed it under a co-equal director of regulation in an office physically located in Bethesda, Maryland, some fifteen miles from the main AEC headquarters in Germantown. Both wings continued to report to the same five commissioners, however. I thought that the AEC did a competent job of regulation, but I recognized the validity of the criticism, and occasionally suggested to my colleagues that the AEC voluntarily take steps to separate the regulatory activity still further. I did not get much support from other commissioners, top AEC staff, or the Joint Committee, however, so I chose not to press the issue. I regret this failure on my part because this perception of an AEC conflict of interest added one more obstacle to the public's acceptance of nuclear power.

There were other failures as well. Perhaps the biggest disappointment of my time at the AEC is how little progress we made in the program to use nuclear explosions for peaceful purposes—Plowshare (from the passage in Isaiah 2:4: "They shall beat their swords into plowshares"). The program never produced much, despite my great hopes and some large expenditures.

One problem that held it back was of our own making. The Nuclear Nonproliferation Treaty committed the United States to making its technology for the peaceful use of atomic explosives available to nonnuclear countries as an incentive to discourage them from acquiring nuclear weapons themselves. But, as I've noted, the final Limited Test Ban Treaty of 1963 prohibited any nuclear explosion that "causes radioactive debris to be present outside the territorial limits of the State under whose jurisdiction or control such explosion is conducted." We should have recognized the effect this restrictive language (it was in our own drafts) would have on Plowshare, but we missed it, perhaps because we expected a Plowshare exemption would be included or perhaps because we were simply asleep at the switch.

For the remainder of my years at the AEC, different government agencies engaged in constant internal debate over the meaning of the word "debris." The State Department and the Arms Control and Disarmament Agency maintained that the clause prohibited the release of any detectable radiation at all, no matter how small, that would cross a territorial border. I thought this interpretation was ridiculous for a number of reasons, a main one being that it ignored the simple truth that whether or not debris was detectable depended not on how much debris was present but on the sensitivity of the equipment used to detect it. According to their way of thinking, a test might be permissible one year and not the next, when a new measuring device was invented, or might be permissible when the wind was blowing in one direction and not when it was blowing in another direction. (For example, we could do more tests at the Nevada Test Site when the wind was blowing from the south because our test site was closer to Mexico than to Canada.) Further, I did not think that a single pulse of radiation could be called "debris." I thought that the word "debris" in the case of radiation referred to an amount that had some practical significance, such as an effect on human health, if it were to be considered "present" under the treaty terms. This was the interpretation I had given to Congress when I testified that the treaty would not interfere with Plowshare (and if I had not given these assurances, it is doubtful that the treaty would have passed the Senate).

The Soviet Union's interpretation varied according to who was doing the testing. When the United States conducted a test and the Soviets managed to detect any radiation, they would  complain, and the State Department would bring this to our attention. It was no more than a diplomatic game, of course, because for their own tests they adopted the more liberal standard I supported. Once, for example, the Soviet Union complained that an American test had caused a two- to fivefold increase in fallout in certain regions. However, since the background radiation there was practically zero, a fivefold increase was still a minuscule amount of radioactivity.

The Plowshare program had been initiated following the Suez crisis of 1956, when the suggestion was made that nuclear explosives could be used to excavate a replacement canal that would be less vulnerable to disruption than the Suez Canal had been. Other projects we studied included proposals to shorten and improve the Santa Fe railroad's route across the Mojave Desert, to remove rapids from two South American rivers, to dig a sea-level canal in Thailand, to excavate several flood control and water management dams, and to study natural gas recovery.

We were enthusiastic about the program because early studies concluded that nuclear excavation offered an enormous cost advantage over conventional methods. As of 1970, it was estimated that ten kilotons of TNT would cost almost fifteen times as much as an equivalent thermonuclear explosive. Two million tons of TNT would cost 1,700 times as much. (The nuclear cost increases very little with yield.) An important factor in the cost comparisons was that the Plowshare program benefited from the weapons program's huge research and development costs. For example, Plowshare scientists could obtain much useful data from underground weapons tests.

Nuclear explosions also had the advantage of speed, accomplishing the job in a fraction of the time needed for conventional methods. They could do work that would be impossible using conventional means. For example, the United States came close to initiating a joint program with Australia in which five nuclear explosives buried under the ocean floor would excavate a narrow harbor on a remote portion of the Australian coast, making possible the shipment of iron ore from an otherwise inaccessible site. That project ended when economic developments made the iron ore no longer worth exporting.

In all, the United States conducted forty-one Plowshare experiments, many of them for studying the possibility of replacing the Panama Canal with a larger, sea-level one through Colombia. (In the 1960s, anti-American riots in Panama made us fear that the canal might be threatened.) The tests focused on developing "clean" devices, free from radioactive fallout, and on learning to predict the size and other characteristics of the craters. In 1960, a study had estimated that a nuclear-excavated canal would cost only one-third the price of one built by conventional means. This sort of estimate made the lure of the program irresistible. Coupled with the incentive of turning the destructive bomb to a beneficial use, it probably made us less than completely objective in weighing the arguments against nuclear excavation.

A study ten years later, however, found that the best nuclear-excavated canal route would cost $200 million more than the best conventional one; the earlier estimates had overlooked many costs of the former. Some of these had to do with the route, which would first require the evacuation of people who lived along it and then the construction of new infrastructure. (By then the situation in Panama had stabilized, so the conventional alternative would escape these costs by following the route of the existing canal.) The new canal would have required three hundred nuclear explosions, with accompanying worries about blast damage and radiation. Some feared the blasts might even trigger a major earthquake, a risk that most geologists considered extremely small but could not rule out. Biologists warned that a sea-level canal would dangerously mix Atlantic and Pacific aquatic species. Although we at the AEC thought it could be managed, radiation probably aroused the greatest concern. In any case, though the government had appointed a commission to study the canal possibilities, the Colombia option never really made it to the level of serious discussion because internal debate over the meaning of the test ban treaty terms led to constant postponements of tests.

We did perform three experimental explosions to stimulate the release of natural gas that was too tightly embedded in hard rock formations to be economically recoverable by conventional means. At the time, there appeared to be an imminent shortage of natural gas. (In 1969, *Oil and Gas Journal* was predicting that U.S. gas reserves would not meet demands by 1974.) The Bureau of Mines estimated that more than 300 trillion cubic feet of gas was potentially recoverable from the Rocky Mountain area if the program was successful.

One test involved a 29-kiloton explosive buried four thousand feet deep in New Mexico. It was very successful inasmuch as a production rate several times greater than that of neighboring wells was achieved, but the gas was slightly radioactive, so none of it was sold commercially. A second explosive, a 50-kiloton device buried eight thousand feet in Colorado, resulted in a copious flow of natural gas: more than 400 million cubic feet of gas was liberated within seventy days, more than had been produced in five years of conventional exploitation of the site. There was a very small amount of radiation present in the gas, well within limits to assure public health, but just the same, it was above zero, so none of this gas was sold commercially either. (The third explosion came in Colorado in 1973, after I'd left the AEC. It was a more complicated scheme and failed to achieve its objectives.)

These experiments proved that nuclear explosives could be useful in natural gas recovery. Of course, the predictions of natural gas shortages proved to be way off the mark, and there ended up being no need for the program.

More important, though, the public was not ready for this use of nuclear explosives. The Colorado tests attracted strong public protest and led to a 1974 amendment to the state constitution requiring a referendum on each nuclear explosion proposed to take place within the state.

Since that 1973 test, the United States has conducted no peaceful nuclear explosions.

Still, Plowshare made significant contributions to basic research, including experiments in producing elements heavier than plutonium, and many heavy isotopes were identified for the first time because of them. But we never succeeded in developing explosives free of radioactivity and could not quell public concern about their use. In retrospect, I believe we spent too much time and money on these doomed experiments.

(The Soviet Union also had a peaceful nuclear explosions program. Theirs began long after ours, around 1968, and continued until Mikhail Gorbachev announced a unilateral moratorium on nuclear tests in 1985. Their projects included construction of a water reservoir in a dry riverbed for storing heavy spring runoff, stimulation of oil recovery from a geologic formation that had been depleted according to conventional standards, and the creation of storage areas in salt formations near petroleum supplies. As late as 1983, the scientific attaché of the Soviet embassy in Washington emphasized to me that his country considered that peaceful explosions would have considerable importance in the future.)

Another issue on which the AEC erred was in dealing with nuclear waste. It left behind a terrible legacy—the massive residue of contaminated wastes at Hanford and other nuclear materials production sites, the full extent of which did not come to light until the late 1980s. The General Accounting Office has estimated that Hanford's waste tanks alone leaked 80,000 gallons of contaminated water into the soil. Department of Energy officials have estimated that cleaning up the complex will take thirty years and cost $100 billion.

The atomic bomb effort was undertaken with frantic haste during World War II. Du Pont, the first contractor, did an excellent job of bringing the project to fruition, following what were then standard industrial practices for waste disposal and storage. As experience began to indicate that improvements were needed, the AEC tried during the 1960s to get better waste tanks built, but the Bureau of the Budget repeatedly denied funds for this work, saying that an upgrade was something that could be deferred "until next year." I regret I did not attach sufficient importance to this problem to make it a subject for appeal to the President. Taking on the work then would have avoided a tremendous amount of environmental damage and later expense.

But all in all, I'm proud of the AEC's record of achievements in the 1960s, a decade when nuclear science made great strides. For instance, an extraordinary number of nuclear-powered naval vessels were launched: forty-four attack submarines, thirty-eight Polaris missile submarines, one aircraft carrier, and three guided-missile cruisers. Nuclear power was an incredible innovation for the submarine. During World War II, a submarine would have to resurface regularly in a time frame measured in days or hours in order to run its engines and recharge its batteries. The nuclear sub made that obsolete; it could live beneath the waves indefinitely. And, armed with nuclear missiles, it made a first strike against the United States something only a madman who accepted the destruction of his own country would try.

This success was of course the work of the brilliant, articulate, and irascible Admiral Hyman Rickover. He was one of the most intense personalities I ever encountered; in a relationship that stretched for decades from the 1940s, I don't think I ever saw him smile. He headed what was supposed to be the joint Navy-AEC naval reactors program, but although we commissioners had good rapport with him, we couldn't claim we gave much direction to his program. The Navy was equally unable to control him, and successive Navy Secretaries engaged in the futile exercise of trying to get rid of him. But he had too much influence and support in Congress. His power was unique, but if he hadn't been as successful as he was, he couldn't have gotten away with it. I never saw any point in challenging his rule of the program—who would you get to run it who was better?

When he finally retired—long past the age for almost everyone else—President Reagan refused to permit a military band to be present at the ceremony because Rickover had somehow slighted him. I found that amusing: I doubt there was a President, Navy Secretary, or anyone else that Rickover hadn't offended at some point.

In the medical sphere, the AEC had helped advance nuclear medicine to such an extent that by 1971 there were about six million applications a year of radioisotopes for a variety of diagnostic and therapeutic purposes. As for the AEC's record in basic and applied science, it was substantial. For example, under its aegis a generator was developed that converts the radioactive energy from a plutonium isotope to electricty. The Apollo 12 astronauts left on the moon an array of instruments powered entirely by this system that are still working thirty years later. And we put tremendous effort into making heavy isotopes, converting a reactor at the Savannah River plant to this use at a cost of hundreds of thousands of dollars. The Joint Committee, suspicious that I was trying to put something over on them by devoting all these resources to research in my own field, grilled me about this effort at times. These suspicions were understandable, but the work put us ahead of the Soviet Union in the heavy isotope field and kept us there, and we're still using the fruits of these reactions in research.

Another of the great research successes of the period was the decision to build a huge accelerator. The process we used to build support for the project deserves some consideration and even illustrates the power for positive social change that these projects can have.

The project got its start in May 1963, when a panel representing the President's Science Advisory Committee and the AEC's General Advisory Committee recommended that the federal government construct a high-energy proton accelerator in the unprecedented energy range of 200 billion electron volts (BeV). (This energy level was a 10,000-fold increase over that of the 60-inch cyclotron built before World War II and about six times more powerful than our most potent accelerator of that time.) The panel's report emphasized the positive effect of the national high-energy physics program on education throughout the country; this went further than the training of graduate and postdoctoral students, because many scientists in high-energy physics had a strong influence on education at all levels. The panel also noted that high-energy physics was receiving great attention abroad, with Europe's CERN 28 BeV proton synchrotron already yielding important scientific data. The United States did not want to fall behind. The cost of the accelerator was estimated at $350 million (in 1960s dollars), so there could be only one such facility in the United States, and it would of necessity be made open to all qualified experimenters.

There was congressional support for such research in the Joint Committee on Atomic Energy, but its members pointed out that without the

President's backing the idea would go nowhere. I forwarded a report, "Policy for National Action in the Field of High Energy Physics," which included the recommendation for the accelerator, to President Johnson, who responded positively. About the same time, the National Academy of Sciences hosted a meeting of twenty-five university presidents at which this topic was on the agenda. That meeting set in motion the formation of the Universities Research Association, which would be under contract with the AEC to construct and operate the accelerator. The idea was soon accepted that we should have a national competition to choose the accelerator site. With miraculous speed, and very early on, the debate had shifted from whether to build the accelerator to where to build it. This was a key to the project's success. The obvious show of support made potential opponents appear out of step with progress.

The AEC quickly compiled a list of criteria for the site, which included suitable geology, availability of electricity and water, adequate space (about 4,000 acres), proximity to a transportation hub and to a large university and research and development base, and quality-of-life aspects that would attract staff. The AEC began accepting site proposals in April 1965, and formed a task group that evaluated two hundred potential locations in forty-six states. This process identified eighty-five possible sites, which were passed on to the National Academy of Sciences for further study that September. Eight teams inspected the sites and gathered more data. The National Academy of Sciences study group then narrowed the choice to six recommended sites by March 1966.

When the civil rights bill had passed, President Johnson had urged everyone in his administration to emphasize—in speeches, in meetings, and at any other opportunity—the need for compliance with the new law. We knew that the accelerator was a plum for whatever area received it, with many short-term construction jobs and, later, long-term, high-quality jobs at the facility; we wanted to make sure that whoever got this prize earned it. So the AEC solicited information from agencies such as the Commission on Civil Rights and the Equal Employment Opportunity Commission on the civil rights status of the sites. The AEC commissioners visited each one, in part to obtain commitments from local authorities and other groups regarding equal opportunity. AEC staff and power consultants met with representatives of utilities that would serve the sites.

President Johnson—in his familiar way of asking "Is it the right thing to do?"—left the decision entirely in AEC hands, despite what must have been some strong political pressures to intervene on behalf of one site or another. In fact, he specifically requested that he not be notified in advance of the public announcement, as an extra shield to show his hands-off approach.

In December, we announced the selection of Weston, Illinois, outside Chicago. But as the time approached to build the accelerator, we ran into a problem: we had not received the commitments on fair housing that we had required from the communities there. Our allies in Congress threatened to stall the authorization for the project. The AEC commissioners met with the mayors of local towns, and I implored them to act quickly to eliminate racial discrimination, because it was still possible that the nation would select another site. The Chicago media characterized my statement as an "ultimatum." The period that followed was agonizing to me because I truly did not want to delay the project or pull it out of Weston. But within months, fourteen communities in commuting distance of Weston announced the enactment of fair housing ordinances.

Robert R. Wilson was named laboratory director—the same Bob Wilson who'd met Helen and me in Santa Fe during the war to transfer the plutonium sample under the protection of his hunting rifle. On December 1, 1968, on a wintry Chicago day with about a thousand people attending the ceremony, Bob Wilson and I broke ground for the project. I said at the ceremony: "Symbolically, we could say that the spade that breaks ground on this site today begins our deepest penetration yet into the mysteries of the physical forces that comprise our universe." Following the suggestion of Congressman Frank Annunzio and others, the National Accelerator Laboratory was named in honor of Enrico Fermi.

Operation began on March 1, 1972, when the laboratory started a successful program of research that did in fact penetrate into the mysteries of the universe as far as a machine of that size could. But, as always, there are more steps along the research road and, eventually, a need for a still larger machine. This was the ill-fated supercollider, and its sad story is in sharp contrast to the planning and execution of Fermilab. We got such a large cross section of people and interests to support the process of competing for the site for the accelerator that they could hardly then turn around and oppose spending the money to build it.

The failure to follow a process like this one killed the supercollider, the last large piece of scientific apparatus that has been proposed in the national arena. Rather than running a fair and open competition, giving as many people as possible a stake in it, the plans for the supercollider gave every appearance of being wired, and President George H. W. Bush's adopted state of Texas was awarded the plum. What a contrast that is to a conversation I had with President Johnson when it appeared that a site possibility in Texas would be eliminated from the accelerator competition early. He remarked to me that early elimination would be an embarrassment to him, yet he thought Texas was really not the right place to build it. When it came time for the supercollider, Texas was still not a good place, and with the siting decision politicized, the whole project seemed like a pork-barrel one. Thus, with Bush out of power and the federal budget tight, a new Congress killed it outright: as a pork-barrel project rather than a project with a large community of scientists and universities supporting it, it was easy to cut.

In better economic times with a more generous federal budget, perhaps the supercollider can be resurrected. Some opponents deride it as now outdated Big Science, but if we want to make advances in particle physics and other areas that concern the most basic building blocks of matter, there is no other choice. Well, perhaps there is the option of saying, "We know enough already, why continue?" I am certainly grateful that Ernest Lawrence did not take this line before the first of the high-tech colliders was developed. Otherwise, we could not now have the many isotopes used in medicine and many other valuable improvements for mankind.

A common question is: What will you find if you build it? Lawrence once answered such a query by saying, "If I knew that, I wouldn't need to build the damn thing." We don't know what we will find. It's a modern version of the saying "Where there is no vision, the people will perish." We need to keep pushing the boundaries. We need to forge ahead with new science.

# NINETEEN

# NUCLEAR POWER: ITS PAST AND FUTURE

Civilian nuclear electric power made great strides during the 1960s, advancing from experimental prototypes to being a reliable supplier of large amounts of electricity. I worked hard to get it moving forward, starting with a time-honored means of making the government act: my administrative assistant Howard Brown and I planted an idea in the White House; President Kennedy responded by asking the AEC to present him with a study, the very one we wanted to do. He directed the AEC to take a "new and hard look at the role of nuclear power in our economy."

The report we wrote demonstrated a growing national and international need for electric power and argued that a vigorous civilian nuclear power program would help fill this need. We pointed out the many advantages of nuclear power: it could extend indefinitely America's fuel reserves (which were believed to be limited), eliminate geographic variations in power costs, place the United States in a position of international leadership, improve its defense posture, and reduce air pollution. I found that last point particularly appealing—one thing that has always excited me about nuclear power is that it is the cleanest form of large-scale electrical generation we know. The report predicted that nuclear power was on the verge of being priced competitively with other sources in high-cost power areas, and had the potential to expand from there. It forecast a nuclear-generating capacity in the United States of 5,000 megawatts by 1970 and 40,000 megawatts by 1980 (for a sense of scale, 1,000 megawatts is enough to supply a city the size of San Francisco), provided there was a vigorous program to which both government and industry contributed. Our report had the hoped-for effect of jump-starting the Kennedy administration's effort.

By 1962, some three dozen experimental nuclear power reactors had been built, testing several competing types. The technology was advancing rapidly, and the research was paying off—in March 1964 Jersey Central Light and Power Company chose nuclear power over competing fossil-fuel alternatives for a new 515-megawatt plant, in a decision based strictly on economics. The president of Jersey Central's parent company called me to break the news, elated that his company had been able to beat the high cost of oil and coal in the Northeast. He predicted that the time had come when nuclear power would be that region's power of choice.

We didn't realize at the time that General Electric had submitted a fixed-price bid on the plant that was below its cost, in the hope of stimulating business and making up any losses by spreading out development costs as more plants were ordered. It certainly stimulated orders. By 1967, more than half the new generating capacity ordered by U.S. utilities was nuclear. In 1966–68, U.S. utilities ordered sixty-seven reactors ranging in size all the way up to 1,100 megawatts. By the time I left the AEC in 1971, there were twenty-five operable units, fifty-two units under construction or being reviewed for operating licenses, and thirty-nine units under AEC review for construction permits. Utilities had signed contracts but not yet filed construction applications for fourteen more. In all, that meant there were 130 nuclear power plants built, under construction, or planned, with a capacity of more than 108,600 megawatts.

The American demand for electricity was growing by leaps and bounds, and nuclear power was there at the right time to meet it. Utilities were looking to build larger plants, which favored nuclear power because it became more economical as plant size increased. Economic projections also favored nuclear power over its competitors. Remarkably, in one generation, this new technology came to supply 20 percent of our electricity. That was as much electricity as the entire country used around 1940, when the discovery of fission sparked our dream of this power source. That's an amazing success story, and it was achieved without cutting corners and without endangering the public.

We nuclear power boosters expected the growth to continue, but as is well known, nuclear power has faltered, if not stopped, in America. No utility has ordered a reactor since the accident in 1979 at Three Mile Island in Pennsylvania, and the industry is commonly considered dead.

But that is hardly the way to describe an industry that continues to supply one-fifth of U.S. electricity and 17 percent of the world's electricity. In some countries it may be disappearing, but it is thriving in nations that have adopted a sound approach. In Japan, it supplies 25 percent of total electricity, a percentage expected to grow to more than 40 percent in the next decade, and it provides 75 percent of France's electricity.

What went wrong in the United States? The answer is more complex than most people think. The environmental movement undoubtedly contributed to the slowdown, but there was much more to it.

The environmental movement broke like a tidal wave. One survey found that in May 1969 only 1 percent of respondents considered the environment the most important issue facing the President. Just two years later this number had climbed to 25 percent. Some 20 million people around the country rallied on the first Earth Day, April 22, 1970. Before then, the only opposition to proposed nuclear plants had been local, based on concern about despoiling natural values, such as the scenery and beaches of the Pacific coastline, or location, such as the safety of nuclear power plants if built near earthquake faults or population centers. Now, however, new opposition began to appear that was concerned with more fundamental ecological problems, such as air and water pollution.

I was somewhat blindsided by the environmental antinuclear movement because I viewed nuclear power as the cleanest and most environmentally benign of our power choices. The first commercial nuclear facility had been a demonstration plant near Pittsburgh, a city historically beset with hideously dirty air from nearby steel plants belching coal smoke. Pittsburgh was implementing pollution abatement programs, and the utility chose nuclear power because it was much cleaner than the other options for large-scale electricity generation.

At the AEC we tried hard to live up to our environmental responsibilities. In November 1970, Dr. Gordon J. MacDonald of the Council on Environmental Quality said, "The AEC has by far the best record of any federal agency in submitting environmental reports under [the National Environmental Policy Act]. The AEC reports are the most complete, the best thought-out, and the most sophisticated of any agency." But if we had made nuclear power live up to its other promises, it is doubtful that environmental opposition would have stopped it.

In his book *Nuclear Renewal*, Richard Rhodes writes, "Everyone who has studied the rise and fall of nuclear power in the U.S. has reached the same broad conclusion: nuclear power stumbled to its present impasse because the technology was commercialized too narrowly [without adequately studying options] and too soon. How manufacturers, government regulators, and utilities all contrived to take such an expensive wrong turn in lockstep is a classic tale of enthusiasm gone awry."

I can't claim to be blameless in that my early boosterism of nuclear power may have contributed to later problems. Because of an impatience to achieve economic benefits quickly, U.S. nuclear plants were prematurely escalated in size to proportions that strained the technology and magnified the potential consequences of an accident, no matter how unlikely. In response to this and other problems, new regulatory requirements were introduced and consequent long delays—either required by regulations or caused by lawsuits—made for such steep escalations in cost that nuclear power no longer seemed able to compete economically with fossil-fuel plants.

In the 1980s, *Forbes* magazine ran a cover story that said, "The failure of the U.S. nuclear power program ranks as the largest managerial disaster in business history." It pointed out that the problem was not necessarily the technology but, rather, the company implementing it: Duke Power built a plant at a competitive cost of $932 a kilowatt, while Long Island Lighting's plant cost more than five times as much. It was the sometimes spectacular failures that gave nuclear power the reputation for being uneconomical.

These peculiarities of the American system blocked nuclear power in the United States, but we need only look to France to see how things could have been different. France entered the nuclear power field relatively late (which allowed it to learn from our experience), but then committed itself to a thorough strategy based mainly on picking a single, standardized reactor design and sticking with it. In the United States, every reactor is redesigned practically from the ground up, which makes each plant present individual design, construction, and regulatory problems, with accompanying cost increases. Nuclear Regulatory Commission chairman Ivan Selin once quipped that in France "there are 365 kinds of cheese and one kind of reactor. In the United States it's the opposite." One consequence is that the French (and Japanese) can build a plant in five years, while in the United States the average is twice as long. That's the main reason their price is competitive. (Long construction periods raise capital costs because a utility must borrow more money and wait longer before receiving a return on its investment.) And, Rhodes reports, "with nuclear power and stringent conservation, the French have been able to reduce their dependence on imported energy sources from 77 to 50 percent (and their air pollution by a factor of five)."

But doesn't France suffer from the commonly accepted environmental "problems" of nuclear power, such as radiation release, accidents, and wastes? Keep in mind that there are more than 300 nuclear plants in operation around the world, and in the almost forty-year history of commercial nuclear power, there has not been a single death or even serious injury caused by an American-style reactor anywhere in the world. And the nuclear industry has a worker-accident rate one-third that of industry as a whole.

The radiation released from a nuclear power plant during normal operation is insignificant in the context of the radiation we all receive every day. (The unit for measuring radiation is called the rem, and is usually referred to in units one-thousandth of that amount, or millirem.) The average American receives a dose of about 350 millirem per year from background radiation. Most of this exposure, 200 millirem on average, comes from radon gas in your home. If you live at sea level, you get another 25 to 30 from cosmic rays; this exposure increases with altitude, so in Denver you receive an extra 50 or so. Sleeping in the same bed with another person can raise your exposure by a millirem; living in a brick house compared with a wooden house can raise it; heating and cooling with natural gas can raise your exposure by 6 millirem.

If you live next door to a nuclear plant, the plant will add less than a millirem to your background exposure. You'll receive more radiation by living downwind from a coal-burning plant (because of radioactive impurities in the coal). You'll be exposed to more radiation (by a factor of 100) from working in the U.S. Capitol building or New York's Grand

Central Station, where the granite walls contain uranium. If you're a good conservationist and caulk your windows and seal your walls, trapping in your house's air will raise your exposure to radiation more than living near a nuclear plant will.

That's fine for normal operation, you might say, but what about accidents? Wasn't a great deal of radiation released in the accidents at Three Mile Island and Chernobyl?

The accident at Three Mile Island, which many people point to as proof that nuclear power is unsafe, actually demonstrated how safe our nuclear plants are. At Three Mile Island, everything that could possibly go wrong went wrong. It's hard to imagine more going wrong. A pressure-relief valve stuck open, so cooling water that should have been pouring into the malfunctioning reactor poured out instead. Unaware of this problem, inexperienced and confused control-room operators shut down the emergency pumps that they should have used to cool the reactor (and that would have done the job without their intervention). There followed an almost contagious combination of other equipment breakdowns and malfunctions as well. With no cooling water, the reactor core overheated and underwent a meltdown, the feared occurrence that nuclear opponents called the China Syndrome because, they said, the core might not stop melting everything in its path until it reached China. But a third of the core melted, and it didn't come anywhere near China. In fact, it never breached its containment. Still, with all these problems combined, the result was a rather mild accident in which no one was hurt. Admittedly, it was disastrous from the point of view of the owner of the plant, who had a huge cleanup job.

Small amounts of radiation were released into the atmosphere. Estimates of the nearby public's radiation exposure range from 1 to 10 millirem. But, because Three Mile Island is located in an area that is naturally high in radon, it's estimated that the average resident's background radiation is 2.5 millirem *per day*. So it's impossible to separate out the dose people received from the accident release from the much higher doses they receive normally in their homes. An exhaustive Columbia University study released in 1990, a decade after the accident, found no correlation between evident exposure of those who lived near the reactor and the development of the types of cancer associated with radiation.

The main effect of the accident, then, was that nuclear regulators and the nuclear industry learned from it; they implemented reforms that improved plant safety.

What about Chernobyl? The Chernobyl reactor design is so different from American ones that worrying about American plants because of Chernobyl is like refusing to ride in a Volvo because the gas tanks in a Ford Pinto are dangerous. Most important, the Chernobyl plant was built without the containment structure that is routinely included in American plants.

My colleague, the physicist Hans Bethe, served on a select scientific panel convened to assess the accident, which concluded, "The Chernobyl disaster tells us about the deficiencies of the Soviet political and administrative system rather than about problems with nuclear power." Other studies have found that (even with the flawed reactor design) a Western-style containment structure would have limited the radioactivity release to little to none. Improvements have been introduced in Soviet-style reactors since then, but the United States and other countries should provide aid so that dangerous reactors there can be decommissioned. Nuclear plants have been and will be built around the world, so the greater the American involvement, the greater the opportunity to ensure that they are built safely.

It's now been two decades since Three Mile Island; nuclear power has kept such a low profile that many people seem to have forgotten it, or have the impression that it just went away. But it still produces 20 percent of our electricity. People remember Three Mile Island, the accident where no one was hurt. Less than two months after it, an airplane crash in Chicago killed 275 people—but who can remember all the airline crashes? We expect that people will die in airplane crashes; we accept the deaths of thousands of people on our highways each year. Yet we worry about nuclear power.

What about the supposedly intractable problem of storing nuclear waste? The problem does not seem so intractable to those who deal with the waste, who believe they have more than one perfectly acceptable solution. The problem is less a technical one than the political one of choosing a solution and implementing it.

I favor the deep-burial plan, in which wastes are locked away deep inside a mountain. Can we be sure the wastes will be safe there for the centuries it takes for them to decay? A precedent actually exists in the Oklo formation in Gabon. When the earth was billions of years younger and the uranium newer, the percentage of fissionable U-235 was much higher, high enough that a natural chain reaction occurred. There was a natural nuclear reactor in this African formation that went on for several hundred thousand years and generated the same kinds of radioactive fission products that are formed in a power reactor. These fission products have long since decayed, but we know they were there because of the isotopes they left. In all this time, almost two billion years since the reaction ended, the fission products didn't migrate, but stayed put in the formation, a few feet underground. So we know that fission products can be held underground in a formation. That's one reason I believe that with the precautions we plan to take at the proposed long-term repository at Yucca Mountain in Nevada, the wastes will be safe for the indefinite future. The advantage of this approach is that if there is a complete breakdown in our civilization and a return to the Dark Ages, the wastes would be out of the way and harmless.

Other countries have found other solutions. In Sweden, for example, they have designed a canister that can contain the wastes long enough for the dangerous elements to decay. In France they reprocess the waste and reuse much of it, greatly reducing its total amount, which they then store in repositories.

The antinuclear forces have an unfortunate tendency to use scare tactics. They emphasize that nuclear wastes are radioactive for thousands of years. What they don't mention is that the really dangerous stuff decays within a few hundred years. That's still a long time, but storing it is not nearly so difficult as trying to keep high-level wastes safe for thousands of years.

What about transporting this waste to the repository—how safe is that? The wastes are transported in casks that have been subjected to rigorous tests (such as tying them to the front of a truck and charging at a concrete wall at 80 miles per hour: the truck was destroyed, the cask slightly damaged). In fifty years of shipping radioactive waste, there has never been a radiation-induced injury to a member of the public. Granted, the transportation of dangerous wastes is not entirely risk-free—and that brings us to the issue of risks. No source of power is risk-free, but nuclear power stacks up well against the other choices. We should assess the risks of nuclear power as we assess the risks in an arms control agreement against doing nothing. Building the plants entails risk, but if we don't build them, if we continue the status quo, we will eventually run up against the greater risks inherent in a continued program of conventional power plants.

The public tends to be illogical in evaluating risks. Many people attach special fear to the hazards of radiation, perhaps because of its association with nuclear weapons, perhaps because of its unseen nature, and perhaps because of a distrust of large-scale, government-sponsored technology. People act as if the source of the radiation is more important than the effects, so are far more accepting of medical X rays, transcontinental flights, and cosmic radiation, for example, and far less accepting of routine power plant releases, than the statistical risks justify. Few people deciding whether to move to Denver or take an airplane trip would factor in the additional radiation exposure in either experience, but many would worry about proximity to a nuclear plant. Small wonder that when using a nuclear magnetic resonance spectrometer to diagnose a patient, doctors have learned to drop the "nuclear" and call it magnetic resonance imaging.

Often those who argue that low doses of radiation are dangerous extrapolate a linear relationship from the problems that high doses cause, which is misleading. True, we still know less than we'd like to about the effects of low doses of radiation—it's so omnipresent that controlled studies are difficult to perform—but there is even some evidence that low doses of radiation could be beneficial. A few studies, for instance on shipbuilders exposed to higher levels of radiation than the general population, found fewer cancers among these people, and there is evidence of fewer cases of some cancer types in the cosmic-ray states of Colorado and Wyoming. We know that larger amounts of radiation can be used to treat cancer by killing the cancer cells; one could speculate that smaller amounts are deterring cancer before it gets started.

Compared with the amount of worry about radiation and nuclear power, the public gives a free ride to competing sources of power such as coal-burning plants. Bernard Cohen, a professor of physics and radiation health at the University of Pittsburgh, calculated the exposures of people worldwide to the radiation spread from Chernobyl, the largest nuclear power disaster in history by far, and figured that over fifty years it will be enough "to cause about 16,000 deaths." That's a tremendously high number, but, Cohen goes on to note, it "is still less than the number of deaths caused *every year* by air pollution from coal-burning power plants in the United States" (emphasis added). Cohen complains that people talk about nuclear waste and ignore "coal waste"—what we more commonly call air pollution. He calculates the lethal toll of additional air pollution caused by coal-burning electricity plants at "30,000 Americans a year." Some estimates put the figure at "only" 10,000, but even this rate means that the fifty-year worldwide Chernobyl toll is equal to the eighteen-month American coal-pollution toll.

Of course, air pollution is only one problem associated with coal-burning plants. There are also the deaths of coal miners from accidents and black lung; the transportation accidents involved in moving tons and tons of coal; the environmental costs of digging the coal. In West Virginia today, whole mountains are being leveled, their tops bulldozed, the valleys filled, altering the topography of huge areas. The state has granted permits allowing 27,000 acres—an area about an eighth the size of Shenandoah National Park—to be razed in this fashion. Burning the coal will pollute the air, and you can imagine what this form of "mining" does to water quality.

Coal is dirty, but at least it's domestic. What about oil? The United States imports so much oil that it puts us in an untenable position—and we recently fought a war to protect our oil supplies, at great cost to the environment. Despite ample experience with our vulnerability on this issue, we import a higher percentage of our oil than we did in the 1970s—more than 50 percent.

Turning away from nuclear power—in part because of worries about potential catastrophes—has led to a greater use of fossil fuels. And now we're seeing that burning fossil fuels can lead to one of the greatest catastrophes ever—the greenhouse effect of global warming and unpredictable climate change. A primary culprit in the greenhouse effect is our addition of carbon dioxide to the atmosphere; a single large coal-burning plant produces 15 tons of carbon dioxide *a minute*. (Most newer plants burn natural gas, which is less polluting than coal but still a greenhouse gas producer.)

Why do we need more power? Why can't we just go with conservation? The oil crisis of the 1970s brought conservation into our consciousness in a powerful way—we increased our energy efficiency and developed a pretty good record in conservation—yet in the fifteen years between 1975 and 1990, our electricity consumption jumped 50 percent. The Department of Energy is still sponsoring conservation efforts; taking these efforts fully into account, it predicts that U.S. electricity consumption will rise another 50 percent in the next twenty years. Where will this power come from?

A country as profligate with energy as the United States can benefit from conservation, but in the developing world there are billions of people who envy our access to abundant energy at the flip of a switch. We take it for granted, and they would like to take it for granted, too. But only energy production, not conservation, can help them raise their standards of living.

The problem with much antinuclear activism is that it is unrealistic (if not elitist) and deals in false choices. By blocking nuclear power plants, many environmentalists seem to think that they are blocking the growth in the demand for power. But that is false. Power plants will be built, and we should not be building environmentally destructive fossil-fuel-burning plants. In my view, an environmentalist blocking a nuclear plant is winning a battle and losing the war. For example, to meet increased suburban demand, power plants are being sited in less populated spots just outside the borders of metropolitan areas' air quality control programs. These locations subject the plants to looser regulations and move the pollution zones farther out from the city centers into the country. Nuclear plants would attract attention and opposition; with fossil-fuel plants there can be an insidious creep.

Another argument favoring nuclear over fossil-fuel power plants is that it is unwise to burn irreplaceable hydrocarbon reserves, which have better uses than generating electricity. We need oil to power our transportation vehicles over air, sea, and ground until a better portable energy system is invented, and natural gas to heat our homes. And we use petroleum's precious organic chemical bonds, made through eons-long synthesis by nature, to manufacture plastics, drugs, dyes, clothing, and a host of other compounds.

What about power sources like the sun and the wind? I'm in favor of using them as much as possible—but they will meet only a small portion of our energy needs. Their proponents always seem to think that a big breakthrough in their use is just around the corner, but their advance has not been limited by a lack of research or technology. The inherent difficulty of using solar energy is that it is so diffuse. If you wanted to build a large-scale electricity-generating plant, it would be so huge that it would create environmental complaints and problems of its own. Solar power can be used in decentralized situations, but in the quarter century since the advent of energy awareness, few have been willing to take the initiative to install solar panels—more people want to be on the grid, not off it.

Hydroelectric power? Not only have most usable sites been taken but there's now movement in the opposite direction—dismantling some dams. And huge facilities, such as the ill-fated proposal for Canada's James Bay, have their own environmental problems.

I'm confident nuclear power will make a comeback when we finally realize its value. Perhaps we will eventually calculate a grim "death per kilowatt-hour" statistic that will convince the public that nuclear power is the safest form of energy available. Perhaps the increasing air pollution will make people reconsider nuclear power, perhaps global warming, perhaps energy shortages. Perhaps inspired leadership will provide a turning point—I have often counseled political candidates that the antinuclear view is a minority one.

When the public does turn back to nuclear power, they will find that the next generation of nuclear power plants will be even safer than the ones in use today. The current generation of reactors achieved a remarkable safety record despite a design that requires active safety systems to shut them down. (That is, if a problem develops, the chain reaction will shut down automatically, but the reactor fuel can continue heating unless cooling water is added.) New plants would be passively safe, in that they would rely on natural forces such as gravity and convection to avoid meltdowns in an emergency, with a minimum of human intervention, just as a circuit breaker prevents electrical overloads.

A new generation of reactors could be priced very competitively if utilities used one standardized design, as the French do. (It's not that French reactor technology is better than ours—their reactors are based on U.S. designs.) Then large portions of the plants would be prefabricated at the factory, where quality control is easier and labor productivity higher, and they could be simpler in design, with fewer pumps, valves, and other appurtenances. The Nuclear Regulatory Commission could give a standardized plant advance certification, eliminating the uncertainties associated with today's custom-built plants. With these improvements and a rational reassessment of its value, nuclear power could return to help meet our growing energy needs.

# TWENTY

# A PROFESSOR AGAIN

In the fall of 1971, I left the AEC and eagerly moved back to Berkeley. I'd received many job offers over the years, including a dozen from universities to be president and one to be vice president of a major corporation, but research and teaching were the loves I wanted to return to. A former AEC chairman returning to teach freshman chemistry was noteworthy enough that *The New York Times* ran a picture of me meeting my first class. (I turned down requests from local television stations to cover it because I didn't want to shortchange the students; a campus public-affairs officer snapped the photo.) The behind-the-scenes story was about how hard I'd worked to get ready for this class.

After more than a decade's absence, it took serious study to get myself back up to speed. To teach, you really have to know your material, and I took preparation for the classroom as seriously as getting ready for a meeting with the President of the United States. At one point, I had to alter my usual open-door policy and ask my assistant to hold my calls while I worked out all the textbook's problems to make sure that I could. When she poked her head in a couple of hours later, she was greatly amused that my only comment was, "This is *hard*."

I taught a freshman chemistry laboratory section for ten years after my return, and my hard work was rewarded with high evaluations from the students. I also took on the job of adviser to a "Freshman Cluster Group." I'd meet once a week for a brown-bag lunch with six to ten students, just to talk about how they were getting along, to bring in other professors for informal talks, and the like. I got acquainted with a lot of students that way, and it was a great pleasure to see more than one of them continue through school, get higher degrees, and even work with me. When it comes to benefits, teaching is definitely a two-way street. I enjoyed the contact with the kids, the enthusiasm of their personalities was infectious, and they kept me alert and intellectually challenged.

I took on some graduate students, and of course resumed research, striking up several partnerships and finding I could still make significant contributions to nuclear science. It was still exciting to me to investigate the nuclear properties of the transuranium elements, to synthesize and identify new isotopes, to study the chemistry of the transuranium elements, and to investigate the dream of finding the superheavy elements—the elements in the region of atomic number 114. The half-lives of the elements were getting shorter as they grew heavier, but I believed there might be an "island of stability" near the end of the row on the periodic table.

I joined Al Ghiorso's group for at least one important project. By now our roles had reversed: he was the team leader, and I was happy just to be included. Al had certainly earned his stripes, coming up with ever more innovative experiments and ever more powerful accelerators. In my absence, Al had continued to push his way up the periodic table, and by then was a co-discoverer of elements 95 through 105, a record number.

In 1974, our group used the heavy ion linear accelerator (HILAC) to bombard element 98 (californium) with element 8 (oxygen), and managed to produce a new isotope. We could show that the new nuclei decayed by the emission of alpha particles (two protons and two neutrons) to a known isotope of element 104, which in turned decayed to a known isotope of element 102. So by establishing this genetic relationship with its daughter (104) and granddaughter (102), we identified the atomic number of the new nucleus as two more than 104—or new element 106. We also obtained a "signature" for our new element by measuring its half-life and the energy of its alpha particles. (The other members of this group were J. Michael Nitschke, Jose R. Alonso, Carol T. Alonso, Matti Nurmia, E. Kenneth Hulet, and Ronald W. Lougheed.) At about the same time, a group in the Soviet laboratory in Dubna announced a similar discovery. They reported bombarding lead (element 82) with chromium (element 24) and obtaining a nucleus with a half-life that was very different from ours (but they did not provide the evidence of a genetic relationship as it decayed, as we had).

The two groups agreed to refrain from proposing a name for element 106 until it could be determined which group had priority of discovery. During this period, I was part of an international group that proposed criteria for establishing the discovery of new chemical elements. One criterion was that no name should be proposed until the observation (claim to discovery) had been confirmed (that is, the experiment had to be replicated by another group). A full ten years later, in 1984, another group at the Dubna laboratory repeated the Dubna experiment of 1974 and concluded that their finding had been in error. Finally, in 1993, almost twenty years after our experiment, a team at the Lawrence Berkeley Lab repeated and confirmed our results.

So we were given credit for the discovery and the accompanying right to name the new element. The eight members of the Ghiorso group suggested a wide range of names honoring Isaac Newton, Thomas Edison, Leonardo da Vinci, Ferdinand Magellan, the mythical Ulysses, George Washington, and Finland, the native land of a member of the team. There was no focus and no front-runner for a long period.

Then one day Al walked into my office and asked what I thought of naming element 106 "seaborgium." I was floored. Al explained that someone had jokingly asked him if he planned to name this new element "ghiorsium." The joke set Al to thinking that maybe we didn't need to look far to find someone to name it after. Without a word to me, he'd approached the other six members of the discovery group and received their unanimous agreement.

I asked for time to think about it, and after discussing it with Helen and others, all of whom were enthusiastic, I assented.

I was incredibly touched. This honor would be much greater than any prize or award because it was forever; it would last as long as there are periodic tables. There are just over a hundred known elements in the universe, and only a handful of these are named after people. Perhaps someday in the future a student would see the name, wonder what it was, and look into my research.

The formal naming process got to be arduous, though, and even a little ugly. There was a large group of elements whose names and discoveries were in dispute, and the name seaborgium was controversial. One committee that passes on names said it was against the rules to name an element after a living person. It was pointed out that no such rule actually existed, so they formulated one and voted in favor of it. (They also ignored the fact that back in the 1950s we had proposed the name fermium while Enrico Fermi was still alive.) But of course, to turn down the name, they also had to ignore the tradition, if not formal rule, that discoverers of an element have the naming rights. During this dispute, one of my favorite remarks came from my old friend Dan Koshland, a member of the Met Lab team who had gone on to great success, including the editorship of *Science* magazine for many years. In an editorial, he said that people really shouldn't hold it against me that I'd failed to die on the correct timetable. With gratifying support for the name from organizations such as the American Chemical Society, it was eventually adopted.

Since two of the isotopes have half-lives as long as tens of seconds, it is possible to study their chemical properties, and seaborgium is known in the literature as a result. Also, because seaborgium is a homolog of tungsten, we have an idea of some of its expected properties, including compounds such as seaborgous bromide, seaborgic sulfate, calcium seaborgate, and so on. Well, perhaps you have to be a chemist to get excited about such a thing.

Despite the controversy, Al let me continue working with him periodically. By 1991, it had been seven years since the last element had been discovered (element 108, hassium, discovered at the GSI laboratory in Germany). The half-lives of the transuranium elements had been decreasing dramatically. Elements 107, 108, and 109 have half-lives measured in thousandths of a second. It takes weeks of bombardment to make a single atom. We expected this to be the case with element 110, and set up an experiment to try to identify it.

This time, Al's group used the SuperHILAC, an even larger, heavier ion accelerator he had designed. The basic experiment was to bombard bismuth (element 83) with cobalt (element 27). A new gas-filled magnetic separator and detector was constructed especially for the experiment.

During a forty-one-day bombardment, one unique candidate was observed with the magnetic rigidity, energy, and energy loss expected for element 110. After four microseconds, the presumed 110 candidate emitted an alpha particle, decaying to element 108. Due to a failure of the electronics, we could not detect the alpha decay of 108 to 106. We could, however, follow other steps of its decay, which ended up at a known isotope of element 103. We thought that we had seen an atom of element 110, but we could not be absolutely certain, and the SuperHILAC was shut down permanently before we could repeat the tantalizing experiment. In 1994, an international group working at the GSI laboratory announced the synthesis and identification of an isotope of element 110 with a half-life of 270 microseconds.

With the pressure from the AEC chairmanship gone, I had time for other activities, including serving as president of the American Association for the Advancement of Science and of the American Chemical Society (in its centennial year). In these capacities, one of my high priorities was working for more international cooperation.

I returned to Washington regularly. I'd become involved with the Science Talent Search, a national science-fair project, and continued acting as a judge for many years. I also served as president of the International Platform Association, a speakers' organization I'd joined when invited by Drew Pearson, the sometimes venomous columnist. Pearson had not written anything too negative about me then, so I figured the discretion-as-the-better-part-of-valor approach would be to go along with his invitation.

Helen and I were members of the initial delegation of scholars that visited the People's Republic of China in the spring of 1973 for the purpose of negotiating exchanges in the fields of physical and biological sciences, social sciences, and humanities. The delegation had an hour-and-a-half negotiating session in the Great Hall at Tiananmen Square with representatives of the Chinese Academy of Sciences and Premier Zhou Enlai. Zhou put on a masterful performance, speaking in Chinese except at times when he grew impatient with his interpreter and switched to English, and when he corrected his interpreter. In a discussion of population control, he mentioned that one method the Chinese used was sterilization. One of our group said that men were not much interested in being sterilized, and Zhou didn't wait for the translation to jump in, saying, "Male chauvinism and inequality. Do you agree?"

Our delegation obtained Zhou's agreement to nine areas of scientific exchanges; he ruled out three of our proposals in the social sciences (China studies, urban studies, and science and technology in China's development), putting them off for "further consideration" in the future, but agreed to exchanges in areas such as plant studies, earthquake prediction, and acupuncture.

As we passed through the receiving line he made comments that perhaps revealed differences in our political systems that he hadn't mastered. He mentioned that our Committee for Scholarly Communication with the People's Republic of China had been in existence since the middle 1960s, but it was only when Nixon made contacts with the Chinese leaders that the committee could be effective. "Doesn't this mean President Nixon has done something good?" he asked, but then he threw his hands up and said, "But oh, Watergate." When our delegation member replied that whatever the outcome of Watergate, he didn't think it would affect U.S.-Chinese relations or the exchange agreements we were negotiating, Zhou happily and vigorously grasped the man's hand with both of his.

At the beginning of my AEC chairmanship, I had once again neglected exercise and begun to pay a price in my health. With my workload and schedule, golf had become more and more difficult to use as an outlet. But then I discovered I could find just as much, if not more, pleasure and relaxation in hiking. We spent many happy weekends enjoying the marvelous system of trails in Shenandoah National Park, a two-hour drive west of Washington. The premier hike near Washington is Old Rag Mountain, with a rock scramble along its ridge and over the top, and we made an annual pilgrimage there around Memorial Day weekend. That grew to be such an event that some fifty people made up the party one year.

On many evenings after work and on weekends we tromped along the peaceful trails of Rock Creek Park, where in a ten-minute drive from our house we could take a walk of several miles, along the White Horse Trail over hills on the west side of the park and the Black Horse Trail along Rock Creek, through forests that seemed hardly touched by humans.

When I returned to our home in Lafayette, I was delighted to find the network of parks that had been created, many of them in the years when I'd been away. The counties of the East Bay had had the foresight to vote for a one-cent-or-so sales tax that went to support parks, and as a result were in the process of building perhaps the premier urban park district in the country. I got to know the head of land acquisition for the East Bay Regional Park District, the affable Hulet Hornbeck, and spent many weekends with him and others scouting out possible purchases and ways to connect parks. (The East Bay was a leader in the greenway movement, for its parks were linked by abandoned railroad lines and old canal rights-of-way that were converted to trails.) In 1972 and 1973 I served on the Citizens' Task Force for the district, chairing its Trails Committee and advising it on a master plan for future expansion and operations. This meant many hikes and exploratory trips with task force members. (The plan was accepted and implemented.) In succeeding years, Helen and I took a multitude of hikes on weekends, often with the Mount Diablo Regional Group of the Sierra Club, and I sometimes served as leader.

As a birthday present, one of my sons gave me a charter membership in the American Hiking Society, a group formed to give a national voice to people who enjoy our nation's trails. Helen and I happened to be in Washington when the nascent society was having one of its first board meetings. We had the afternoon free, and took a cab out to Vienna, Virginia. The small group was discussing a proposal to sponsor a cross-country hike as a way to heighten its profile and dramatize the need for trails. They were proposing starting in Los Angeles when I piped up and volunteered that if the route began in San Francisco instead, I'd be willing to plan the route through California. The group was not about to let a volunteer slip by. So Helen and I spent almost every free weekend for a year scouting and laying out the path for the hike across California. We greatly enjoyed that task, discovering wonderful places to hike and making friends with people involved in the history of the Pony Express Trail (part of which we followed through the Sierra Nevada).

We laid out a route about 265 miles long, designed to be traversed in twenty-one hiking days. The hikers would cover about thirteen miles a day, and there had to be a site where a large group could camp at the end of the day.

The project was given the name HikaNation, and to start it out with a bang, we obtained permission to walk across the Bay Bridge from San Francisco to Oakland (it took an act of the legislature, something our friend Mike McReynolds took the lead in obtaining), the first time this had ever been done. Seven thousand people turned out early on the morning of Sunday, April 13, 1980, to walk across the bridge. It was a glorious blue-sky and crystal-clear day, and a thrill to walk across the bridge. But it was a tough day for the backpackers, because we had to keep to a fast pace to get across the bridge in time for it to be reopened, and then it was a good distance to an appropriate camping spot—an arduous breaking-in, with more than its share of blisters. The hikers jokingly (I think) accused me of underestimating the actual mileage, and added a term to their lexicon—"Seaborg miles"—for miles that seemed (or were) much longer than expected.

A group ranging from one to two hundred people hiked across California; Helen and I hiked with them on weekends and whenever else we could, and a core group of about forty hikers made it all the way across the country. Helen and I flew east to join the HikaNation group at Harpers Ferry, West Virginia, the following May, and hiked with them down the towpath of the Chesapeake and Ohio Canal to Washington.

A decade later, my son Eric and his (now) wife Ellen Dudley were recruited by the American Hiking Society and *Backpacker* magazine to scout the route of the American Discovery Trail, the first coast-to-coast trail. That route incorporates the one Helen and I scouted from Berkeley to Sacramento, a contribution that made us proud.

Of course, the big issue of the 1970s was the energy crisis, when Middle Eastern countries embargoed and increased the price of oil. One of the lessons of this time that I'm not sure we fully appreciate yet is modern culture's total dependence on energy. The great inflation of the 1970s was tied at least somewhat to the increase in the price of energy. Everything we do is based on energy, so if you increase its price, the price effect ripples through the economy. Questions of changes in fiscal policy notwith-standing, if you look at the inflation trends in a broad view, the biggest inflation jumps began with the increase in energy prices (which quintu-pled over time) and didn't let up until energy prices stabilized.

As energy costs jumped, conservation became more attractive; both government policy and the marketplace encouraged it, which led to a drop in the growth of demand. The lessening of the growth in energy consumption was an important factor in limiting the spread of nuclear power. Much has been made of the fact that many utilities canceled their orders for nuclear power plants, but the utilities canceled a similar num-ber of fossil-fuel plants. Higher oil prices could have made nuclear power even more attractive as an option, but conservation and limited growth held it back.

In 1973 and 1974 I gave some thirty lectures on the energy crisis and the future, emphasizing the importance of conservation, of moving to-ward what I termed a "recycle society" (in which almost everything will be reused over and over, and virgin resources will become a thing of the past), and advocated the continued development of nuclear power and alternative sources such as solar and geothermal energy.

When President Gerald Ford signed the Energy Reorganization Act of 1974, the AEC went out of existence, and in its place came the Energy Research and Development Administration and the Nuclear Regulatory Commission. This reorganization made sense; it was time for an overall energy policy administration, and nuclear energy was now largely ready to stand on its own. Continued public confidence demanded that the reg-ulatory work be split off and done by a separate commission. I'd advo-cated the creation of an energy agency, along with the adoption of an overall energy budget. As part of a national energy policy, Americans would determine how much energy was needed (an energy budget) and how to meet the need. I had a chance to pass some of these thoughts on to then–Vice President Ford when I introduced him at a World Future Society conference in April 1974. (We'd become acquainted during the 1960s, when he was a congressman and I was AEC chairman, and we discovered a common bond in our interest in sports. On one occasion in 1965, at a Gridiron Club dinner when we were both seated at the head table, we each noticed that the other was restless. We discovered it was for the same reason: the NCAA basketball final that night featured Ford's alma mater, the University of Michigan, versus my alma mater, UCLA. We stole upstairs to find a television set, joining Michigan governor George Romney to watch UCLA's victory. We returned to the banquet, where no one seemed to have missed us.)

When Jimmy Carter came into office he struggled toward an energy policy of his own. Much of what he accomplished was laudable, but there was much that I disagreed with. I always thought that Carter underemphasized the need for production and relied too much on conservation to do it alone.

Because he had a background as a nuclear engineer in the Navy, I thought that would give us a common bond, which in some ways it did, but his opposition to nuclear power was disappointing, and he made some mistakes that I believe cost us dearly in later years. (Throughout his presidency I kept in touch with him through our mutual friend Sol Linowitz, then ambassador to the Organization of American States and chief negotiator of the Panama Canal treaty. I'd known him for years in his various public-service capacities, and asked him to pass on to the President suggestions regarding nuclear power, arms control, and a comprehensive test ban treaty. Alvin Weinberg, longtime director of the Oak Ridge National Laboratory among many other accomplishments, reported a conversation in which Carter said that his involvement in cleaning up after a nuclear accident while in the Navy had prejudiced him against nuclear power thereafter.)

One major mistake was his decision to stop research aimed at perfecting the fast breeder reactor, a breeder reactor being one that creates more fissionable material than it consumes. (For instance, a reactor that runs on enriched uranium 235 can also turn its unusable uranium 238 into plutonium 239, which can in turn be used as fuel. Thus, breeders can create an almost inexhaustible supply of fuel.)

Another major mistake was the decision to have no civilian reprocessing of spent fuel from nuclear reactors. Once a reactor's fuel rods have been used up ("spent"), they still contain plutonium and other fuel that can be reclaimed and reused as fuel—the reclamation is known as reprocessing. However, because plutonium is involved, reprocessing raised worries that reprocessed fuel could be diverted to weapons use, and thus that reprocessing could contribute to nuclear proliferation. So President Carter decided that the United States would set an example for the world, and refused to allow the reprocessing of fuel, in hopes that other countries would follow suit.

Predictably, no other country in the world paid any attention to our example (except West Germany). Britain, France, and Japan perform commercial reprocessing (and reprocess for other countries). In reprocessing, the usable fuel is chemically extracted and turned into new fuel rods; the process can even capture products with medical and industrial uses, while the unusable fission products are concentrated in a very small volume and transformed into a stable solid form for long-term storage. In contrast, U.S. nuclear plants use their fuel once, with spent fuel destined for a repository. However, because we have failed to settle on a repository, this waste is piling up around nuclear plants in liquid form, which presents hazards of leakage. A big side effect of this policy is that it makes it appear that nuclear power plants produce more waste than necessary, and it drives up the cost of nuclear power. The American failure to reprocess nuclear fuel is a principal reason why so many people find the nuclear fuel problem so intractable.

Whenever I had the chance to talk with politicians, I tried to impress on them that the antinuclear stance was neither a winner with the people nor sound public policy. Being antinuclear won the loyalty of a limited segment of people, the committed activists, but it was not the position of most Americans, who want a more sound, broad-based energy policy.

Today's period of energy stability should be viewed as a temporary rather than a permanent state. We still need better energy planning and could still use a national energy policy. We must decide on a rational basis whether it makes sense to continue the helter-skelter building of fossil-fuel plants according to the vagaries of expediency or whether we should make a real effort to figure out what approach makes the most sense.

One day in the summer of 1981, I received a phone call from Ronald Reagan's Secretary of Education, Terrel Bell. He was calling to tell me of the formation of the President's Commission on Excellence in Education, which would present recommendations on the renovation of pre-college education. Bell invited me to serve on it, but I turned him down because I thought I didn't have the time. Besides, I suspected either a whitewash or a stalking horse for the Reagan administration's conservative views on education (such as abolishing the Department of Education and instituting prayer in school).

I'd known Ronald Reagan since his days as governor of California in the 1960s. He was a man of great charm, in private just as amiable as in public, quick in repartee, always ready with a quip or an anecdote, although the relevance of what he said to the issue at hand was often lost on me. One time when we'd met in an informal setting, we got to talking about exercise. He described a system of exercises he followed religiously to keep himself in shape. In case I had any doubts about their effectiveness, he challenged me to hit him in the stomach with as much force as I cared. I demurred, but he was insistent, so I punched. It was rock hard; I think it hurt my fingers more than it hurt him.

Reagan's treatment of the University of California when he was governor was anything but good, and it was the sort of treatment I expected education would receive during his administration.

Two days after Bell's call, I received a call from David Gardner, the commission's chairman. I'd known David Gardner since the 1950s, when he'd been on the staff of the UC alumni association. He'd traveled with me when my duties as chancellor required attending alumni events. He'd risen quickly through the administrative ranks of the University of California, to vice president, when he was hired away to be the president of the University of Utah (where he was doing a spectacular job). He was calling to ask me to reconsider my refusal to serve on the President's commission; he explained that he had accepted the chairmanship on the assumption that I'd be a member, and that he'd used my name to recruit others. Under the circumstances, I could hardly refuse a friend, and I could be certain that under his leadership the commission would be serious in its evaluations.

The Soviet Union's launch of the Sputnik satellite in 1957 had shocked the United States into putting more emphasis on education. The Defense Education Act had put more money into schools, particularly in better science programs. Educators had explored creative new methods of teaching, including the use of television. I had chaired a committee that developed a creative new high school chemistry curriculum with an emphasis on audiovisual advances. New national tests were developed to keep watch over student performance. But this boom became a bust about the time Neil Armstrong walked on the moon in 1969. It was if we had patted ourselves on the back for accomplishing our mission and then turned to other concerns. Issues like the Vietnam War and Watergate pushed public education off the national agenda, and we went through a period of neglect.

By 1981, when the National Commission on Excellence in Education was convened, average high school achievement test scores were lower than when Sputnik was launched. Science achievement scores of seventeen-year-olds declined steadily in the national assessments held in 1969, 1973, and 1977. Mean math scores on the Scholastic Aptitude Test dropped from 502 in 1963 to 466 in 1980. More than 20 million Americans were functionally illiterate, including about 13 percent of American seventeen-year-olds, with the greatest problems among minority youth.

The committee operated for eighteen months, holding eight meetings as well as a dozen public hearings, panel discussions, and symposia, including testimony from some 250 experts. We commissioned about fifty studies by educational experts. (Most of the commission's members could already be considered experts in education; members included the immediate past president of the San Diego school board, the president of Yale, the superintendent of schools of Albuquerque, two high school principals, and the reigning winner of the National Teacher of the Year award.)

I believe that before we started we were all concerned with the state of education, and we were all familiar with the problems. Still, we were shocked by some of our findings, which revealed not simply a problem but a looming crisis. The problems were especially acute in science education, an area that has been historically neglected in a way that has always upset me.

Enrollment in remedial math courses at four-year public colleges increased 72 percent between 1975 and 1980 (in the face of a 7 percent overall enrollment increase). Remedial math made up 25 percent of all math courses at those institutions. At community colleges, 42 percent of math classes covered only secondary-level material. In 1971–80, the number of secondary school science and mathematics teachers in training dropped by 65 and 75 percent, respectively. A 1981 survey found a shortage of secondary school chemistry teachers in thirty-eight states and a shortage of physics teachers in forty-two states. The Navy reported that a quarter of its recent recruits could not read at the ninth-grade level, the minimum level necessary to understand simple written safety instructions.

After our hearings, meetings, study of reports, and discussions, the commission's staff drafted a report that surprised me with its blandness—almost as if they expected the commission to be so polite it wouldn't rock the boat. We told them to rewrite it, but although they improved it, it still did not do justice to the scope of the problem and the urgency of the need for solutions.

I was convinced we had to do something dramatic to get people's attention. Another complaint about the state of education would do little good. As the deadline approached, I told David Gardner that if the report's language wasn't strengthened, I'd issue my own minority report, even if I was a minority of one. I was the best-known member of the panel; we both knew that if I took the extraordinary step of disowning the majority report, my own views might overshadow it in the media.

On the last evening before the report was due, I continued to hold out for language that would be strong enough to be acceptable to me, and we had an involved discussion about it. Somewhat exasperated, David said, "Glenn, you sound as if you are negotiating with the Russians." His analogy was more apt than he could know, because to me it was every bit as important as if I *were* negotiating with the Russians, and the overarching message of the report was the importance of education to national well-being and national security. The text we finally agreed on contained strong, militaristic phrases like "an act of war" and "unilateral educational disarmament."

Here's how "A Nation at Risk" started:

> Our Nation is at risk. Our once unchallenged preeminence
> in commerce, industry, science, and technological innova-
> tion is being overtaken by competitors throughout the

world. This report is concerned with only one of the many causes and dimensions of the problem, but it is the one that undergirds American prosperity, security, and civility. We report to the American people that while we can take justifiable pride in what our schools and colleges have historically accomplished and contributed to the United States and the well-being of its people, the educational foundations of our society are presently being eroded by a rising tide of mediocrity that threatens our very future as a Nation and a people. What was unimaginable a generation ago has begun to occur—others are matching and surpassing our educational attainments.

If an unfriendly power had attempted to impose on America the mediocre educational performance that exists today, we might well have viewed it as an act of war. As it stands, we have allowed this to happen to ourselves. We have even squandered the gains in student achievement made in the wake of the Sputnik challenge. Moreover, we have dismantled essential support systems which helped make those gains possible. We have, in effect, been committing an act of unthinking, unilateral educational disarmament.

Our society and its educational institutions seem to have lost sight of the basic purposes of schooling, and of the high expectations and disciplined effort needed to attain them.

The report, which we considered an open letter to the American people, argued that "history is not kind to idlers." Education could not be regarded as easy; the country could not coast on its prosperity and expect it to continue:

Secondary school curricula have been homogenized, diluted, and diffused to the point that they no longer have a central purpose. In effect, we have a cafeteria-style curriculum in which the appetizers and desserts can easily be mistaken for the main courses.

Twenty-five percent of the credits earned by general track high school students are in physical and health education, work experience, remedial [subjects], and personal service and development courses, such as training for adulthood and marriage.

We had entered an era of low expectations in which schools sent students the wrong signal about the need to work hard:

The amount of homework for high school seniors has decreased (two-thirds report less than 1 hour a night) and grades have risen as average student achievement has been declining.

"Minimum competency" examinations fall short of what is needed, as the "minimum" tends to become the "maximum," thus lowering educational standards for all.

One-fifth of all four-year public colleges in the United States must accept every high school graduate within the State regardless of program followed or grades.

Textbooks were being "written down" to ever lower reading levels; expenditures for textbooks had declined by 50 percent in the preceding seventeen years. And American students were studying less than students in other countries: in England and elsewhere, students in academic high schools spent eight hours a day at school, 220 days per year, compared with the American standard of six hours a day for 180 days a year. Teachers were poor and underpaid: "Too many teachers are being drawn from the bottom quarter of graduating high school and college seniors. The average salary after 12 years of teaching is only $17,000 per year."

The report concluded with a set of five recommendations. The first recommendation was on content:

We recommend that State and local high school graduation requirements be strengthened and that, at a minimum, all students seeking a diploma be required to lay the foundations in the Five New Basics by taking the following curriculum during their four years of high school: (a) four years of English; (b) three years of mathematics; (c) three years of science; (d) three years of social studies; and (e) one-half year of computer science. For the college-bound, two years of foreign language in high school are strongly recommended in addition to those taken earlier.

The second recommendation was on standards and expectations:

> We recommend that schools, colleges, and universities adopt more rigorous and measurable standards, and higher expectations, for academic performance and student conduct, and that four-year colleges and universities raise their requirements for admission. This will help students do their best educationally with challenging materials in an environment that supports learning and authentic accomplishment.

The third recommendation dealt with time: "We recommend that significantly more time be devoted to learning the New Basics. This will require more effective use of the existing school day, a longer school day, or a lengthened school year." The fourth included seven points about teaching, with recommendations that teachers meet higher educational standards and be paid better, among other things. The fifth recommendation concerned leadership and fiscal support: "We recommend that citizens across the Nation hold educators and elected officials responsible for providing the leadership necessary to achieve these reforms, and that citizens provide the fiscal support and stability required to bring about the reforms we propose."

The commission presented its report to President Reagan at a White House ceremony in April 1983. The President said he endorsed our efforts, but then he gave a speech that made me wonder if we were talking about the same report. He said it was a "call for an end to federal intrusion . . . consistent with our task of redefining the federal role in education." He added, "We'll continue to work in the months ahead for passage of tuition tax credits, vouchers, educational savings accounts, voluntary school prayer, and abolishing the Department of Education."

(He also mentioned that Eureka College had recently awarded him an honorary degree, which he thought he didn't really deserve because when he'd graduated he considered the degree they awarded him then to be an honorary one.)

After the ceremony, reporters asked me to identify the places in the report where we advocated vouchers and prayer in school. I replied as diplomatically as possible that our report made no reference to any such issues. When pressed for further reactions, I simply replied that the President had embraced the main thrust of our report, and that's all that mattered to me. Fortunately, the news reports ignored Reagan's attempt at putting his own spin on it.

Copies were sent to every member of Congress, all state governors, state legislatures, heads of teachers unions, school administrator organizations, the Chamber of Commerce, and many more. Commission members traveled around the country to encourage implementation of the recommendations, and "A Nation at Risk" ignited a movement, drawing almost unprecedented attention from educators, parents, the public, and the press. When President Reagan saw how popular the report was, he began to embrace it, and it became a little harder for him to continue his calls to abolish the Department of Education. He may have hoped his commission would promote his education agenda, but he'd created something he couldn't control.

"A Nation at Risk" was followed by more than a hundred reports from a wide spectrum of organizations that emphasized the deplorable state of precollege education in science and mathematics in the United States. And our schools made some progress in the ensuing years. As of 1990, thirty-seven states required four years of English, twenty-eight required three or more years of social studies, and ten required three years of mathematics. But only four states had upgraded their requirements to three years of high school science, and many other states still fell short of our recommendations.

Longer school days were reported in 40 percent of high schools, 30 percent of middle schools, and 34 percent of elementary schools. A longer school year had been established in 17 percent of high schools, 16 percent of middle schools, and 18 percent of elementary schools. More homework was required in 27 percent of high schools, 30 percent of middle schools, and 32 percent of elementary schools.

The number of science centers in the United States had nearly doubled to serve the education community.

But all of this fell far short of what we wanted. Half the newly hired teachers of mathematics, sciences, and English were not qualified to teach those subjects. Fewer than a third of U.S. schools had qualified physics teachers. Small wonder that 30 percent of U.S. high schools offered no course in physics, 17 percent none in chemistry, and 70 percent none in earth or space sciences. And no wonder our students' math and science test scores continued to be among the lowest in the industrialized world. Too many people are being left behind in our increasingly technological world. The lack of science literacy continues to threaten the efficient functioning of our democracy in this scientific age.

The intractability of the problem was evident to me again when I recently served on a California commission on education. Other members fought my ideas for high standards, saying I was expecting too much. But I believe that we *must* expect much.

Two basic reforms would do the most good. First, we obviously need more qualified math and science teachers. Our colleges and universities should establish a system in which students majoring in science or mathematics can obtain teaching credentials in a four-year curriculum without the extra year of methods courses traditionally required by schools of education. (Cooperation between science and math departments and education schools to include the methods courses in the four-year curriculum should make this possible.) Similarly, efforts to modify teacher credentialing should be expanded to permit retired industrial and military scientists to augment the science teaching force.

Second, the federal government needs to provide leadership in improving science education. There is still resistance to federal involvement in what is viewed as a local issue, but this position ignores the past—and our best hope for the future. Historically, the federal government has instigated major reforms in education. The Morrill Act of 1862 established the land-grant universities; the World War II–era "G.I. Bill" began the now prevalent federal financial help for college students; the creation of the National Science Foundation in 1950 led to an effective system of support for graduate (and more recently undergraduate and precollege) education in science; the Sputnik-inspired National Defense Education Act gave money to states to build and equip high school and elementary school laboratories.

It's amazing to me that the federal government has not undertaken a program to meet the current crisis in science education. It should establish national goals and standards in concrete terms for precollege education. It should also take the lead in curriculum reform and modernization, and it should greatly increase its financial support.

Perhaps the most important step is to attract qualified science majors to teaching, which can only be done by raising salaries dramatically. As the columnist Mark Shields has observed, if we paid teachers at the level we pay members of Congress, our education problems would be over. Teachers are motivated by love of their work, but that is not enough. We expect doctors to love medicine, but we don't expect their devotion to be their only motivator; we pay them well.

Effective raises nationwide would cost tens of billions of dollars annually and can happen only with federal help. But to put education expenditures in perspective, they should be considered not as an expense but as an investment. The return on investment is illustrated by a Committee for Economic Development report that found that each year's class of dropouts costs the nation about $240 billion in crime, welfare, health care, and services. For every dollar spent on education, it costs nine dollars to provide services to dropouts. About 80 percent of prison inmates are school dropouts, and each inmate costs the nation about $28,000 per year.

The business community can help out, too. For example, the Lawrence Hall of Science and San Francisco Bay Area companies collaborate to select excellent teachers to work in well-paid industry positions during the summer in order to familiarize them and their summer employers with each other's needs, problems, and successes. Industry could also make its workforce more available to help schools.

Ronald Reagan's two presidential terms are remembered for his emphasis on national defense centered on arms buildups and anti-Soviet posturing, but in my view the report of the President's commission on education was the most important contribution to national security that his administration made.


The concern with national defense was accompanied by an obsession with secrecy that knew no bounds. Let me give an example. During my years as AEC chairman, I had systemized a process I'd maintained since the age of fourteen: I wrote a diary each evening at home, and supplemented it with copies of correspondence, announcements, minutes of meetings, and other relevant documents that crossed my desk each day. I carefully excluded any classified information. I thought I was in a position to make, for historians and other scholars, a unique record of what occurred at high levels of the government in this important time, a record that might not be available anywhere else. Over ten years, I accumulated some 18,000 pages of material. That the information I was keeping was unclassified was confirmed in 1965 when the AEC historian microfilmed what I had done thus far for public access in the Kennedy and Johnson presidential libraries. And as a double check on myself, before I left the AEC I had the journal vetted by the AEC Division of Classification, which cleared it virtually without deletions. I received no written confirmation of this action because I never dreamed it would be needed—after all, you can't get a statement that information is declassified if it was never classified in the first place. Another obvious sign that it was not considered classified came when the AEC shipped one copy to my office at the university and another to my home in California. I made these copies accessible to scholars for the next twelve years.

In July 1983, the chief historian of the Department of Energy asked to borrow a copy for use in the history division's long-term project of writing a history of the AEC. Volume IV was to be devoted largely to the period when I was chairman. The historian promised to make copies and return the journal within three weeks.

When the University of California historian learned I was shipping the journal from my office to DOE, he warned me that DOE was likely to find classified material in it and hold it indefinitely, pending a complete classification review. Since the journal had never contained classified material and had been cleared, his worry seemed overblown, but perhaps he knew how much times had changed. In any case, despite my repeated entreaties, the DOE historian did not return my journal in three weeks, or in three months, or in a year and a half. Nor would he give me any explanation for the delay. Finally, I was told in February 1985 that the journal was being held because it had been found to include classified material, and the DOE ordered its San Francisco area office to pick up my home copy, too, so it could be subjected to classification review.

When I responded that I would not allow this, I was told they had the legal right to seize my journal and arrest me if I resisted. Faced with this threat, I acceded to a compromise whereby DOE gave me a locked storage safe (complete with burglar alarm) so that I could continue to have access to my journal, which I was preparing for publication. It was no longer, however, to be available for use by scholars. A few months later, DOE's San Francisco area manager told me he'd been instructed to do a classification review of this copy at my home, and said that if I did not agree, the FBI would seize the papers under court order. He said there was no record that the AEC had ever declassified the journal, so I could be accused of having illegally removed classified material when I left the AEC. If it came to legal proceedings, he knew of no case like this, he said, where the government, with all its resources, had lost.

Given this ultimatum, I agreed to a classification review with the understanding that it would be completed within ten days. Instead of the promised ten days, the reviewer worked in my home for several weeks and came up with the deletion of 162 words, phrases, sentences, and paragraphs affecting 137 documents.

Then I learned that the copy the DOE historian had borrowed was itself undergoing classification review—which required some five months and led to deletions from 327 documents; worse, an additional 530 documents were removed entirely, pending further review by DOE and other agencies. I can at least be thankful that my home auditor, reviewing the exact same material, chose to delete a much smaller portion.

During this time, yet another review was taking place in Bethesda, Maryland, at the home of Benjamin Loeb. Ben and I were collaborating on a book about arms control in the Johnson administration, and I'd sent him some portions of the journal relating to this. Six classification specialists sat around his dining-room table for a few days, choosing a large number of documents to take back with them to DOE headquarters. Most of these were returned with deletions, and some were not returned for four years.

I thought that three reviews would be enough, but in October 1986 the DOE classification people told me they wanted to do another review of my home copy in order to "sanitize" it. Had the first reviewer gotten it dirty? They would take it to the Livermore Lab, where eight to twelve people would do the job, which would take three to six weeks. When they returned the "sanitized" version almost two months later, there had been about a thousand deletions, including the removal of about five hundred documents for review by other U.S. or British agencies. Over my objection, an unsightly declassification stamp was placed on every surviving document.

Finally, the DOE sent to the Lawrence Berkeley Laboratory a team of about twelve people to begin an itemized listing of all the personal correspondence I had brought from the AEC and of the contents of my journal and files for the twenty-five years of my working life *prior to* becoming AEC chairman! This team spent about two weeks on its work, and a year later another DOE group came for about a month to complete the catalogue. They never told me their motive for compiling this catalogue, but of course in the process they uncovered additional "secret" material.

My grammar school, high school, and university student papers are stored in another part of our home, where they were somehow overlooked by the DOE classification teams.

My journal was finally reproduced in January 1989, in twenty-five volumes, averaging about 700 pages each, many of them defaced with classification markings and with large gaps where deletions had been made. In June 1992 a twenty-sixth volume was added, containing documents initially taken away for classification review and returned (with deletions) after the other volumes had been produced.

Here's a verbatim example of the kind of document that was too hot to be released in 1989 but deemed ready for declassification by 1992. The stationery is from "The White House":

October 23, 1961

## MEMORANDUM FOR THE CHAIRMAN, ATOMIC ENERGY COMMISSION

The President approves your proposal to tell Sir Roger Makins, Chairman of the United Kingdom Atomic Energy Authority, that from the point of view of technical feasibility, the United States sees no objection to the detonation of a small-yield U.K. device during the current U.S. underground test series, as described in your letter of October 19, 1961.

A decision as to whether or not to make public British participation in the test can be delayed until it is known that the test will definitely take place.

You are also authorized to explore with Sir Roger the possibility of our using Christmas Island and its facilities in the event that the United States decides to implement plans now being prepared for the resumption of atmospheric testing.

McGeorge Bundy

I think anyone would agree that, more than twenty-five years after the fact, it's hard to imagine the release of this document posing much of a threat to national security. But here's the kicker: my "letter of October 19, 1961," referred to by Mac Bundy, which contains essentially the same information as in his memo and more, including the positions of the Defense and State Departments, was allowed to stay in the journal all along (with the deletion of one small sentence)!

The successive reviews of my journal at different places by different people resulted in widely varying types and numbers of deletions. Some were utterly ludicrous, such as the deletion of my description of accompanying one of my children trick-or-treating on Halloween (thank heavens the Soviets didn't know about that!) or of Helen's visit to the Lake Country in England.

A particular specialty of the reviewers was to delete items that were already in the public record. A favorite target was the code names of nuclear weapons tests—despite the fact that in 1985, the year before they began the review, the DOE had issued a public report, "Announced United States Nuclear Tests, July 1945 through December 1984," that included these code names. I'd already published much of the deleted material in a book I wrote in 1981 on the test ban treaty.

Another category concerned entries that might have been politically or personally embarrassing to individuals or groups but had nothing to do with national security.

The twenty-six expurgated volumes are available in the Manuscript Division of the Library of Congress. I requested repeatedly that an unexpurgated copy of the journal be kept on file somewhere, in the hopes that, especially with the end of the Cold War, sanity might return to the classification system. I have been told that DOE's history division does maintain such a copy for its own use, and eventually they agreed to transfer a copy to a classified area of the Library of Congress.

Despite this horror story, I did receive sympathetic treatment from many people in DOE who made it clear to me that they did not agree with this treatment of me and my journal. And more than one person has told me that evidence does indeed exist that my journal was cleared back in 1971.

The treatment of my journal is just one example of how, during the Reagan years, the security classification system became arbitrary, capricious, frivolous, and virtually devoid of objective criteria. This treatment is particularly ironic when you consider how long I have worked for more government openness. At its beginning in 1947, the AEC had initiated a progressive program of declassification that recognized the need for such information in America's open, and increasingly scientific, society. And throughout the 1960s, the program served our country well. But in the 1980s it took a wrong turn, and indeed retrogressed to the point where it even reversed many of its own earlier declassification actions. This is secrecy taken to its illogical extreme.*

What are the costs of excess secrecy? Is it better to be safe than sorry when it comes to protecting our secrets? In his excellent book *Secrecy*, Senator Daniel Patrick Moynihan blames government secrecy for the colossal failure of our intelligence agencies to foresee the downfall of the Soviet Union. We spent billions and billions of dollars in an arms race with a nation that was falling apart under the strains of its own unwork-

---

*There was some positive movement in the early 1990s. Energy Secretary Hazel O'Leary renamed the Office of Classification the Office of Declassification. But with the hysteria surrounding the charges of Chinese spying, her successor Bill Richardson instituted new security measures and changed the name of that office again, to the Nuclear and National Security Information Office.—E. S.

able system. People with no access to classified information could pick that up with their own eyes and ears, but at the highest levels of government, "top secret" and even more secret reports that focused on the narrowest areas of Soviet strength served as blinders that gave their readers tunnel vision. Moynihan shows convincingly how secrecy can be and has been used for political ends rather than for its avowed purpose: to protect our national security. As I write, the government continues to withhold from the public scrutiny of its citizens more than 1.5 billion pages of documents that are more than twenty-five years old.

Moynihan has been a champion of openness, and a champion of my particular cause, even introducing a bill that would declassify my journal. He chaired a Senate panel on secrecy which pointed out that it is much harder to protect the few secrets that count when almost everything is considered secret. Secrecy is really another form of government regulation, it suggested, and the current capricious system should be replaced with a strict legal framework. Statutory standards should be set for declaring information classified, and classifications should have a fixed lifetime, so that declassification is automatic—unless there is some demonstrable national security need.

It is interesting that the people who argue most strenuously for government deregulation of the marketplace are often the same people who guard government secrecy most strenuously, even though the latter is really government regulation of the marketplace of ideas and information. When information is secret, it is secret not only from foreign enemies but also from citizens who need to make decisions. Whenever you talk about the usefulness of secrecy with scientists and others who develop weapons, they advocate more openness and speak of the futility of classifying information. It is the politicians (particularly those trying to paint themselves as tough on national defense) and bureaucrats with their own agendas who gain from advocating secrecy.

The secrecy obsession was one aspect of the Reagan administration's overemphasis on national security—another part was a huge arms buildup. Jimmy Carter had sought to reduce tensions by negotiating the second Strategic Arms Limitation Treaty (SALT II) and by making great progress toward a comprehensive test ban agreement. Unfortunately, Reagan reversed these policies. Although some progress was made on arms limitation—the Intermediate-Range Nuclear Forces Treaty, eliminating American and Soviet land-based intermediate-range missiles, was signed in 1987, and the Strategic Arms Reduction Talks were held—the primary feature of Reagan's administration was the huge, destabilizing, and budget-busting arms buildup. Its centerpiece was the Strategic Defense Initiative, the Star Wars program that Reagan introduced as a domelike shield against all incoming missiles.

From the start, it was a fantasy; I never understood how he was able to sell it to the American people. One of my favorite comments on SDI came from Arthur Laron, a former Eisenhower assistant, who likened the difficulties to those in a story from the humorist Will Rogers. During World War I, Rogers had a suggestion for how to deal with the German submarine menace: we should simply raise the temperature of the Atlantic Ocean to the boiling point. How could we do this? "Well, that is a technical question for the scientists," he said. Unfortunately, there was a scientist who seemed to think that with a little ingenuity we *could* boil the ocean—Edward Teller convinced Reagan of SDI's technological feasibility.

Teller was somewhat of an anomaly in the scientific community. For most of us, weapons research and development had been an unwanted necessity, but Teller was driven to devote a large part of his life to it by his virulent anticommunism—almost a paranoia—that evidently stemmed from his early days in Europe. In his book *Dark Sun*, about the making of the H-bomb, Richard Rhodes described him well: "Edward Teller became the Richard Nixon of American science—dark, brooding, indefatigable." After his testimony against Robert Oppenheimer in the 1950s, some scientists wanted nothing to do with him, but I never saw the value in that approach—I had to work with him at the Livermore Laboratory. However, our views on what constitutes national security have been diametrically opposed: he was against the Limited Test Ban Treaty and any other agreement that would limit the ability of the United States to build as many weapons as it could. Sometimes we debated these points in public. He is a brilliant and articulate speaker.

Once, at a dinner party at the home of the president of the University of California, Teller was a minority of one in a spirited debate on arms control and Star Wars. I remember him still, sitting at the table after everyone else had gotten up, his head in his hands, shaking his head. It was a picture of loneliness, or perhaps a kind of desperation that he was surrounded that evening by people whom he could hardly accuse of being uninformed or unintelligent but who could not see the threats he believed we must respond to. Yet there's some disagreement among scientists as to whether Teller really considered SDI possible. Al Ghiorso maintains that he's too smart to have really believed this, and that there must have been more to his agenda. But I thought his anticommunist drive was so strong that he could talk himself into almost anything.

I've never forgotten my first encounter with him during World War II. He stopped by my office and confidently offered to calculate anything I needed, including information about the chemical reactions of plutonium. I told him that we knew so little of the chemistry of plutonium that I doubted our problems would lend themselves to solution through calculation. What would there be to calculate? This objection raised not the slightest doubt in his mind about his ability to solve our problems. As it happens, the chemistry of plutonium turned out to be so surprising that any calculations he might have made would have been futile. Similarly, his claims about the feasibility of SDI have proven unrealistic, being based on a judgment clouded by anticommunism, coupled with an immense belief in his own ability to do anything. His certitude, along with Reagan's well-known natural optimism (the President kept a sign on his desk displaying the motto "It CAN be done"), made for a dangerous combination.

When SDI was proposed, I thought of the lessons we should have already learned during the Cold War. First, I thought of the failed antiballistic missile defense system the United States had deployed in 1974 to protect our missile launchers in North Dakota. It had cost some $7 billion (in 1974 dollars), but the system was deactivated two years later because it was considered ineffective. It now stood on the plains as a monument to the futility and wastefulness of the arms race.

Second, I remembered the U.S. response when the Soviet Union began to deploy an antiballistic missile system around Moscow in the late 1960s. Despite our own studies, which showed that we would be unable to build a workable defensive system, we approached the issue as if the Soviets could. President Johnson and Congress agreed that the U.S. should develop "a complete new generation of weapons for the strategic offensive forces"—the next destabilizing step in the arms race. Wouldn't the Soviet response to any defensive system we tried to deploy be the same—and lead to another lesson in how bigger weapons lead to less security instead of the greater security their proponents contend they will give us?

The natural response to any defensive system is to figure out how to overwhelm it. American weaponeers came up with the idea of arming missiles with many warheads—so-called multiple independently targeted reentry vehicles (MIRVs)—that could separate to attack various targets. If we put many warheads on each missile, we would need to launch fewer missiles but could still rain down more warheads than a defender could ever hope to intercept. Eventually, the United States and the Soviet Union signed the Anti-Ballistic Missile Treaty, which greatly limited missile defenses, and one of the main arguments for MIRVs disappeared. Although MIRV opponents argued that it would be smarter to follow up this agreement with one banning MIRVs, by then the idea had too much momentum to stop. President Nixon, a MIRV proponent, wrote in his memoirs: "I believed that the only effective way to achieve nuclear arms limitation was to confront the Soviets with an unacceptable alternative in the form of increased American armaments and the determination to use them."

Of course, the Soviets were no more willing than we would be to negotiate from weakness. They matched us by developing MIRVs of their own before talking about arms limitations, even doing us one better by building larger, more powerful missiles.

The deployment of MIRVs made an already dangerous situation even more so, because they made a first strike more tempting. If each side has an equal number of missiles with one warhead each, it makes little sense to attack your opponent's missile sites, because you won't be 100 percent effective. Say you and your opponent each have one hundred single-warhead missiles and you launch fifty of yours at your opponent's missile silos. If you have a "kill rate" of 50 percent, you'll knock out twenty-five of your opponent's missiles. Thus, you'll have fifty missiles left to your opponent's seventy-five. Assume, on the other hand, that you have ten warheads on each missile. This time, you need launch only five missiles (with a total of fifty warheads) to knock out twenty-five of your opponent's. In this scenario, you have ninety-five missiles left to your opponent's seventy-five.

McGeorge Bundy called the fixed missile with MIRVs "a good killer but not a good survivor." That's why MIRVs were destabilizing in an already tense situation—they could increase the incentive for a first strike because you were better off launching first and trying to take out the other side's missiles before it could get them launched.

The Soviet MIRVs posed a severe threat to our principal land-based weapons, the Minuteman missiles, and led us to develop a new generation of more powerful missiles we hoped would be less vulnerable—another round in the arms race. But even this missile—the MX—was delayed because of fears of its vulnerability. The Carter administration proposed an ill-fated shell game of moving them around out West so the Soviets wouldn't know where they were. The Reagan administration had its own problems with deployment logistics. And as the Soviets built more MIRVed missiles, President Reagan spoke of a "window of vulnerability" that required yet another response.

This progression was predicted in advance by arms control experts, but their concerns were brushed aside in the rush to more arms, a rush that is always hard to resist. When the Seabed Treaty, which banned the emplacement of weapons of mass destruction on the ocean floor, was being considered in the late 1960s, the Joint Chiefs of Staff initially opposed it. The United States had no plans to put weapons on the ocean floor, had no technology to do so, and would gain no strategic or tactical advantage from such weapons. I could understand no reason for the Joint Chiefs' opposition other than its being a knee-jerk reaction against any limits on their armamentarium. The Pentagon always wants more weapons, and we think they are the experts, so they generally get their way. But they are military experts, not experts in nonmilitary solutions. Yet they are accorded respect well beyond this area of expertise. Generals know what can go wrong with their arsenals, so they tend to lack complete confidence in them. And they feel a professional responsibility to take a worst-case view of a potential opponent's capabilities and intentions—it's been said that each side looks at the other's forces through the small end of a telescope and at its own through the large end. Each therefore seeks enough weapons to prepare for extreme contingencies.

It is indeed a technical matter to design a new weapon, requiring expert knowledge. But the decision on whether to deploy a weapon or to enter into an arms control agreement instead is not primarily a technical but a policy issue, and the judgments that have to be made are political, psychological, moral, and philosophical. President Kennedy once observed that experts are essential, but one has to be alert to the potentially crucial factors they leave out of account. The deference we pay to military and other experts on questions concerning nuclear arms seems to be based on the presumption that such matters are too complicated to be understood by the average citizen or political representative, yet the unbiased perspective of the well-informed nonexpert may in fact be the most trustworthy.

During the period when President Reagan's arms buildup was beginning, I had a memorable chat with the Soviet ambassador, Anatoly Dobrynin. He said that the strategy (alluded to in the quote from Nixon's memoir) of first building up nuclear weapons stocks in order to negotiate a cutback later made no sense. He cited as examples the American introductions of Trident submarines and of MIRVs. In both cases, the Soviet Union matched the U.S. buildup and no cutback followed on either side. Nor would there be any reductions in this case, until relations between the two countries had radically changed.

That's where defensive systems had brought us in the past—into another turn of the arms spiral. Now here was the Strategic Defense Initiative, and despite the fact that it was never more than a science-fiction fantasy, SDI took on a life of its own, epitomizing the dangers of the military-industrial complex that President Eisenhower had warned of in his farewell speech. The defense industry uses what could be described as a spread-the-wealth strategy. Huge weapons programs are broken down into components, with enough components put into enough congressional districts so that a critical mass of members of Congress will vote their districts' pork-barrel job interests rather than the nation's interest. When spending projects are cloaked in the guise of the national defense, even so-called small-government advocates like Ronald Reagan can support them. This happened with Reagan's SDI, and after years of unsuccessful tests and nothing to show for our investment, by the end of the 1990s we were still wasting $4 billion a year on it. A recent survey showed that many Americans believe that we actually deployed some sort of Star Wars defense; others probably forgot that Congress and the Pentagon were spending these vast sums of taxpayer money on a fantasy.

SDI changed over time, a transmogrification that was a thing to behold. Its proponents quickly scaled back their hopes from the perfect shield to one that was only partially effective. The most optimistic proponents talked of an effectiveness rate of 90 percent. It astonished me that people could still support SDI at this level, because given the size of the Soviet arsenal, that success rate would allow five hundred bombs to land in the United States—about ten per state, with each bomb large enough to obliterate a large metropolitan area.

By the 1990s, the impervious outer-space shield had been all but forgotten, replaced by a proposed national missile defense which, instead of giving perfect protection from a massive attack by the Soviet Union, would provide limited protection from a few missiles (and perhaps to only a few places). So far, there has been no evidence that it would work even in this limited capacity. In Desert Storm the Patriot missiles were largely ineffective against the rather primitive Scud missiles, and subsequent tests of other systems have been no more encouraging.

But I wonder if anyone really expects a missile defense system ever to work. Historically, missile defenses have provided better political defense than military defense; they deflect the charge of being "soft on defense" without ever deflecting a missile.

And even if we could invent a system capable of stopping those few missiles from a rogue state, would it do any good? Most experts agree that the attacker always has the advantage because it can come up with ways to confuse the defense with a plethora of dummy warheads, or even flak and balloons. Alternatively, couldn't a country with the sophistication to build a weapon of mass destruction and an intercontinental delivery system easily deliver a bomb by other means? It could smuggle a bomb in the same way that tons of drugs are delivered every year; it could smuggle in parts for assembling a bomb; it could explode one offshore and set off a tidal wave.

The national missile defense is Star Wars come to earth, with about as much likelihood of succeeding. But its continued development would be more than a waste of money. Instead of increasing our safety level, it is likely to increase our danger level. Terrorists and rogue states are the most commonly mentioned threats (although they have no weapons or means to deliver them), but there is only one country today against which a missile defense could be potentially effective. The Chinese have perhaps two dozen ICBMs, enough to make them confident that the United States would never attack for fear of receiving unacceptable damage in return. If the United States began to deploy a missile defense, it would upset that balance. Presumably the Chinese would react the same way the United States reacted when it was worried about the Soviets' deployment of a missile defense: they would expand their arsenal in order to overwhelm the U.S. defense. It might take years, but with their fast-growing economy and increasing technological ability, it would be a rational response—in other words, another arms race.

But there is an alternative. We could rein in missile-defense development and use the other tool at our disposal to prevent new arms races and the further proliferation of nuclear weapons—and that is the comprehensive test ban.

Back in the 1980s, as the arms buildup intensified, the arms control agreements being discussed were immensely complex, involving issues that negotiators could be stuck on for years, such as whether the unit of counting should be missiles or warheads, whether British and French weapons should be included on the U.S. side, and whether weapons the Soviet Union had aimed at Asia should be counted in the total. In the years it would take to work out these kinds of questions, both sides would build new, more dangerous weapons. But in contrast, the comprehensive test ban was simplicity in itself—both sides would simply quit testing. And because it was so simple, U.S., British, and Soviet negotiators had agreed on the main outlines of a comprehensive test ban in 1980. The key issue that had killed the comprehensive treaty in the 1960s— our inability to agree on verification procedures to make sure there was no cheating—grew closer to resolution with each passing year. By 1982, we were fairly confident of detecting tests above 1 kiloton through seismic, satellite, and intelligence sources. (For comparison, the Hiroshima bomb was 20 kilotons.)

I thought that the test ban was a more useful avenue than another popular concept of the time—a nuclear freeze, in which each side would maintain its forces at the current levels—because this would also require verification procedures that would take years to work out.

At one point, I had the idea of having all the living former presidents endorse the test ban as a way of getting President Reagan's attention. But this approach never quite panned out, so I worked toward having the ban added as an amendment to the Limited Test Ban Treaty as an easier way of getting it done. But the Reagan administration was simply not interested. I hoped for better luck with the Bush administration.

One morning in 1989, I went for breakfast at Millie's Kitchen, where I was a regular. A waitress called me to the phone. It was the White House asking me to fly east immediately to brief President Bush on cold fusion. A couple of days earlier, the University of Utah electrochemist Stanley Pons (working with a Brigham Young University physicist, Steven Jones) had announced at an American Chemical Society meeting that he had discovered a process he called cold fusion, which miraculously released energy. Several network news shows had featured the story, suggesting that here was a breakthrough that could lead to an unlimited power supply.

Now, of course, any of us familiar with the field and with the laws of thermodynamics were pretty doubtful that such a reaction was possible. Fusion is the act of combining two nuclei into one, a phenomenon in which the force of nuclear binding results in a tremendous energy release. The only fusion reactions we were familiar with were terrifically violent and powerful, and involved such high temperatures as to be essentially uncontrollable. It is the fusion of hydrogen nuclei into helium that creates the energy emanating from the sun—and from a hydrogen bomb. Scientists have been trying to tame fusion for human use in power production for more than a generation, and we always seem to be about twenty years away from any practical application. Now these scientists were saying that through a simple experiment, the electrolysis of deuterium oxide, they were seeing a fusion reaction that released a great deal of energy at manageable temperatures.

In Washington I met first with White House Chief of Staff John Sununu, who, with his engineering background, seemed to follow quite well my explanation of why I doubted the announced findings, and he asked some penetrating questions. My skepticism notwithstanding, I said that the cold-fusion claims needed to be investigated, and recommended that an investigatory panel be appointed. Secretary of Energy James Watkins said that was being done. (About six months later, the panel's report disputed the Utah scientists' contentions and gave more conventional explanations for the phenomena seen.)

I then repeated my explanation for President Bush. A personally rewarding aspect of that meeting was that I was able to tell the President I'd discovered the radioactive iodine being used to treat his wife, Barbara, for her thyroid problem. He joked that Barbara was now radioactive, so she was not allowed to kiss their dog, which implied that the safety concern did not extend to him. (Two years later, President Bush would undergo the same treatment.) But my efforts to convince the Bush administration to support a comprehensive test ban were unsuccessful. They were still worried about such nonissues as verification and "proof testing"—the testing of weapons to make sure they work.

I've always found this proof-testing argument somewhat disingenuous. In my ten years with the AEC, we did not conduct a single proof test. As Norris Bradbury, former director of the Los Alamos laboratory, has said, historically we have checked the operability of stockpiled weapons not by setting them off but "by meticulous inspection and disassembly of the components." If the government has ever used proof tests, disclosing that information would help inform the debate without endangering national security, but it's doubtful this information would ever be declassified. In any case, a bomb that you explode to make sure that it works is of little future use—and the test still doesn't tell you if other bombs in your stockpile will work unless you inspect them to ensure they are in similar condition.

The only reason to test is to improve your capacity. A country that has a newly developed nuclear weapon will want to test it. And a country trying to make improvements needs confirmatory tests. The United States hardly needs to worry about improving its technology at this point. As the world leader in nuclear armaments, the United States has the most to gain from a test ban because it would freeze nuclear weapons development to our advantage.

Conversely, the country that could perhaps benefit most from testing is China. Given time and money, and the incentive of trying to protect itself because of a U.S. missile-defense effort, China could develop a nuclear capacity much more threatening to us that its current minimal one. Yet the Chinese are willing to stop testing. What message are we sending?

In the 1960s we listened to the hard-liners, who said that the only way to maintain our advantage was to continue building weapons as fast as we could. But the Soviets were just as determined, and our advantage disappeared. Do we learn from that, or do we listen to the hard-liners repeating the mantra about never foreclosing a weapons option?

For those still worried about the need for proof testing, the country that should perhaps be most concerned about the continued long-term viability of weapons stockpiles is Russia. Russia lacks our technological testing capacities; its economic problems make good upkeep of its system problematic. Yet Russia is willing to sign the treaty. In the future, if our relations deteriorate and Russia wants to rebuild its nuclear weapons capacity, it will be interested in testing. Will we look back and wish we'd implemented this treaty?

Because of pressure from Congress, President Bush finally agreed in 1992 to initiate a moratorium on nuclear weapons testing, and Russia, Great Britain, France, and China all agreed to participate.

When Bill Clinton took office, his administration actively worked on behalf of a nuclear test ban treaty, and on September 11, 1996, the Comprehensive Nuclear Test Ban Treaty was endorsed by the U.N. General Assembly. Thirteen days later, representatives of the five acknowledged nuclear powers signed it. President Clinton was the first to sign, calling it "the longest-sought, hardest-fought prize in the history of arms control." It promised to finally reverse the failure that President Eisenhower called "the greatest disappointment of any administration of any decade of any time and of any party." It was a moment of elation for me, a goal that took thirty-three years after the signing of the Limited Test Ban Treaty for the world to achieve. Now another 146 countries have signed the treaty, and 41 have ratified it. To go into force, the treaty must be ratified by 44 specific countries—all the countries with nuclear power reactors or nuclear research facilities. And that includes us: the treaty does not go into force for any country until the U.S. Senate ratifies it.

The nuclear tests by India and Pakistan in the spring of 1998 underscored the need for U.S. ratification of the treaty. In the 1960s, the treaty would have helped slow the arms race between the superpowers; now its main thrust will be to stem the proliferation of nuclear weapons. Even though countries like India and Pakistan have gone nuclear, a cessation in testing can help to keep the danger level from rising further because these two wouldn't be able to improve their weapons. We must do all we can to persuade these countries to join in—and they certainly won't if we don't ratify it ourselves.

The United States must show leadership, as we finally have in taking seriously our commitment under the nonproliferation treaty to move toward disarmament. With the end of the Cold War, the United States and Russia agreed to dismantle thousands of warheads. Ironically, dismantling warheads can lead to another danger as the large amounts of plutonium taken from these weapons are put into storage. With the collapse of the Russian economy, the security of their stockpile is a serious question. Every day it stays in storage there is the possibility it could be stolen, or simply reassembled into the weapons from which it came. This vast quantity of surplus plutonium is perhaps the most serious nuclear threat in the post–Cold War world. The question is how to dispose of it—the Russians made it clear that they would not destroy their plutonium unless we destroyed ours in a manner acceptable to both countries.

The simplest solution would be to immobilize the plutonium and store it as we would long-term radioactive waste. But the Russians objected that this did not put the plutonium out of reach for future use. In addition, plutonium is expensive to make and usable as fuel in nuclear reactors. Given the state of the Russian economy, they couldn't afford to throw away this valuable resource. They proposed using it for fuel—"burning" it in electricity-generating reactors—but only if we did the same with ours. After it had been through the reactor, the plutonium would be considered unusable in a weapon because of the intense radiation of the fission products mixed with it. Given the situation, the Clinton administration concluded this would be the most acceptable solution for both countries.

While this program sounds technical and exotic, it is of vital importance that it be carried out as quickly as possible. For instance, there can be local opposition to using the plutonium in a reactor—but it is safe to do so, and if we delay, so will the Russians. In addition, we must provide as much aid as Russia needs—such as helping them build the specialized facilities—but this sort of help is delayed by misinformed charges that it is questionable "foreign aid."

In our rapidly changing world, the United States must provide leadership on these kinds of issues—complex technical problems that require an informed citizenry. Are we prepared for the challenge? Our citizens must be well enough acquainted with the general principles of science to be good judges of policy based on them, or at least to be able to reject spurious policies founded on pseudoscience and nonscience.

I have led a fortunate life; I was given a chance through an excellent system of public education, and I did my best to make the most of my opportunities. I worry now that this system of education is faltering just when we need it the most.

I often liken the role of the scientist to that of a mountain climber who with great care and exertion reaches some high prominence from which he or she is able to perceive new vistas that are hidden from the sight of those in the valley below, even though many in the valley may have better eyesight. To be fortunate enough to behold one of these vistas is exhilarating indeed, and, as never before, the world needs climbers willing to set their goals high, then work to achieve them.

Let's hope we see many such climbers in the next generation; our progress depends on it. Many young people express curiosity about a career in science, but seem intimidated by it, fearing that it requires some unusual aptitude or innate talent. Students have asked me so often about what it takes to succeed as a scientist that I put my thoughts down in the following "letter" decades ago. My advice remains the same today as when I first wrote it.

## LETTER TO A YOUNG SCIENTIST

Dear Student,

I understand you may be interested in a career in science. Perhaps it will be helpful if I share with you some of my thoughts on the value and rewards of such a career. I remember well the influences and considerations that led me to turn in this direction as a very young man.

My own history in this respect has both unusual and usual aspects. Up until the time I entered high school, I had no exposure to science and, therefore, little knowledge of its possibilities. I chose literature as my major subject, and I took no science until my junior year when, in order to meet the college entrance requirement, I took a chemistry course. Largely due to the enthusiasm and obvious love of the subject displayed by my teacher, Dwight Logan Reid of David Starr Jordan High School in Los Angeles, chemistry captured my imagination almost immediately. I had the feeling, Why hasn't someone told me about this before? From that point forward, my mind was made up. I felt I wanted to become a scientist and bent all my efforts in that direction. I have never been sorry, for I have found in science a life of adventure and great personal satisfaction.

In considering a career in science, you may ask yourself whether you really have the qualifications. You may feel—and many might try to tell you—that you need to be a genius. This is not true. While great advances have been made by our greatest minds, such as Einstein, Rutherford, or Edison, most scientific discoveries have been made by men and women who, while of better-than-average intelligence, were by no means in the genius category.

We have so many tasks that need doing in all phases of medicine, public health, agriculture, industry, and basic research that we cannot hope to carry them out without help from people of many levels of ability. Furthermore, many discoveries are made by men and women whose scientific effectiveness came as a result of a combination of qualities. In a particular instance, manual dexterity, special experimental technique, a freshness of viewpoint, or an insight gained from past experience may be decisive. Science is an organized body of knowledge and a method of proceeding to an extension of this knowledge by hypothesis and experiment. By learning the fundamental principles, by mastering the elements of the scientific method, and by acquainting yourself with the experimental techniques available to the modern scientist, you can proceed with near certainty to significant scientific advances and to achievement that may exceed that of many mental giants of a generation ago.

My advice is this: Do not worry too much about your intelligence, about how you compare with your contemporaries, but concentrate on going as far as possible with the basic endowments nature has given you. Don't underestimate yourself. Some young people are probably somewhat more confident—or cocky—about their abilities than their years warrant, but if I may judge from my own experience in talking with young people, many lack self-confidence and are somewhat hesitant in visualizing themselves as potentially important scientists. You should have no hesitation at all about doing this. Set yourself a high goal of achievement and exert yourself to advance toward this goal. The development of your abilities will be most marked if you strike out steadfastly for a goal that may even be high enough that you never quite achieve it.

I would like to emphasize a particularly necessary element in the makeup of a good scientist: simple hard work. Many a person of only better-than-average intelligence has accomplished, just on the basis of work and perseverance, much greater things than some geniuses. Such a hardworking individual will succeed where a lazy genius may fail. Some scientific discoveries are made by armchair research, but most of them require considerable experimental work and represent a lot of perseverance and perspiration, as well as a properly conceived method of attack. Many people of quite superior promise never have that promise realized unless they are fortunate enough to be in an environment where they are continually prodded into activity. People differ enormously in this quality, as in other respects: some are self-starters and have great physical endurance, some work best alone, and others are most effective in a team effort. You will have to evaluate your own characteristics and try to place yourself in the environment most likely, as a routine result, to draw hard work from you.

This matter of hard work runs counter to the trend of modern times, with its emphasis on leisure, shorter workweeks, and more leisure-time activities. I am in sympathy with these developments in society, generally, but I cannot feel that the 35-hour workweek has much relevance for a creative scientist. The greater effort expected of a scientist, however, is seldom extracted against her will. The great gift is the ability to secure employment that allows the opportunity to do work she genuinely loves; she does not work simply because it is necessary in order to live. We live in a money-oriented society, but I think that personal success in money matters is often overrated as the reigning monarch of our standard of values. I believe that every person has a deep psychological need to feel that what she is doing is of some importance, aside from the money being paid for doing it.

The scientist has the satisfaction of this need built into her life, and this gives zest and motivation to the efforts over an indefinite period of time. The intellectual satisfactions, the thrill of discovery, and the sense of worthwhile effort are a rich reward and a strong stimulus to continued work. Scientists and engineers are definitely not clock-watchers. Most of my scientist friends work in establishments where the doors of the laboratory are never locked and the lights frequently burn late into the night.

Scientists would feel a sense of purpose and inner satisfaction even if their efforts were not important to the world in which we live. In actuality, of course, there is no group of persons on whom society as a whole depends so heavily. Science has exciting challenges to meet. Great discoveries with great benefits to human beings everywhere are much closer than the far horizons, and the technology necessary to utilize these great discoveries for the better health and quality of life of mankind offers an immense field for your efforts. In view of this, there can be no question as to whether a career in science would be interesting—even more than interesting: exciting. Science is like the exploration of new countries or adventures on oceans never traveled before. The scientific discoverer is the first to see or to know a really new thing: she is the locksmith of the centuries who has finally fashioned a key to open the door to one of nature's secrets. This age of discovery has opened up new frontiers in space, medicine, biology, artificial intelligence, new sources of energy—the possibilities are almost limitless.

You can be part of it.

BY ERIC SEABORG

At the age of eighty-five, my father was still putting in a full day at his office, continuing research, writing books, working with various organizations, and pursuing his many interests. In 1997, when California began drafting its first academic standards for precollege education, two organizations applied to do the work on the science standards, and my father became the most visible member of one of them—thirty or so scientists and educators who called themselves the Associated Scientists. The other group, organized by the Institute for Science Education at California State University, San Bernardino, was largely composed of education professors and teachers.

When the state standards commission gave the job to the San Bernardino group, a furor erupted—in part because the Associated Scientists (which included several Nobel laureates) had offered to do the job for free, as opposed to the $180,000 fee charged by the San Bernardino group, and in part because a commission member had remarked that the Associated Scientists "wouldn't know a classroom if you put it in front of them."

The outcry forced the state commission to ask the groups to work together, and Governor Pete Wilson appointed my father to chair the committee that would reconcile the approaches. It was a challenging position because the two groups represented two sides of a deep philosophical disagreement. The San Bernardino group thought that science teaching was too elitist; the Associated Scientists thought teaching had already been "dumbed down" too much. The San Bernardino group thought the

Associated Scientists' standards contained too much technical language, which teachers wouldn't understand. To the Associated Scientists, this very concern was a symptom of a problem: if you can't handle the basic vocabulary of the subject, how can you teach it?

The Associated Scientists group thought, for example, that children should be taught that all substances are made of molecules, and worried that educational "reformers" would oversimplify this concept to "big things are made up of small things." In a letter accompanying his group's proposal, my father wrote: "Educational content is continually diluted in a failed effort to produce palatable bits of information for progressively less skilled students. It is essential that we take a stand and insist on educational standards with greater content."

Over several months in 1998, my father went regularly to Sacramento to preside over the hammering out of standards that both groups could accept. In the end, he was still not satisfied that the agreed-upon standards were "world class," and when he presented them to the full commission, he voiced his concerns as to why. For example, one of his major goals had been to have the high school graduation requirement raised to include three years of science, with a year-by-year progression specified: biology in the ninth grade, chemistry in the tenth, physics in the eleventh, and earth science in the twelfth.

Just weeks after that presentation, in August, he flew east to the American Chemical Society meeting in Boston. ACS presented him with a special award because its membership had voted him one of the top three chemists of the past seventy-five years. He spoke at and attended symposia, and at the end of a long day that would have tired a man half his age, he followed his usual routine when traveling: he walked up and down the hotel stairs to get his exercise. There he suffered a massive stroke. After several months of being bedridden, wracked by severe arthritis that made any movement painful, he decided "the only way out" was to stop taking in food. He died at home in February 1999.

My father just missed sharing in the excitement of some scientific news he had been anticipating since the 1960s. As new elements have been found, they have become shorter- and shorter-lived, on the order of milliseconds and microseconds, a trend that if continued would preclude the discovery of more elements. But calculations predicted that a confluence of factors might make some of these superheavy elements more stable, meaning that they might last seconds or even minutes. For years nuclear scientists had debated this idea of an "island of stability" around element 114. My father was a proponent of this theory, Al Ghiorso was a skeptic, and they had a long-standing bet about it.

In early 1999, scientists at a laboratory in Dubna, Russia, announced the discovery of element 114. Energized by this news, Al Ghiorso and his team wanted to replicate the Dubna group's procedure but lacked the needed supplies and equipment. Instead, they used the materials at hand to design their own experiments. By bombarding lead (element 82) with krypton (element 36), they were able to form element 118, which soon decayed into element 116, which in turn decayed into element 114. Thus, in one fell swoop they found two elements and further evidence of element 114—and, perhaps more important, data indicating that the island of stability does indeed exist. They immediately began planning further experiments designed to find even more elements. Evidently, it's still not safe to name an element "ultimium," as nuclear science continues to expand the frontiers of knowledge.

My father also missed news that would have disappointed him considerably—the rejection of the Comprehensive Nuclear Test Ban Treaty by the U.S. Senate, in marked contrast to the success of the Limited Test Ban Treaty during the Kennedy administration. Republican Senate leaders had kept the treaty bottled up for two years, holding it hostage to unrelated issues. When President Clinton would not agree to their terms, they suddenly held only three days of hearings and then rushed it to a vote. All the Democrats voted in favor of ratification (with one abstention); all the Republicans except four voted against it. Evidently, the Republican leaders acted swiftly in 1999 to avoid being on the wrong side of the issue in the election year of 2000—polls show that 80 percent of the public favors a test ban.

President Clinton failed to mobilize this supportive public and rally it to the cause. His passivity contrasted sharply with Kennedy's dedication to the earlier treaty. Kennedy faced an unenthusiastic Senate, but he took the offensive, marshaling the vocal support needed to gain ratification. Yet despite the current setback, the Comprehensive Nuclear Test Ban Treaty still bears the signature of the President of the United States and the country continues its moratorium on testing. Perhaps, with changes in its membership, the Senate can be convinced to take up the treaty again and deal with it in a more serious and responsible fashion.

In the debate over California school standards, the charges of elitism must have seemed ironic to my father, considering how much energy he had always devoted to the cause of making science accessible to the public in every way possible, including his beloved Lawrence Hall of Science. Even in his eighties he worked at this. When he was invited to visit a couple of elementary schools, one in Colorado attended by his granddaughters, another in his neighborhood in California, he prepared with his customary care. He consulted with the director of the Great Explorations in Math and Science (GEMS) project at the Lawrence Hall of Science, who supplied him with the materials for a simple experiment: Ziploc bags, calcium chloride (the salt commonly spread on sidewalks to melt ice), baking soda, and phenol red (a dye that changes color in the presence of acids or bases).

The students put the baking soda and calcium chloride in a Ziploc bag. When they added the phenol red solution, the brew heated up, gave off bubbles, and turned from bright pink to orange to yellow. This was an exciting way to learn about the concept of a chemical reaction. The experiment progressed amid squeals of delight and then my father got the students to discuss what caused the heat, the color change, and the bubbles.

At the beginning of the demonstration, my father had asked how many of the students wanted to be scientists when they grew up, and a few tentative hands went up. At the end, he posed the question again. All the children in the class raised their hands.

# ACKNOWLEDGMENTS

There are many people to thank and acknowledge for help in a wide variety of capacities in moving this book from idea to reality.

Ellen Dudley provided her irreplaceable editing, perspective, and advice on everything from the proposal to the final manuscript, and put up with inordinate disruption in her life. Lynne Cobb contributed page-by-page professional-equivalent editing. Helen Seaborg and Bill Jenkins read the entire manuscript and made valuable comments. Darleane Hoffman, Stanley Schneider, Arnold Fritsch, and Bernard Cohen shared their expertise and special knowledge on sections of the manuscript. Dan Koshland and Jeanette Bonniksen shared important memories and background. Albert Ghiorso helped with memories, comments, and access to records. Mary Jane Gore provided emergency support. Kristin Balder-Froid provided wonderful ideas, coordination, and support. Tammera Campbell and Marilee Bailey in the photo lab and archives of the Lawrence Berkeley National Laboratory were amazingly responsive in locating and providing photographs. Pam Patterson at LBL made their contributions possible. Janice McGee and Nancy Tallarico disrupted their own work in the office of lab director Charles Shank to help in locating research materials. Other photo and research help came from Margaret Brown at the American Chemical Society, Steve Koppes of the University of Chicago, Jerry Lubenow and Maria Wolfe of IGS Press, and Ray Colvig. And, finally, thanks to the helpful people at Farrar, Straus and Giroux: Nina Ball-Pesut and Jack Lynch, and especially Elisabeth Sifton for her immense patience and deft editing.

Grateful acknowledgment is made to the following sources for permission to reprint photographs:

Lawrence Berkeley National Laboratory: Glenn Seaborg at eight months; Glenn and Jeanette Seaborg, 1916; Glenn with family in South Gate, 1925; Glenn with parents and Jeanette in South Gate, 1929; Dwight Logan Reid; UCLA campus, 1929; Seaborg in East Hall, 1937; Seaborg and Jack Livingood; old Rad Lab; G. N. Lewis; Seaborg and Helen Griggs, 1941; Seaborg with daughter Dianne, 1961; Seaborgs at new home in Washington, 1961; Lawrence, Seaborg, and Oppenheimer with cyclotron controls, 1946; Livingston and Lawrence with cyclotron, 1934; beam of 60-inch cyclotron; Wahl and Seaborg with cigar box; room 307, Gilman Hall; Seaborg with Geiger counter, 1941; Werner and Cunningham in Jones Laboratory; balance with sample holder; aerial view of Hanford, 1944; Hanford mess hall; Hanford waste tanks; Seaborg on *Quiz Kids* show; Isadore Perlman, 1942; Albert Ghiorso, 1950; americium compound with needle for scale; heavy ion linear accelerator (HILAC); inside HILAC; 184-inch cyclotron; Seaborg receiving Nobel Prize; Thompson and Seaborg with centrifuge, 1948; U.S. Junior Chamber of Commerce's Ten Outstanding Young Men of 1947; Seaborg at blackboard with student, 1972; Zhou Enlai greeting Seaborg in China; the discoverers of element 106; Seaborg in 1986; Seaborg pointing to seaborgium on periodic table

Lawrence Berkeley National Laboratory/U.S. Department of Energy: Soviet representatives exchanging gifts with Seaborg family, 1971

University of Chicago and Argonne National Laboratory: Arthur Holly Compton

Fritz Goro/TimePix: Ghiorso and Jaffrey at Met Lab; Stanley Thompson working with mirror and lead bricks

Ted Shreshinsky: Clark Kerr and Seaborg

Jon Brenneis: Seaborg with football players; Berkeley Nobel laureates

John Fitzgerald Kennedy Library, Columbia Point, Massachusetts: Seaborg at Kennedy cabinet meeting

Office of the Naval Aide to the President, Washington, D. C. (photo by R. L. Knudsen): Kennedy and Seaborg at Nevada Test Site, 1962

Lyndon Baines Johnson Library, Austin, Texas (photo by Y. R. Okamoto): Seaborg and Johnson in Oval Office

U.S. Department of Energy, Germantown, Maryland: Oppenheimer receiving Fermi award, 1963

Wide World Photos, Inc.: Adlai Stevenson and Seaborg at United Nations anniversary, 1965

Nixon Project, National Archives: Seaborg with Nixon, 1970

Ronald Reagan Library/The White House: Reagan presenting Seaborg with plaque

George H. W. Bush Presidential Library: Seaborg briefing Bush on "cold fusion"

The White House: Seaborg and Clinton with 1993 Westinghouse Talent Search finalists; Seaborg with Al Gore

# PERIODIC TABLE OF THE ELEMENTS TODAY

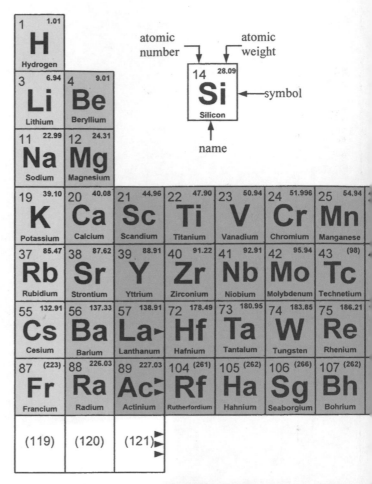

| 1 1.01 **H** Hydrogen | | | | | | |
| 3 6.94 **Li** Lithium | 4 9.01 **Be** Beryllium | | | | | |
| 11 22.99 **Na** Sodium | 12 24.31 **Mg** Magnesium | | | | | |
| 19 39.10 **K** Potassium | 20 40.08 **Ca** Calcium | 21 44.96 **Sc** Scandium | 22 47.90 **Ti** Titanium | 23 50.94 **V** Vanadium | 24 51.996 **Cr** Chromium | 25 54.94 **Mn** Manganese |
| 37 85.47 **Rb** Rubidium | 38 87.62 **Sr** Strontium | 39 88.91 **Y** Yttrium | 40 91.22 **Zr** Zirconium | 41 92.91 **Nb** Niobium | 42 95.94 **Mo** Molybdenum | 43 (98) **Tc** Technetium |
| 55 132.91 **Cs** Cesium | 56 137.33 **Ba** Barium | 57 138.91 **La▸** Lanthanum | 72 178.49 **Hf** Hafnium | 73 180.95 **Ta** Tantalum | 74 183.85 **W** Tungsten | 75 186.21 **Re** Rhenium |
| 87 (223) **Fr** Francium | 88 226.03 **Ra** Radium | 89 227.03 **Ac▸** Actinium | 104 (261) **Rf** Rutherfordium | 105 (262) **Ha** Hahnium | 106 (266) **Sg** Seaborgium | 107 (262) **Bh** Bohrium |
| (119) | (120) | (121)▸▸▸ | | | | |

Silicon box key:
14 28.09 **Si** Silicon — atomic number, atomic weight, symbol, name

**Lanthanide series** ▸

| 58 140.12 **Ce** Cerium | 59 140.91 **Pr** Praseodymium | 60 144.24 **Nd** Neodymium | 61 (145) **Pm** Promethium |

**Actinide series** ▸

| 90 232.04 **Th** Thorium | 91 231.04 **Pa** Protactinium | 92 238.03 **U** Uranium | 93 237.05 **Np** Neptunium |

**Superactinide series** ▸ (122-153)